Advances
in COMPUTERS

VOLUME 4

Contributors to This Volume

DAVID R. BENNION
HEWITT D. CRANE
WILLIAM A. CURTIN
H. H. GLAETTLI
WILLIAM C. McGEE
HOWARD E. TOMPKINS

Advances in
COMPUTERS

edited by **FRANZ L. ALT**

National Bureau of Standards
Washington, D. C.

MORRIS RUBINOFF

University of Pennsylvania
and
Pennsylvania Research Associates
Philadelphia, Pennsylvania

associate editors **A. D. BOOTH**

R. E. MEAGHER

VOLUME 4

Academic Press • New York • London •1963

ACADEMIC PRESS, INC.
111 Fifth Avenue, New York, New York 10003

United Kingdom Edition published by
ACADEMIC PRESS, INC. (LONDON) LTD.
Berkeley Square House, London W.1

LIBRARY OF CONGRESS CATALOG CARD NUMBER: 59 - 15761

Second Printing, 1969

PRINTED IN THE UNITED STATES OF AMERICA

Thielman 20 J 69 HEW/Math

Contributors to Volume 4

DAVID R. BENNION, *Stanford Research Institute, Menlo Park, California*

HEWITT D. CRANE, *Stanford Research Institute, Menlo Park, California*

WILLIAM A. CURTIN, *Radio Corporation of America, Defense Electronic Products, Moorestown, New Jersey*

H. H. GLAETTLI, *IBM Research Laboratory, Zurich, Rüschlikon ZH, Switzerland*

WILLIAM C. McGEE, *Thompson Ramo Wooldridge, Inc., Canoga Park, California*

HOWARD E. TOMPKINS,* *National Institutes of Health, U.S. Department of Health, Education and Welfare, Bethesda, Maryland*

*Present address: Department of Electrical Engineering, University of Maryland, College Park, Maryland.

Preface

Reflecting the decision reported in the preceding volume of "Advances in Computers," the present volume takes a first step toward broader coverage of the different aspects of the computer field. Included are substantial presentations on computer applications, computer hardware, computer system design, and computer education.

The computer applications article discusses the formulation of data processing problems. It describes procedural and nonprocedural programming languages, generalized data processing routines, and the growing trend toward standardization. A chapter is devoted to data organization and discusses rectangular arrays, trees, and other methods of data description.

The volume contains two articles on computer hardware, one on all-magnetic circuit techniques and the second on all-fluid digital logic elements. The former describes the various methods for designing switching and memory circuits using only magnetic devices. The superior reliability and environmental properties of all-magnetic circuits are discussed as well as operational and compatibility considerations. The article on digital hydraulic and pneumatic circuits provides a comprehensive description of all the present approaches to the design of these novel devices and evaluates their performance and potential.

The system design article discusses multiple computer systems. It begins with a definition of such systems and outlines the motivation for their development. The significant features of such systems are listed and exemplified in detail through description of a hypothetical design. Consideration is given to the methods for scheduling programs on multiple computers. The article concludes with a description of four existing machines: PILOT, LARC, GAMMA 60, RW-400.

The article on computer education surveys its growth in industry, universities, high schools, and throughout the American community. A large number of educational programs is described, including those under professional society auspices and courses by volunteer individuals and groups. The place of programmed instruction in computer education is also described.

The diversity of the articles is apparent. We hope that this volume will, in fact, serve as an "antidote to specialization."

FRANZ L. ALT
MORRIS RUBINOFF

October 1963

Contents

The Formulation of Data Processing Problems for Computers

WILLIAM C. McGEE

All-Magnetic Circuit Techniques

DAVID R. BENNION and HEWITT D. CRANE

Computer Education

HOWARD E. TOMPKINS

Digital Fluid Logic Elements

H. H. GLAETTLI

Multiple Computer Systems

WILLIAM A. CURTIN

Contents of Volume 1

Contents of Volume 2

Contents of Volume 3

Tentative Contents of Volume 5

Advances
in **COMPUTERS**

VOLUME 4

The Formulation of Data Processing Problems for Computers

WILLIAM C. McGEE

Thompson Ramo Wooldridge, Inc.
Canoga Park, California

1. Introduction

Since the introduction of computers for commercial use in the early 1950's, a considerable technology has emerged from the application of computers to data processing problems. In Volume I of this series, Gotlieb [1] points out that the chief characteristic of data processing is that any particular problem is not self-contained, but rather is one of a number of interlocking problems in a large data-handling system. As a result, the technology has produced not only techniques specific to computers such as programming and operation, but also techniques in a wide variety of related activities, such as systems analysis, procedures, data preparation and distribution, data control, and auditing.

1

In spite of this considerable activity, there does not exist a very substantial or definitive literature on data processing technology.[1] A large number of papers have been published describing the application of specific computers to specific problems, but such papers individually do not lend insight into the basic nature of data processing, nor do they suggest the best way to implement slightly different problems on the same or slightly different computers. Perhaps the best place to obtain such information is from the several books on data processing programming which have appeared in recent years. These include books by Canning [2], Chapin [3], Gotlieb and Hume [4], Gregory and Van Horn [5], Ledley [6], Martin [7], and McCracken, Weiss, and Lee [8]. Each of these books is primarily an introduction to computer programming for persons with no prior knowledge of the field. However, they also attempt in varying degrees to distinguish between data processing, which is their primary concern; and the historically older field of scientific and engineering computation. To this extent, they serve to define the characteristics of data processing, and thus provide a good starting place for the reader interested in the fundamental aspects of this activity.

In the last three or four years, there has been an increasing interest in the fundamental aspects of data processing. This interest has arisen from a general dissatisfaction with the conventional methods of defining computer processes, principally on the grounds that such methods are machine-dependent and cannot therefore be used effectively by persons without computer training, nor can they be used to exchange techniques among users of different computers. One result of this dissatisfaction has been a considerable effort to remove conventional programming languages even farther from the machine language level, with the aim of making such languages machine-independent. Typical of this work is the development of the COBOL programming language, which, by virtue of its acceptance by a large number of computer manufacturers, is rapidly becoming an unofficial standard data processing programming language.

Other investigators are convinced that the conventional type of programming languages, however far removed from machine-language, can never be entirely machine-independent because they are basically *procedural*. As a result, a number of *nonprocedural* languages have appeared, which attempt to define computer processes explicitly in terms of the results to be produced rather than implicitly in a procedure. While the end results of both approaches are the same, the proponents of nonprocedural languages hold that only their approach has a chance of being truly machine-independent.

Basic to both approaches is the question of the data upon which processes

---

[1] Notable exceptions are the literature on *sorting* and on *addressing quasi-random access devices*, which is quite extensive.

operate. It is now generally recognized that the data involved in data processing applications is much more poorly "structured" than that of the usual scientific or engineering application, and that special techniques are therefore required for describing data to a compiler and for storing data in machine-language media. In addition to the work of implementing such techniques in existing compilers, a fair amount of effort has been expended in studying the basic nature of the data for data processing applications, and in particular the relationship of such data to the even more poorly-structured data of such applications as information retrieval and artificial intelligence.

Finally, the last several years have seen an increasing interest in *data processing theory*. The apparent lack of success in developing a truly machine-independent programming language is held by some to indicate a basic ignorance of what data processing is all about. Others conclude that standardization, either in computers or computer languages, will be impossible until suitable theoretical foundations have been established. A small number of investigators are now working to provide such a foundation. A theory as such has not yet emerged, but some significant achievements have been made in providing the *tools* upon which a theory may be based.

The purpose of this article is to review the developments of the last several years in the areas alluded to above. In order to provide an adequate appreciation of these developments, some of them will be described in considerable detail. However, these descriptions should not be considered definitive; and the reader interested in such a description should refer to the indicated reference. It is hoped that this review will be helpful to programmers and analysts responsible for implementing data processing applications and programming systems, as well as to computer managers and designers wanting to keep abreast of recent developments in computer programming.

2. Procedural Programming Languages

2.1 Development

The evolution of programming languages for data processing problems has closely paralleled that for scientific and engineering problems. For the most part, the pattern of this evolution has been dictated by computer characteristics and capabilities. The very early electromechanical computers had rather extensive facilities for parallel operation, but with the advent of high-speed random-access memories these facilities had to be abandoned for economic reasons: it was just too expensive to provide multiple channels to a high-speed memory. The result was the sequential

3

computer of the type proposed by Burks, Goldstine, and von Neumann, after which the overwhelming majority of present-day computers are patterned.

The "von Neumann" computer concept, as it turned out, was quite acceptable for the uses to which it was originally put, namely, scientific and engineering computation. Such applications are inherently sequential in nature, and there was a natural parallel between the steps of a computational procedure or algorithm on the one hand, and the discrete operations of the computer on the other.

Whether or not a sequential computer is "best" for solving scientific and engineering problems, or any kind of problem for that matter, the concept has had a pervading influence on the evolution of programming languages. These languages almost invariably have taken the form of step-by-step procedures, and for this reason have come to be called *procedural programming languages.*

The development of procedural programming languages has been well documented, for example, by Orchard-Hays [9] and Jenkins [10]. The main motivation in this development appears to have been the desire to turn over more and more of the clerical aspects of programming to the computer, so that the programmer may write programs more rapidly and accurately. Thus, we find machine language being progressively replaced by mnemonic operation codes, relative or regional addresses, subroutines, mnemonic addresses, macro-instructions, and most recently mathematical or "English-language" procedure statements. Programming languages have thus come to look progressively less like machine language. Despite this, they have remained essentially procedural. Part of this may be due to the fact that the agency (assembler, compiler, etc.) which translates source programs into machine-language programs is considerably simpler if some correspondence is maintained between the elements of the "source" program and the elements of the "object" program. Mostly, however, it is due to the pervading influence of the von Neumann computer concept.

The evolution of procedural programming languages for scientific and engineering computation on the one hand, and data processing on the other hand, followed almost identical paths up until about 1955. At that time the number of business data processing applications of computers had increased to the point where a language especially tailored for this type of application was needed. Remington Rand was the first to recognize this need, and under the direction of Dr. Grace Hopper developed the FLOW-MATIC programming system [11, 12]. A companion development was that of the AIMACO system [13, 14] of the USAF Air Materiel Command. Both systems are "English-language" programming systems, permitting the programmer to state procedures in sentences constructed from a restricted set of English-language verbs and connectives, and

4

arbitrary nouns for the objects to be operated upon (fields, records, etc.).

The development of FLOW-MATIC and AIMACO laid the groundwork for a number of similar programming languages. Among the better known of these are the FACT system of Minneapolis-Honeywell [15]; the Commercial Translator system (COMTRAN) of IBM [16]; the COBOL system, sponsored by the U.S. Department of Defense [17]; and the NEBULA system of Ferranti, Ltd. of Great Britain [18]. Each of these systems is an extension of the basic idea behind the FLOW-MATIC system, so it is not surprising to find that they have many characteristics in common. Also, there has been an extensive exchange of ideas among the developers of these systems, to such an extent that the same terminology occurs frequently in the different systems.[2]

In the following section an attempt is made to briefly describe the more important facilities provided by the recent data processing programming languages, with illustrations drawn where appropriate from the FACT, COMTRAN, and COBOL systems. For definitive descriptions of these systems the reader should refer to the previously cited sources. In addition, references [20–23] may be useful for additional information on COBOL.

2.2 Characteristics of Recent Procedural Languages

In each of the recent procedural languages, a program is composed of two major parts: one specifying the procedure to be followed by the computer in the running of the problem, the other defining the symbols which the programmer uses in the procedure to denote the data to be operated upon. In COBOL terminology, these program parts are called the *procedure division* and the *data division*, respectively. In addition, if the language is intended for use on a variety of computers or on a computer having a variety of configurations, an *environment division* is usually included to describe, to the compiler, the computer system on which the source program is to be compiled and the computer system on which the object program is to be run. Finally, an *identification division* is sometimes included to provide a place for the programmer to identify himself and the program he is writing.

The problems of data description are shared by procedural and nonprocedural languages alike, so a discussion of these problems and the facilities provided in programming systems to handle them is deferred to Section 4. This section will cover principally the facilities provided in the procedure division of a program.

A characteristic of the recent procedural languages is the facility provided for writing procedures in a form as close to natural English as pos-

---

[2] A comparative study of some eight recent data processing languages, four of which were developed in England, is given in [19].

sible. Thus we find that these languages have the same grammatical units as natural languages: clauses, sentences, and paragraphs.

The clause is the basic grammatical unit, and may take two forms: *imperative* and *conditional*. The imperative clause is used to direct the computer to carry out some operation. It consists of a verb in the imperative mood, followed by one or more objects and connectives as required by the verb. For example, to add the number A to the number B, the following imperative clause might be used:

(FACT)	ADD A TO B
(COMTRAN)	ADD A TO B
(COBOL)	ADD A TO B

The *conditional clause* serves to direct the computer to take one of two alternative actions, depending on the truth or falsity of a *condition* appearing in the conditional clause. The conditional clause has the general form

IF (condition)

and is used in compound clauses of the general form

IF (condition) (clause 1) OTHERWISE (clause 2)

The convention followed is that if the specified condition is *true*, clause 1 is executed; but if the condition is *false*, clause 2 is executed. For example:

(FACT)	IF A EQUALS B, ADD C TO D, OTHERWISE SUBTRACT C FROM D
(COMTRAN)	IF A = B THEN ADD C TO D OTHERWISE SET D = D − C
(COBOL)	IF A EQUALS B ADD C TO D; OTHERWISE SUBTRACT C FROM D

Note that, in general, either clause in a compound conditional clause may itself be a compound conditional clause, thus giving rise to a potentially endless "nesting" of compound conditional clauses. In practice, such nesting is rarely carried beyond two levels since the result rapidly becomes unreadable beyond that point.

The conditions appearing in the conditional clauses generally refer to the relation between two operands, one or both of which may be variable. The relational operators provided are equivalent to *less than, less than or equal, equal, greater than or equal, greater than*, and *not equal*. Compound conditions may be formed by joining simple conditions with the connectives AND and OR, such as in

A EQUALS B AND C IS ZERO

Such conditions are "evaluated" by the object program by the usual rules of Boolean algebra.

The *sentences* of a procedure are composed of one or more clauses, which are separated by such symbols as commas or semicolons, and terminated by a period. Sentences provide, as in natural languages, for the expression of "one complete thought," an interpretation which may be useful to the programmer but which means nothing to the compiler. Sentences are generally the lowest grammatical unit which may be referred to by other parts of the procedure.

The largest grammatical unit of a procedure is the *paragraph* or *section*, and consists of one or more sentences preceded by a *name*. The purpose of such units is to permit reference to groups of sentences by other parts of the procedure; hence, paragraphs require names. Paragraphs may also be used as they are in natural languages, to delineate separate groups of thoughts. In some languages paragraphs may be "nested" (in the form of paragraph, sub-paragraph, sub-sub-paragraph, etc.) to provide convenient reference to different parts of a paragraph from different parts of the procedure.

The procedures expressible in a program are largely determined by the *verbs* provided for use in imperative clauses. Verbs may be classified by the general function they perform: *data value assignment; input-output;* and *program control.*

Data value assignment verbs are used to change the value of specified data types in computer memory. When this involves merely copying new values over old values, verbs of the "move" type are used:

(FACT)	PUT A INTO B.
(COMTRAN)	MOVE A TO B.
(COBOL)	MOVE A TO B.

In such sentences, A and B may refer to "elementary items," or they may refer to groups of elementary items. In the latter case, the sentences cause each item in the group to be moved. Some systems provide for automatically rearranging and editing the items as they are moved from their source to their destination, on the basis of definitions supplied the programmer in the data division of the program. This facility is useful when the *form* of an item must be changed for purposes of computation or output.

More complicated forms of data value assignment are provided through arithmetic assignments. In some systems, the type of arithmetic to be performed is specified by the verb. Each of the following replaces C by $2 \times C$:

(FACT)	MULTIPLY C BY 2.
(COBOL)	MULTIPLY C BY 2.

Some systems provide the alternate or additional facility of replacing a given number by the value of an arithmetic expression of arbitrary complexity:

(FACT)	SET C TO $2 * C$
(COMTRAN)	SET C $= 2 * C$
(COBOL)	COMPUTE C FROM $2 * C$

Operations permitted in arithmetic expressions generally are addition, subtraction, multiplication, division, and exponentiation. In most systems, arithmetic is performed as if all factors were integers, and automatic truncation (or, optionally, rounding) is provided to align the implied decimal points of the calculated quantity and the receiving field. A standard "overflow" condition is generally postulated to facilitate the detection and correction of results which exceed the size of the receiving field.

The input-output functions of a program are accomplished through input-output verbs. Principal among these are the verbs used to read and write the *logical records* of files. Records are the largest unit of data in a file, and are defined by the programmer in the data division of the program. As a result of this definition, the compiler reserves areas in memory for holding records (generally just one for each file) as they are input and before they are output. For example, if MASTER RECORD is the name of a record type in an input file called MASTER FILE, the sentences

(FACT)	GET NEXT MASTER-RECORD.
(COMTRAN)	GET MASTER.RECORD.
(COBOL)	READ MASTER-FILE RECORD.

cause the next logical record in the MASTER FILE to be entered into its assigned area in memory where it can be processed by succeeding sentences. Similarly, the sentences

(FACT)	FILE NEW-MASTER-RECORD.
(COMTRAN)	FILE NEW.MASTER.RECORD.
(COBOL)	WRITE NEW-MASTER-RECORD.

cause the record which has been developed in an assigned area to be released to the output file NEW MASTER FILE. The read and write verbs are sufficiently general that they are used to transfer information between computer memory and a number of different kinds of peripheral devices. It is the function of the compiler to deduce, from the definition of the file, the type of device being referred to and to generate instructions appropriate to that device.

It might be pointed out that the read and write verbs do not necessarily cause the physical transfer of data when they are executed. For reasons of processing efficiency, such transfers are usually effected by an interme-

8

diary "input-output system" which resides with the object program in memory. The input-output system "delivers" input records to the object program when called for by read verbs, and "receives" output records when called for by write verbs. These input-output systems generally use relatively large areas of memory as buffers (usually not accessible to the programmer) for holding blocks of logical records for the object program. Input-output systems of this type have found extensive use in the past [24–27]. Their specific application to COBOL has been studied by Bouman [28] and Mullen [29].

Although intended to be general, there are certain types of input/output for which the read and write type of verbs are not suitable, particularly, the input and output of low-volume operating type information. For such operations, special input and output verbs are usually provided.

The final function performed by verbs is program control. Program control verbs may be used for (1) altering the normal sequence of sentence execution, either unconditionally or conditionally, so that program execution continues at an arbitrary sentence; (2) altering the normal sequence of sentence execution so that an arbitrary procedure, located elsewhere in the program, may be performed before control is passed to the next sentence; and (3) stopping program execution.

The first of these uses is referred to as branching. To illustrate, the sentences

(FACT)	GO TO PAY-CALCULATION.
(COMTRAN)	GO TO PAY.CALCULATION.
(COBOL)	GO TO PAY-CALCULATION.

cause the computer to proceed to the paragraph identified as "PAY CALCULATION" before resuming program execution. The sentences

(FACT)	IF HOURS-WORKED IS GREATER THAN 0,
	GO TO PAY-CALCULATION.
(COMTRAN)	IF HOURS.WORKED GT 0 THEN GO TO
	PAY.CALCULATION.
(COBOL)	IF HOURS-WORKED IS GREATER THAN 0
	GO TO PAY-CALCULATION.

cause the same kind of branching, but only if the indicated condition is true. Otherwise, control passes to the next sentence in the normal manner. Note that a special verb is not required for conditional branching; instead the use of an unconditional branch verb is made conditional by the conditional clause construction.

A common requirement in many programs is to make an unconditional branch to one of two or more alternate paragraphs, depending on the value of some computed variable. Such branching is called "n-way" branching and is handled as follows:

(COMTRAN)	GO TO (ROUTINE.A, ROUTINE.B)
	ON INDEX.
(COBOL)	GO TO ROUTINE-A, ROUTINE-B
	DEPENDING ON INDEX.

In both sentences, control will go to ROUTINE A or ROUTINE B according as INDEX has the value 1 or 2.

An equivalent facility is provided in COBOL through the ALTER verb. If paragraph P reads

P. GO TO ROUTINE-A.

then the execution of the sentence

ALTER P TO PROCEED TO ROUTINE-B.

will cause the computer, the next time it encounters paragraph P, to branch unconditionally to ROUTINE-B.

Perhaps the most powerful feature of the recent data processing languages is the facility for calling for, with a very concise sentence, the execution of a procedure of virtually unlimited length and complexity. In general, such procedures may be called for implicitly by some feature of the language; or explicitly by means of special clauses.

The ordinary verbs of the language are, in a sense, a means of calling up implicit procedures, but are not ordinarily viewed as such since their scope, from the standpoint of the programmer, is fairly limited. Some verbs, however have considerable scope and might be viewed as legitimate procedures. For example:

(1) The EXAMINE verb in COBOL scans a specified field from left to right, tallying the number of occurrences of specified characters and/or replacing specified characters with other specified characters. This verb gives editing facility in addition to that built into the MOVE verbs.

(2) The SORT verb in FACT actually performs a full sort of a specified file when encountered in a source program. If feasible, the sentences preceding the sort verb are compiled with the first phase of the sort program while the sentences following the sort verb are compiled with the last phase of the sort program.

(3) The UPDATE verb in FACT creates a program for updating a master file with a detail file. The program contains some 8 undefined procedures, such as "matched-master procedure," "updated-new-master procedure," etc., which are supplied by the programmer using conventional FACT language. The update program automatically provides for the input of master and detail records and the output of updated master records.

However, the programmer has considerable latitude in other phases of the process, and may in fact create any number of error files, report files, etc., simultaneously with updating. Sentences preceding and following the update sentence are used to perform operations which logically precede and follow the updating operation.

(4) The WRITE verb in FACT causes one or more lines of a specified report to be written to a report file. The correspondence between items to be printed and their eventual location and format on the report is established in advance by the programmer through the use of report definition forms. By means of these forms, headings, page numbers, and other indicative information may be conveniently specified, as well as the formation and printing of many levels of totals, including final totals. In general, one WRITE sentence will cause one detail entry (one or more lines) to be written to the report file, plus whatever heading and total lines are triggered by this action. (A similar facility has been suggested for COBOL by Donally [30].)

At least one language (COBOL) permits the programmer to define his own verbs, and use them just as though they were part of the built-in repertoire. Assume, for example, that a procedure repeatedly required the evaluation of the *diminish function* of two arguments X and Y, defined by

$$z = x \ominus y = \begin{cases} x - y & \text{if } x > y \\ 0 & \text{if } x \leq y \end{cases}$$

To save himself some writing, the programmer might define a new verb DIMINISH as follows:

DEFINE DIMINISH WITH FORMAT DIMINISH X BY Y
    GIVING Z.
    MODEL. IF X IS GREATER THAN Y COMPUTE Z = X − Y;
    OTHERWISE MOVE ZERO TO Z.

Now, whenever he requires the diminish operation in his main procedure, for example, to calculate overtime hours, he simply has to write:

DIMINISH HOURS-WORKED BY 40 GIVING OVERTIME-HOURS.

The DEFINE verb in the above example is an illustration of a "compiler-directing" verb. It does not result in any object code which is executed directly, but merely guides the compiler in generating appropriate coding wherever the verb being defined does appear in the main procedure.

A roughly equivalent method for extending the "vocabulary" of the compiler is provided in COMTRAN, by means of a feature which allows the programmer to use arbitrary (single-valued) *functions* wherever data-

11

names can be used. The function is defined as the output of a "dummy" routine:

> DIMINISH.ROUTINE. BEGIN SECTION USING X, Y
> GIVING DIM.
> > IF X IS GREATER THAN Y THEN SET DIM $= $ X $-$ Y
> > OTHERWISE MOVE ZERO TO DIM.
> > END DIMINISH.ROUTINE.

Later in the program, if the programmer wishes to calculate overtime pay, he merely has to write

> SET OVERTIME.PAY $=$
> OVERTIME.RATE $*$ DIM ((HOURS.WORKED, 40)).

By this means the programmer can avoid developing overtime hours explicitly.

Most languages provide a means for explicitly calling for the execution of a procedure which appears elsewhere in the program. This type of call differs from the ordinary transfer of control, in that once the called procedure has been executed, control passes to the next sentence in sequence in the normal fashion. The manner of program linkage is, in fact, entirely analogous to that used with subroutines.

Calls for the execution of procedures are accomplished by certain verbs provided explicitly for this purpose, followed by the name of the procedure to be executed. For example,

> (Fact)   SEE EXCEPTION-PROCEDURE.
> (Comtran) DO EXCEPTION.PROCEDURE.
> (Cobol)   PERFORM EXCEPTION-PROCEDURE.

all cause the computer to execute the EXCEPTION PROCEDURE and then go to the sentence following the call. The group of sentences which can be executed in this manner is limited either to that grammatical unit (sentence, paragraph, section, etc.) which is identified by the specified name, or to an arbitrary group of sentences which are "bracketed" by such words as BEGIN and END. For further flexibility, the languages generally provide for the calling of two or more (usually sequential) groups of sentences by means of sentences such as

> (Fact)   SEE PROCEDURE-A THRU PROCEDURE-K.
> (Cobol) PERFORM PROCEDURE-A THRU
> PROCEDURE-K.

(Comtran does not require this facility since it allows unlimited "nesting" of bracketed sentence groups.)

The utility of a procedure is greatly enhanced if the data it is to operate

12

on and the location of the results it is to produce can be specified in a convenient way in the calling sentence. By this means, the same procedure can be called on from two or more different places, and produce results which are unique to the particular call. For example, suppose that a COMTRAN program contained the DIMINISH. ROUTINE as shown on p. 12. Then the call sentence

> DO DIMINISH.ROUTINE USING HOURS.WORKED, 40
> GIVING OVERTIME.HOURS.

will cause the computer to substitute HOURS WORKED, 40, and OVERTIME HOURS for X, Y, and DIM, respectively, in the diminish routine and then perform the routine. Somewhere else in the program, the sentence

> DO DIMINISH.ROUTINE USING OVERTIME.HOURS, 8
> GIVING DOUBLETIME.HOURS.

will do the same thing, with OVERTIME HOURS, 8, and DOUBLETIME HOURS now replacing X, Y, and DIM.

The final facility provided through the explicit call of procedures is that for *repeating* a procedure a specific number of times. This facility is called *looping*, and is useful when the same procedure is to be used on arrays of data or on data values which are to be incremented or decremented in a systematic manner. For procedures to be used on arrays of data, the language must provide a convenient way for referring uniquely to any data in the array. This is usually done by giving a name to the general item in the array, and by using *subscripts* following this name to refer to a particular item in the array. For example, an input record might contain five occurrences of a field named DAILY-HOURS corresponding to the hours worked by an individual on each of five days in a week. The hours worked on the 3rd day of the week would be referred to as DAILY HOURS (3). To obtain the total hours worked during the week, the following (COBOL) procedure might be used:

> MOVE ZERO TO WEEKLY-HOURS. PERFORM WEEKLY-
> HOURS-CALCULATION VARYING I FROM 1 BY 1 UNTIL
> I = 6. GO TO PAY-CALCULATION.
> WEEKLY-HOURS-CALCULATION. ADD DAILY-HOURS
> (I) TO WEEKLY-HOURS.

The first sentence resets the value of WEEKLY-HOURS to zero. The second sentence causes the paragraph named WEEKLY-HOURS-CALCULATION to be executed repeatedly, the first time with I = 1, the second time with I = 2, and so forth. On each repetition, a value of DAILY-HOURS is accumulated in WEEKLY-HOURS, so that by the time I reaches 6, all five values for the week have been accumulated.

13

2.3 The Trend Toward Standardization

The almost identical facilities provided by current procedural programming languages has been interpreted by some as indicative of the feasibility of developing a universal programming language. This in fact has been the motivation behind the development of COBOL. Judging from the willingness with which computer manufacturers have accepted COBOL as standard software, COBOL is rapidly becoming an effective, if unofficial, standard data processing programming language. According to Promberg [31], as of September 1961 some 12 computer manufacturers were implementing COBOL for 30 different computer systems. Whether or not COBOL best serves the interests of the data processing industry, there can be no doubt that its influence will be felt for many years to come.

As with similar efforts at standardization, COBOL has been the subject of considerable criticism. A principal point of contention seems to be the requirement in COBOL for expressing all parts of a program in free-form restricted English, and the amount of writing this entails. In [32], Hughes points out that in using an English-language compiling system, the programmer must make a conscious effort to restrict himself to "computer English" and he cannot take advantage of the redundancy present in natural languages. As a result, programs are longer than warranted by their information content. Hughes feels that such systems are really sales features for upper management and are not suitable for professional programmers.

Essentially the same view is expressed by Humby [33] in a report on the development of the RAPIDWRITE system at International Computer and Tabulators. (This same work has also been reported by Ellis [34].) ICT is providing with its 1301 and later computers a COBOL processor which accepts not only COBOL 60, but an abbreviated form of COBOL in which environment and data division statements are rendered as tabular entries on pre-printed forms, while procedure division statements are written on IBM cards, one card per statement, containing printed statement types and "noise" words. A processor is then used to reconstruct and print the full COBOL program. The method purports to satisfy both the professional programmer (who writes) and the systems analyst (who reads).

It might be pointed out that most English-language compiler systems other than COBOL use tables for the data division. At least one group, the Systems Group of CODASYL, has proposed the substitution of a tabular data division for the free-form data division in COBOL [59].

In addition to the use of tables in the environment and data divisions, there is at least one instance of their use in the procedure division. In

[35], Longo gives an example of programming for the SURGE system, using a problem coded in COBOL by Mackinson [36]. The SURGE system (for Sort, Update, Report Generate, Etc.) was developed originally as a cooperative venture of IBM 704 users, and has now been implemented for the IBM 709/7090 at General Electric in Evendale. The point of Longo's article is to show how a tabular, or "check-off" form of the procedure division can substantially compress the bulk of a source program. The result is not as readable, but, in Longo's opinion, readability should be secondary to programmer, compiler, and object program efficiency.

Another point of contention is COBOL compatibility, i.e., the ability to compile the same source program on different computers and obtain object programs which produce the same result. The developers of COBOL made explicit recognition of this problem by providing an *environment division* for programs, into which as many as possible of the machine-dependent aspects of a process are collected. Thus, to use a different compiler on a source program, only the environment division need be changed; the data and procedure divisions do not have to be modified.

Despite this objective, some observers are dubious about its practical realization. In particular, Lippitt [37] and Mullin [38] have reported on some of the problems of making COBOL universal and at the same time efficient. Mullin suggests that the only way of achieving this is with an introspective software system which observes object programs as they are run and modifies them to make them more efficient. On the brighter side of the compatibility question, Bromberg [39] reports a successful "live" demonstration of COBOL compatibility, using UNIVAC COBOL and RCA 501 COBOL Narrator on identical problems.

One British view of COBOL, which is critical, has been reported in the *Computer Bulletin* [40] and in Volume 2 of *Automatic Programming* [41]. The latter reference also contains an instructive comparison of FACT with COMTRAN and COBOL [42].

Instead of pointing out the deficiencies in existing procedural languages, some investigators have taken the more positive approach of specifying what a good procedural language should consist of. Perhaps the earliest of these is a checklist by Bemer [43]. A similar list is given in the Comment Section of *Data Processing Digest* [44]. In a recent article [45], Cantrell proposes various criteria for programming languages and compilers, and reports on how well current languages, particularly COBOL and ALGOL, · measure up to these criteria.

3. Nonprocedural Programming Language

Despite their prevalence and unquestioned utility, procedural programming languages have been subjected in the past few years to increasing criticism. In [46, 47], Lombardi cites the following shortcomings of procedural languages:

(1) Procedural programming requires the specification of detailed procedure which in most cases could just as well be left to the compiler. In certain arithmetic processes, detailed procedures are critical to the success of the application (e.g., to insure convergence, or control round-off error) and are better left to the programmer. In other applications, and particularly in data processing applications, such detailed procedures can be supplied just as effectively and much more efficiently by the compiler.

(2) In procedural programming, the detailed definition of a process is implicit in a procedure, and is not easily reconstructed once the initial thought processes which went into the procedure have been forgotten. The spectacle of trying to reconstruct, for example, certain payroll practices from a dump of the payroll program is one that is all too familiar.

(3) In procedural languages, input-output operations are controlled, directly or indirectly, by explicit statements. As a result, the compiler often cannot make efficient use of the central processor and/or the input-output devices. By removing the constraint imposed on the compiler by the appearance of explicit input-output statements, the compiler might be able to produce more efficient programs.

In addition to the above, it is Lombardi's contention that a procedural statement of a process is unavoidably influenced by the agency which carries out the procedure, i.e., by the computer. From this he concludes that a universal programming language cannot possibly be a procedural programming language.

In answer to these shortcomings, a number of *nonprocedural* programming languages have appeared in recent years. Some of these languages have actually been implemented, others are just proposals. In contrast with the procedural languages, which are beginning to fall into a definite pattern, the nonprocedural languages each seem to approach the problem in a basically different way. The following sections give some examples of nonprocedural programming, and describe some specific nonprocedural languages.

3.1 Nonprocedural Aspects of Procedural Languages

In most programming languages which are nominally procedural, there are nonprocedural elements present to varying degrees. A good illustration is the formula or arithmetic expression which is allowed in assignment-type statements of procedural languages, such as

$$(\text{COMTRAN}) \qquad \text{SET A} = (\text{B} + \text{C}) * \text{D}$$

In such statements, the procedure by which the value of the expression on the right hand side of the equals sign is to be obtained is not stated

16

explicitly; rather, it is inferred by the rules of ordinary algebra. An extension of this idea, which is used in ALGOL, is to make the evaluation of the right hand side conditional. In a data processing language this might take the form

SET Z = IF X GT Y THEN X — Y OTHERWISE 0.

An even more compact representation is proposed by Lombardi [48]:

$$Z \leftarrow (X - Y)[X > Y], 0[X \leq Y]$$

where the bracketed expressions are conditions to be met before the associated unbracketed expression is used in the computation.

Another example of non-procedural elements in a procedural language is the provision for looping. The COBOL sentence

PERFORM WEEKLY-HOURS-CALCULATION VARYING I
FROM 1 BY 1 UNTIL I = 6.

does not describe explicitly how the looping is to be done. Instead, the procedure is determined by certain conventions adopted by the compiler implementer. In COBOL, for example, the previous sentence is interpreted as being equivalent to the following set of sentences, in which the looping procedure is explicit:

```
              MOVE 1 to I.
   LOOP.      IF I = 6, GO TO EXIT.
              PERFORM WEEKLY-HOURS-CALCULATION.
              COMPUTE I FROM I + 1.
              GO TO LOOP.
   EXIT.      (Next Sentence)
```

In a procedural language, any verb or statement which results in a sequence of computer instructions whose correspondence to elements in the statement is not simple might be viewed as a nonprocedural element. In many cases their distinction is neither clear nor useful, but in a few cases it is. Cases in point are the complex procedures called up certain built-in verbs, such as SORT and UPDATE in FACT. These procedures are usually so extensive that they dominate the entire program, and in a sense these programs become more non-procedural then procedural.

3.2 Generalized Data Processing Routines and 9PAC

It has been recognized for some time that conventional data processing applications can be synthesized from a small number of generalized data processing routines. The most prominent of such routines is the generalized sort routine which is capable of sorting any file (within broad limitations) on the basis of parameters which are supplied to it. Gen-

17

eralized sort routines have been developed by virtually all manufacturers of data processing equipment and used by virtually all users of such equipment.

The notion of generalizing other data processing operations was apparently first put into practice at General Electric's Hanford Atomic Products Operation [49, 50], where generalized routines were developed for *file maintenance* and *report generation*. These routines were later taken over by the SHARE users' organization, where they are now known as the SHARE 7090 9PAC System [51].

The 9PAC System consists of two generating routines: the file processor and the reports generator. Both routines accept parameters supplied by the programmer defining the particular process to be carried out, and generate an equivalent object program which carries out this process. Generated programs may be executed immediately, or they may be saved for use at a later time.

The principal function of the file processor is to generate object programs for the updating of a magnetic tape master file. In addition to the master file, one or more files of "change data" may be input to the object program for purposes of updating the master file. Changes to the file may take the form of insertion of new records, deletion of existing records, and modification of existing records. Output consists of the updated master file; an optional *activity file* reflecting changes made to the file; and an *error file* reflecting erroneous data and errors in the programmer's specifications.

Processing is controlled by means of parameters supplied by the programmer. Parameters are entered on standard tabular forms and are keypunched into "change packets." To accommodate varying operational requirements, three types of change packets are provided.

(1) The *vertical* change packet may be used to delete master file records according to a constant criteria, or to make uniform changes to selected master file records. In the latter case, the change data is carried in the packet itself.

(2) The *update* change packet is used to insert, delete, or modify master file records of a given type on the basis of records in a specified change file. Provision is made for selecting records of a given type in the change file, and for verifying the data in the change file before applying a given change file record to the master file.

(3) The *horizontal* change packet serves the same function as the update change packet, except that the change file records may contain, in addition to the change data, the identification of the master file record field to be changed and the type of change to be made. The horizontal change is useful for handling small-volume, miscellaneous changes to a master file.

For a given processing, any number of packets of the above types may

18

be used. Each packet carries a "priority number" which determines the order in which the packets will be applied when they affect the same master record. Thus, an update change packet with priority 01 and action code I (for insert) will insert a record from a given change file when the key in the latter is "low" relative to the master file. A horizontal change packet with priority 02 and action code M (for modify) will modify master records whose keys match those in records in a second change file. The packet will also modify matching master records inserted by the priority 01 packet, since it carries priority 02 and is thus applied after the priority 01 packet. In general, the basic cycle consists of

(1) determining if any of the current records from the change files match the current master record;

(2) if not, applying any relevant vertical packets, writing the current master record, and reading the next master record;

(3) if one or more matches, processing the packets which correspond to the matching change files, in packet priority order, and reading the next change records from these files.

Other features of the file processor include provision for generating change report file records under the control of each change packet; provision for changing the dictionary of the master file and making the corresponding changes in the master file itself as the processing proceeds; and provision for creating a new master file from one or more detail files.

The reports generator generates object programs which will produce printed reports and magnetic tape files for subsequent processing. Files of arbitrary format may be input to the object program, although special facilities are provided for addressing fields within files having 9PAC-type dictionaries (e.g., updated master files and change report files from file processor runs).

Output from the report generator object program is one or more magnetic tape files which may then be used for off-line punching or printing or for subsequent computer processing. Each output report file is specified by a parameter packet which defines the various types of lines to appear on the printed report, the input file quantities which are to be placed in these lines, and their position and punctuation. One or more fields of the input file may be designated as control break fields at any of up to nine levels, so that when the values of these fields change, the associated total lines will be issued. Output record files for subsequent computer processing are defined by similar parameter packets.

The essence of the generalized routines is that they in effect transform a general purpose computer into a special-purpose computer whose parameters are set by the user. The utility of such special-purpose computers was recognized even before the generalized routines came into being. Canning [52] has suggested the desirability of a special purpose "electronic

19

sorter" with the ability to compare selected portion of records from two or more input magnetic tape files, and to distribute these records to two or more output files according to the results of the comparisons. A common use for such a device is sorting by merging. Another common use, illustrated in Fig. 1, is the simultaneous merging of two master files, and the

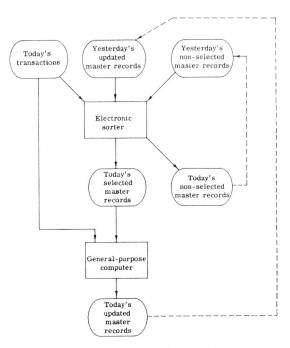

Fig. 1. Simultaneous merge-extract with a special-purpose computer.

extraction from the merged file of records which match records in a transaction file. The extracted master records are then input to a general-purpose computer for updating, and in the next cycle are merged back into the main master file. The intent of this procedure is to reduce the number of master records which must be processed by the general purpose computer, which is presumably much more expensive than the electronic sorter. Two examples of special purpose devices of this type are the Bizmac Sorter and the Elecom File Processor, described by Gotlieb and Hume in [4].

A weakness which is shared by the generalized routines and the special-purpose processors, and which may explain why the latter at least have not become more popular, is that they are too specialized and cannot be used more flexibly. This weakness is overcome to some extent in the generalized routines through the provision for the programmer to insert

20

hand-written code at strategic points in the program created by the generator. By such means the programmer is able to specify special processing (e.g., input editing) which is not provided by the generator. (The provision for hand-written code is an essential feature of the UPDATE technique in the FACT system—see Section 2.2.)

A more restrictive shortcoming lies in the *structure* of the generated program. In most applications, processing is limited by magnetic tape transfer rates and it is therefore important to do as much as possible with the data on tape as it passes through the computer. The generalized routines are limited, for practical reasons, in the variety of structures which can be generated, and they may not be able to generate programs which utilize magnetic tape data as efficiently as hand-coded structure. As a result, two or more passes may be required using generalized routines where a single pass may suffice with hand-coded routines. This in itself does not mean that generalized routines are inferior, since the effort required to use them is substantially less than that to prepare hand-coded routines. In certain situations, the consequent savings in programming time may offset the loss of machine time.

3.3 Logic Tables and DETAB-X

Data processing procedures are characterized by the conditional nature of the steps to be carried out: the validity of an input field is conditional upon its containing all numeric characters; the disposition of an input record is conditional on the type code that it contains; the format of an output line is dependent on its position on the page; and so forth. While such conditions individually are not complicated, they are generally strung together in such long chains that the correspondence between an action and the condition upon which it is contingent is often difficult to trace in a flow chart or a procedural program. In an attempt to solve this problem, the Manufacturing Services group of General Electric Company devised the TABSOL method [53, 54] of expressing the logic of decision making in tabular form. Essentially the same technique was developed by the Large Steam Turbine-Generator Department of General Electric under the name of LOGTAB [55], and TABSOL is currently being implemented by the GE Computer Department for integration into its compiler for the GE 225 [56]. Other descriptions and uses of the logic table technique are given in [57, 58].

The major current effort in logic tables is being conducted by the Systems Group of CODASYL (Conference on Data Systems Languages). This group has developed a version of logic tables called DETAB-X [59] and is proposing that the facility be incorporated in the next version of COBOL. For this reason it may be well to explore the logic table concept (using DETAB-X as a model) and how it relates to a procedural language like COBOL.

21

A procedure expressed in DETAB-X is a set of rules of carrying out certain actions. A rule is expressed as a set of actions together with a set of conditions which must all be satisfied before the actions of that rule are carried out. Conditions, in turn, are based on the variables of the process. The logic table technique takes advantage of the fact that in many processes, the variables or conditions on which one rule is based will also be relevant to other rules. Similarly, certain of the individual actions will be shared by different rules. The logic table permits this logic to be displayed in a compact, systematic way.

The configuration[1] of a DETAB-X logic table is shown in Fig. 2. The right-hand portion of the table is divided into columns, one column for

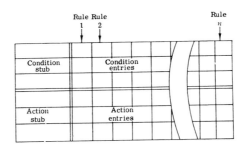

FIG. 2. DETAB-X logic table.

each rule. The conditions for the rule are entered in the upper part of the columns, while the actions are entered in the lower part. The condition stub and action stub are used for entering the "common" parts of conditions and actions, respectively.

Two types of condition entries are allowed. In the *limited entry*, the entire condition is expressed in the condition stub, and the entry consists merely of Y (for take the condition as is); N (for negate the condition before testing); or hyphen or blank (meaning ignore this condition). Conditions are written in COBOL. For example, if AGE is a data-name and PROGRAMMER is a condition-name, two condition entries might appear as follows:

	1	2
AGE GT 25	N	Y
PROGRAMMER	N	—

---

[1] An alternate arrangement is sometimes used in which rules are written in horizontal rows with conditions in the left part of the row, actions in the right part, and corresponding stubs above. See for example [54].

Rule 1 is followed if AGE is not greater than 25 and the variable with associated condition-name PROGRAMMER is not set to PROGRAMMER. Rule 2 is followed simply if AGE is greater than 25.

In the *extended entry*, part of the condition (the first operand or the first operand and a relational operator) is written in the stub and the remainder is written in the entry proper. For example:

	1	2
AGE	LE 25	GT 25
SEX EQ	M	F

Rule 1 applies if AGE is less or equal to 25 and SEX is male. Rule 2 applies if AGE is greater than 25 and SEX is female.

Action entries may similarly be of limited or extended form. In limited form, the entire action is written in the action stub, and the entry consists merely of X (meaning perform this action if the rule applies); or hyphen or blank (meaning do not perform this action if the rule applies). Again, actions are expressed as COBOL statements:

	1	2
AGE	LE 25	GT 25
SEX EQ	M	F
DO TAB 030	X	—
SET PREM EQ	1.5	1.3

In this example, the first action is a limited entry, causing a return-jump to TAB 030 if rule 1 applies. The second action is an extended entry in which the variable PREM is set to 1.5 or 1.3 according as rule 1 or rule 2 applies.

The proposed method of incorporating logic tables into a COBOL source program is to permit the use of tables where conventional COBOL paragraphs would normally be used. Tables are given names in the same way as paragraphs, and may be entered from GO TO or PERFORM statements. When in a table a rule is encountered which applies, the action statements of that rule are executed in the order listed. Among these statements must be one which causes control to leave the table; or, alternatively, a single statement of this type may be provided for all rules. In addition, an "exception exit" may be specified in case none of the rules in the table applies.

Taken by itself, the logic table is a form of nonprocedural programming, since the procedure by which the computer tests conditions and finds whether they are "true" is not specified by the programmer; rather, it is

23

supplied by the compiler which converts logic tables into machine code. This aspect of logic tables accounts for at least one of their advantages over procedural languages, namely, that the detailed definition of at least a portion of the process has been made explicit. Other advantages commonly cited are that the method "forces" the analyst to make a complete and accurate statement of the problem; that errors are easily detected and corrected; and that the language is amenable to mechanization. On the negative side, it has been observed that tables are sometimes awkward to prepare. Further, the definition of a process in table form usually contains many redundancies, and unless these can be removed by the compiler, the resulting object code will use storage space extravagantly. Perhaps most significantly, however, the conciseness and completeness of the method can prove to be a disadvantage to the unwary programmer, since he is required to grasp the entire procedure much earlier than he is accustomed to with conventional flow charting. Eventually, this characteristic of logic tables may prove to be their biggest advantage.

3.4 The Algebraic Data System Language

In [48], Lombardi proposes a nonprocedural language called the Algebraic Data System Language. The language borrows heavily from the notation of ALGOL, and provides three main facilities: (1) means for expressing general data manipulation, an example of which was given in Section 3.1; (2) means for describing *tables*, and for specifying operations on tables (this work is treated more fully in [60]); and (3) a means for expressing the rules by which the flow of data through a computer is to be controlled by an object program. The latter facility is a result of Lombardi's observation that data processing problems should be specified directly in terms of their "issues," rather than in terms of the procedure by which these issues are produced. The technique is sufficiently different that it is worthwhile describing at least its essential features.

Lombardi conceives of a data processing program as consisting, in part, of a set of *flow control expressions*, one or more for each file to be created. Flow control expressions take the form

$$A[E]$$

where A is the name of an output file, and E is a Boolean expression having at any moment the value *true* or *false*. Processing is visualized as occurring in a series of *pulses*, such that on each pulse, records are entered from input files according to a standard scheme, the flow control expressions are scanned, and for each expression which is "true" a record is issued to the corresponding output file. The process assumes that the input files are *equi-ordered* (i.e., use the same data type for key), and that the records in each input file are in order on this key. A sequence of one or more pulses in which all input records and output records having the same key are

24

processed is called a *phase*. By properly stating the conditions under which output records are to be issued, the programmer can specify the order in which records are written to output files. The *content* of these records is presumably specified elsewhere in the program.

To facilitate the statement of conditions under which output records are issued, a number of *binary indicators* are postulated for each input and each output file. Principal among these are the existence indicator, the input/output indicator, the left indicator, and the right indicator, defined as follows:

Indicator	Input file	Output file
Existence	At least one record has been entered in the current phase	At least one record has been issued in the current phase
Input/Output	A record has been entered on the current pulse	A record will be issued on the current pulse
Left	The first of one or more records with identical keys has been entered on the current pulse	The first of one or more records with identical keys will be issued on the current pulse
Right	The last of one or more records with identical keys has been entered on the current pulse	The last of one or more records with identical keys will be issued on the current pulse

These indicators may be referred to in the flow control expressions. For example, if a record is to be issued to output file OF only if a record was entered from input file IF on a given pulse, the flow control expression for OF would be

$$\text{OF} \left[\text{IF} \& \text{I} \right]$$

where IF & I denotes the input indicator for file IF.

Indicators for input files are set during the automatic input procedure at the beginning of each pulse. On the first pulse of a phase, the lowest of the keys of the next-in-line records of each input file is determined and set into a current key register (CKR). A single record is then entered from each file whose next-in-line record has a key equal to the CKR. On each subsequent pulse of the phase, a single record is entered from the file having the highest *logical order* (specified by the programmer), and whose next-in-line record still matches the CKR. Thus, if input file A precedes input file B in logical order, and both files have multiple records with the same key, a record from each of A and B will be entered on the first pulse of the phase; then all remaining A records with the same key; then all remaining B records with the same key. Whenever a record is entered, the existence and input indicators for the corresponding file are set to 1; if a record is

25

not entered on a given pulse, the input indicator is set to 0 but the existence indicator is not changed. In addition, if a record entered is the *first* of one or more records in the same file having identical keys, the *left* indicator is set to 1; otherwise it is set to zero. Similarly, the *right* indicator is set to 1 when the *last* of one or more such records is entered.

Once the input file indicators have been set, the flow control expressions are scanned and the output file indicators are set. Expressions are scanned in the programmer-specified logical order of the corresponding output files. If two or more expressions refer to the same file, they are scanned in order of appearance. If an expression is true, the output and existence indicators for the corresponding output file are set to 1. In addition, the left or right indicator for this file is set to 1 if the record to be issued to this file is the first or last to be issued in the current phase. If an expression is false, the output indicator is set to zero and the remaining indicators are unchanged. When all expressions have been determined to be true or false, records are issued to those files whose output indicators are set to 1.

In general, the condition in a flow control expression will be a function of the output file indicators as well as the input file indicators. This means that the flow control expressions must in general be scanned repeatedly until no further conditions are found to be true, since the condition in one expression may depend on some later condition being true or false. Obviously, impasses of the form "After you, Alphonse," "No, after *you*, dear Gaston" may inadvertently be specified by the programmer and have to be detected by the compiler.

The use of flow control expressions may be illustrated by deriving expressions appropriate for the simultaneous merge-extract process of Fig. 1 (Section 3.2). In this process, an old selected master file (OSM) is to be merged with an old master file (OM), and any records in the merged file with keys matching records in a transaction file (T) are copied to a new selected master file (NSM). Any unmatched records in the merged files are to be copied to a new master file (NM). For simplicity, we will assume that OSM and OM have no records with matching keys, and that neither contains records with duplicate keys. However, T may have records with duplicate keys, and may have records for which there are no matching records in either OSM or OM. A third output file (ER) will be created to hold matched transaction records with duplicate keys and unmatched transaction records.

The flow control expressions for this process are as follows:

NM [(OM & E OR OSM & E) AND NOT T & E]
NSM [(OM & E OR OSM & E) AND T & L]
ER [(NOT OM & E AND NOT OSM & E) OR NOT T & L]

The first of these expressions states that a new master record will be issued on any pulse during which an old master record or an old selected master record "exists" *and* a transaction record does not exist. The second expression is similar, except that a new selected master record is issued only when the matching transaction record is the first of one or more such records in a phase (T & L = 1). Finally error records are issued when neither an old master record nor an old selected master record exists (unmatched transaction), or when a duplicate transaction is discovered (T & L = 0).

The flow control expression technique is noteworthy because it permits a very compact and precise expression of a significant and often hard-to-express portion of a file processing procedure. The technique is similar to that of the 9PAC routines and the UPDATE function in FACT, in that a conceptual model of a computer is used as the basis for stating processes. Unlike 9PAC and FACT, however, the model is quite general, requiring only that files be placed in logical order; no special significance is attached to the fact that one input file and one output file are master files, except insofar as the programmer wishes to attach such significance. The technique is therefore capable of expressing a wide variety of processes on a single pass of the input files.

The flow control expression technique borrows from logic tables the notion of actions which are based on explicitly stated conditions. Instead of being expressed in tabular form, however, decision rules are stated in a form similar to Boolean algebra, hence are considerably more compact.

4. Data Organization and Description Methods

Perhaps the most distinguishing feature of data processing applications is the character of the data to be processed. Unlike numerical applications, whose data can be conveniently represented in a small number of standard forms, data processing applications must contend with data which has many forms. The principal reason for this is the prominent role which people play in data-handling systems. While it might in principle be possible to code all data into a small number of standard forms, to do so would place an unreasonable burden on the people who prepare data for input to the computer and who interpret data output from the computer. Instead, the computer is called upon either to process and output data in the form in which it is input, or else to convert input data to a more convenient form for processing and then reconvert it before output. These functions place special requirements on the computer, and account in part for the evolution of the so-called "business data processors" whose chief characteristic is their ability to process arbitrary-length strings of 6-bit "characters."

Data processing applications must also contend with highly elaborate data *structures*. This characteristic stems from the fact that there are normally very large amounts of data flowing through the computer, and that the data often must be organized in a special manner in order to achieve reasonable processing efficiency. The result is data structures which require special techniques to describe and process.

The following sections summarize the facilities which have been provided in recent programming languages for organizing and describing the data of data processing applications.

4.1 Elementary Items

Elementary items of data are strings of "particles" (characters, digits, etc.) which are always referred to in a program as integral units, i.e., which do not have to be referred to in terms of their component particles. An elementary item is normally the *value* of some characteristic or *property;* thus 123.45 might be the value of the property *weekly salary.* An elementary item is referred to in a program by means of a *name* which is assigned to the corresponding property. Thus, if the name WEEKLY-SALARY is assigned to the property *weekly salary,* then values of weekly salary are referred to by statements of the type

ADD WEEKLY-SALARY. . . .

Note that such references do not mean "add the property named WEEKLY-SALARY," which would be meaningless; but rather, "add the value currently associated with the property named WEEKLY-SALARY." This semantic hair-splitting is generally of no concern in the so-called problem-oriented languages, but can be essential in programming languages where property names become synonymous with memory addresses and operations on addresses are required.

The association of names with properties is one of two principal functions of the *data division* of a program. The other principal function is to define the form or forms which values of properties can assume. Most data description techniques provide for describing elementary items in terms of the following characteristics:

> *Class* (alphabetic, numeric, alphanumeric)
> *Size* (number of characters or digits)
> *Sign* (signed or unsigned)
> *Justification* (left or right)
> *Position of Assumed Decimal Point* (for automatic scaling)
> *Synchronization* (correspondence between item value and computer words)
> *Punctuation* (position of editing symbols, etc.)

In COBOL, an entry in the data division might appear as follows:

> WEEKLY-SALARY; SIZE IS 5 DIGITS; SYNCHRONIZED
> RIGHT; POINT LOCATION IS LEFT 2 PLACES; CLASS
> IS NUMERIC.

From such information, the compiler is able to reserve space for the item in computer memory when the compiled program is run, and to generate the machine instructions required to manipulate the item correctly.

The assignment of names to elementary items provides a facility for referring to these items individually. In addition, it is frequently desirable to be able to refer to a *group* of elementary items with a single name. For example, it may be desired to group the elementary items MONTH, DAY, and YEAR and refer to them collectively as DATE. Similarly, it may be desired to group DATE with other groups and/or elementary items and refer to them collectively as PAY RECORD. In some languages, the number of levels at which data may be named is arbitrarily fixed; for example, 9PAC provides four levels of naming: sub-field, field, record, and file. In other languages such as COMTRAN and COBOL, an effectively unlimited number of levels may be used, up to the level of the *logical record*. A similar facility exists in FACT, except that levels may be used up to the level of the *file*.

The level at which a name is defined must be indicated to the compiler. In some systems this is done by listing names in outline form, with level indicated by degree of indentation. In other systems, names are given explicit *level numbers*. For example, three levels of naming would be indicated in COBOL as follows (indentation is for readability only):

01 PAY-RECORD.
   02 NAME; CLASS IS ALPHABETIC.
      03 FIRST-INITIAL; SIZE IS 1 CHARACTER.
      03 MIDDLE-INITIAL; SIZE IS 1 CHARACTER.
      03 LAST-NAME; SIZE IS 15 CHARACTERS.

   02 DATE; CLASS IS NUMERIC.
      03 MONTH; SIZE IS 2 CHARACTERS.
      03 DAY; SIZE IS 2 CHARACTERS.
      03 YEAR; SIZE IS 2 CHARACTERS.

The facility for naming data at different levels provides a simple way of referring unambiguously to different items even though they have the same name. All that is required is that such items belong to groups which have unique names at some level. The technique is called *name qualification* and consists of preceding or following the given data name with the names of its higher level groups until the entire name is made unique. Thus, if DATE appears in both PAY RECORD and UPDATED PAY RECORD, the phrases

(FACT)   PAY-RECORD DATE
(COMTRAN)   PAY.RECORD DATE
(COBOL)   DATE IN PAY-RECORD

may be used to indicate that the DATE desired is the one in PAY RECORD, not the one in UPDATED PAY RECORD.

4.2 Rectangular Arrays

In Section 2.2 it was pointed out that procedural languages often provide facility for repeating the execution of a procedure a specified number of times (i.e., the facility for looping). Such a facility will generally be meaningful only if different data values are used or created on each repetition of the procedure. One way of achieving this is to store all of the data values to be used or generated in the procedure in some systematic way in the computer, and to indicate to the compiler that it is to generate machine instructions which will step systematically through the different data locations on successive repetitions of the procedure. The data structures required for this purpose are known generally as *rectangular arrays*, and the technique of stepping through successive data location is called *indexing*.

A rectangular array may be viewed as a set of data strings of identical length. Each string contains, in the same relative position, the data values of one or more properties which we may call *array properties*. In addition, with each string is associated a value for each of n *dimension properties*, these values being determined by the *position* of the string in the set of strings.

To illustrate, suppose a list is to be stored which contains the number of employees and overhead rate in each of seven labor categories (1 through 7) within each of three departments (1 through 3):

	Number of employees	Overhead rate	
	XXXX	XXX	(labor category 1)
	XXXX	XXX	(labor category 2)
(Department 1)	.	.	
	.	.	
	.	.	
	XXXX	XXX	(labor category 7)
	XXXX	XXX	(labor category 1)
(Department 2)	.		
	.		(etc.)
	XXXX	XXX	
	XXXX	XXX	
(Department 3)	.		
	.		
	XXXX	XXX	

This list may be regarded as a 2-dimensional rectangular array, in which *number of employees* and *overhead rate* are the array properties and *department number* and *labor category* code are the dimension properties. Note that values of the dimension properties do not appear explicitly in the list; instead, they are implied by the position of an item in the list.

Rectangular arrays are defined in the data division of a program by assigning a name and form to each of the array properties, as in the definition of elementary items; by assigning a name at a higher level to the group of elementary items; by assigning a name at a still higher level to the group of the first groups; and so forth. Each higher level of naming corresponds to a different dimension property, and is accompanied by an indication of the number of different values which the dimension property can assume. In COBOL, the previous array might be defined as follows:

01 TABLE
    02 DEPARTMENT-ENTRY; OCCURS 3 TIMES.
        03 LABOR-CATEGORY-ENTRY; OCCURS 7
           TIMES.
           04 NUMBER-OF-EMPLOYEES; SIZE IS 4
               CHARACTERS; CLASS IS NUMERIC.
           04 OVERHEAD-RATE; SIZE IS 3 CHARAC-
               TERS; CLASS IS NUMERIC.

The number of dimensions which a rectangular array may have is usually limited to 3.

A particular value in an array is referred to in a program by giving the name of the corresponding array property; and by indicating, usually with *subscripts*, the values of the dimension properties corresponding to the particular value sought. Thus, the number of employees in labor category 7 in department 2 would be referred to in a COBOL procedure as

NUMBER-OF-EMPLOYEES (2, 7)

When array values are to be used in a repeated procedure, arbitrary names may be used for subscripts to denote a "general" array value. These same names are then used in the statement which initializes, tests, and increments subscript values. For example, to obtain the total number of employees represented in the previous list, the following COBOL procedure could be used:

MOVE ZERO TO TOTAL-EMPLOYEES. PERFORM EMPLOYEE-
COUNT-ROUTINE VARYING DEPARTMENT FROM 1 BY 1
UNTIL DEPARTMENT = 4 AFTER LABOR-CATEGORY FROM
1 BY 1 UNTIL LABOR-CATEGORY = 8. GO TO NEXT-STEP.
EMPLOYEE-COUNT-ROUTINE. ADD NUMBER-OF-EMPLOYEES
(DEPARTMENT, LABOR-CATEGORY) TO TOTAL-EMPLOYEES.

Note that the higher-level names used to define a rectangular array are not required in referring to individual array values (except when qualification is necessary). They may be used, however, to refer to groups of array values, to groups of these groups, and so forth. To move all the array values corresponding to department 2, for example, the following statement could be used:

MOVE DEPARTMENT-ENTRY (2). . . .

4.3 Trees

An important characteristic of the rectangular array is that a string of array property values of the same length and format must be present for every combination of dimension property values. There are two situations where this characteristic can result in wasted space. The first situation occurs when one or more of the array properties have the same value in every string corresponding to a given dimension property value. For example, if *department name* were included in the previous list:

	Depart- ment name	Number of employees	Overhead rate	
	XXX	XXXX	XXX	(labor category 1)
	XXX	XXXX	XXX	
(Department 1)	.			.
	.			.
	.			.
	.			.

then it is apparent that the value of *department name* will be the same in every string for department 1, the same for every string in department 2, and so forth. This array is wasteful of space because it contains *redundant* data.

The second situation occurs when one or more array properties are not *relevant* for all combinations of dimension property values. Suppose, for example, that department 1 did not have a labor category 2. Obviously nothing meaningful can be supplied as values for *number of employees* and *overhead rate* in the string corresponding to these dimension property values; nor is it permissible to omit entering anything for these values, since otherwise the procedure for locating other array values would "get out of step." Instead it is customary to enter some "null" representation (such as blanks) for these values:

32

Depart- ment name	Number of employees	Overhead rate	
XXX	XXXX	XXX	(labor category 1)
XXX	(blanks)		(labor category 2)
XXX	XXXX	XXX	.
.		.	
.		.	
.		.	
.		.	

(Department 1)

Again, this array is wasteful of space because the null representation takes more space than actually required to indicate the nonrelevance of the array values.

If a rectangular array contains many redundant data values, or many null representations of data values, a good deal of storage can be wasted. A more economical means of storing the equivalent data is the *tree structure*. In [61], McGee gives a general procedure for organizing data into a tree structure. This procedure consists of (1) grouping properties into classes such that the relevance of any property in a class implies the relevance of all other properties in that class; and (2) deriving dependence relationships among the classes such that one class is dependent on another if the relevance of the former implies the relevance of the latter. To illustrate, the properties *department number, department name, labor category, number of employees*, and *overhead rate* of the previous example might be grouped into two classes, as follows:

Class 1:   department number, department name
Class 2:   labor category, number of employees, overhead rate

where the indentation of Class 2 denotes its dependence on Class 1. Class 1 is called the *parent class* of Class 2.

A number of schemes may be used for storing tree structures in a computer. Perhaps the simplest is the one governed by the following rules:

(i)   Occurrences of a given class always follow an occurrence of their parent class.

(ii) Occurrences of a given class follow their parent in order of the value of one or more "identification" properties in the given class.

(iii) Occurrences of two or more different classes of the same level follow their parent in an arbitrary but fixed order.

33

If we assume for the moment that all seven labor categories are relevant to each of the three departments in the example, the application of the above rules results in the following structure:

De- part- ment number	De- part- ment name	Labor cate- gory	Number of em- ployees	Over- head rate	
X	XXX	X	XXXX	XXX	(labor category 1)
		X	XXXX	XXX	(labor category 2)
			.		.
			.		.
			.		.
			.		.
		X	XXXX	XXX	(labor category 7)
X	XXX	X	XXXX	XXX	(labor category 1)
			.		.
			.		.
			.	etc.	.

(Department 1) brackets the first group; (Department 2) brackets the second group.

This tree is an example of a class of trees in which the structure of the data below each instance of a repeated class is identical. (Note that seven instances of class 2 follow each instance of class 1.) In [62], Hoffman describes a technique for storing such trees in computer memory and for referring to items in the tree. In Hoffman's method, the above tree would be defined by the expression

CLASS-1 (3, DEPARTMENT-NUMBER (1), DEPARTMENT-NAME (3),
CLASS-2 (7, LABOR-CATEGORY (1), NUMBER-OF-
EMPLOYEES (4), OVERHEAD-RATE (3)))

in which the first integer within paired parentheses denotes the number of occurrences of the class defined by the remaining names within the same parentheses; and the integer following a property name is the number of data "particles" in the corresponding property value. Individual data values are then referred to by a sequence of n expressions of the form

(class name, occurrence number)

where n is the level of the class in which the referenced value resides; followed by the name of the property whose value is sought. Thus, the value of *department name* for department 1 would be referred to by

(CLASS-1, 1), DEPARTMENT-NAME

34

while the overhead rate for labor category 7 within department 2 would be referred to by

$$(\text{CLASS-1, 2}), (\text{CLASS-2, 7}), \text{OVERHEAD-RATE}$$

Hoffman gives an algorithm for calculating the address of a data value from its reference expression, and shows how the corresponding algorithm for locating values in a rectangular array can be produced as a special case of the general algorithm. As might be expected, the general algorithm is considerably more complicated than the special one.

The above tree illustrates how a tree structure may be used to eliminate redundancy. Tree structures may also be used to eliminate null representations, simply by omitting occurrences of classes which are not relevant. Suppose for example, that the departments had relevant labor categories as follows:

Department	Relevant Labor Categories
1	1, 2, 4
2	3, 6
3	2, 5, 7

The tree would now take the following form:

	De- part- ment number	De- part- ment name	Labor cate- gory	Number of em- ployees	Over- head rates	
(Depart- ment 1)	X	XXX	X X X	XXXX XXXX XXXX	XXX XXX XXX	(labor category 1) (labor category 2) (labor category 4)
(Depart- ment 2)	X	XXX	X X	XXXX XXXX	XXX XXX	(labor category 3) (labor category 6)
(Depart- ment 3)	X	XXX	X X X	XXXX XXXX XXXX	XXX XXX XXX	(labor category 2) (labor category 5) (labor category 7)

Note that any "regularity" which was previously present in the tree is now gone. In general this means that it is not possible to develop an algorithm for calculating the address of an arbitrary item in the tree. Instead, items may generally be located only be scanning the tree, which in turn implies that each occurrence of a class in the tree be explicitly identified.

35

Tree structures can be considerably more complicated than the one illustrated, but the difference between the tree structure and the rectangular array is readily apparent. In tree structures, data may appear at any level, while in rectangular arrays data may appear only at one level even if redundant data values must be used. In tree structures, data values may be omitted if they are not relevant, whereas in rectangular arrays, some representation of irrelevant data must be present. Tree structures thus conserve space, but at the price of more complicated procedure for referring to arbitrary data items.

None of the recent data processing languages provides for defining and referring to trees which are stored in random access memory, perhaps because it is felt that the increase in processing time required to refer randomly to values in a tree outweighs any space saving which the tree achieves. If the tree can be processed *sequentially*, however, the access problem is virtually non-existent and the case for the tree structure is much stronger. The classic example of sequential data processing, of course, is the processing of files which are too large to be accommodated in random access memory, and which are consequently recorded on a serial-access medium such as magnetic tape. Like internal data arrays, files on magnetic tape can be structured as trees. Not only can this result in a substantial saving in tape, but, more significantly, in a substantial saving in tape processing time.

The facilities in recent languages for handling files which are structured as trees are varied. Both COMTRAN and COBOL, for example, provide facility for defining logical *records* which are defined in a procedural sense as that unit of information which is taken from an input file or released to an output file with read verbs and write verbs, respectively. Facility is provided, as noted earlier, for defining rectangular arrays *within* such logical records, but no facility is provided for imposing on files a logical grouping more comprehensive than the record. This is not to say that files organized as tree structures cannot be processed with these languages, but simply that it is the responsibility of the programmer to state explicitly the processing logic which such a structure implies.

The FACT system and the 9PAC system, on the other hand, permit a file to be defined as a tree structure and provide for the implied processing automatically. In FACT, occurrences of a class are called *groups* and in 9PAC they are called *records*. The essential feature of these systems is the automatic distribution of groups or records to different input and output areas depending on the type of group or record involved, and the control of output operations required to maintain the tree structure of output files. For example, the FACT statement

GET NEXT GROUP OF (file name) FILE

obtains the next group of an input file and stores it in an area reserved for groups of its type. The statement

$$\text{FILE (group name)}$$

releases to an output file a group of the specified type plus any dependent groups which have been developed in the corresponding output areas. Similar facilities are provided in 9PAC, except that input-output operations are controlled by a program generated from parameters rather than by explicit statements.

The use of tree structures for serial-access files can result in significant savings in processing time, but at the same time can raise some problems not encountered with conventional files. The problem of sorting a tree-structured file, for example, is quite different from sorting a conventional file. The sorting technique used in the FACT system has been described by Glore [63].

4.4 Other Methods

The techniques of the previous sections do not of course exhaust the possibilities for organizing and describing data. There are, for example, a number of techniques in which information about the data structure is carried along with the data itself. Representative of these techniques is the Variable Information Processing System described by Kosakoff and Buswell [64], in which explicit field and record delimiters are used in the data structure. (The advent of "variable word length" computers with hardware delimiters is making such schemes seem more attractive.) The list structure of the Information Processing Languages [65] is another example in this class, and permits the representation of structures of considerable generality, of which the tree structure is actually a special case.

The problem of poorly-structured data is present in applications closely related to data processing. In [66], Colilla and Sams comment on the hierarchal nature of data (particularly the tree structure) in information retrieval applications. Gower [67] describes a mapping scheme for storing "n-way tables" which are used extensively in statistical applications. A novel application of tree structures to *sorting*, which apparently originated in England, is reported by Windley [68].

Finally, mention should be made of schemes in which information is represented by its *position* in an array rather than by digital values. The classic example of such schemes is the Peek-A-Boo system [69, 70] in which positional representation is used to facilitate the manual extraction of records meeting certain criteria. A machine version of the Peek-A-Boo technique has been proposed by the Jonker Business Machines Company in their Termatrex System [71, 72]. A further extension of the technique to computer memories has been described by Fredkin [73].

5. Developments in Data Processing Theory

Despite the rapid growth of computer technology and some phenomenal successes in the development of truly useful computers and computer programs, there is growing concern that the technology does not yet have a suitable theoretical foundation; and that as a result, long-range progress will be impeded. This concern is expressed in a variety of ways:

The difficulty in setting standards in computer languages is taken by some as evidence of a lack of understanding of the fundamental nature of computing.

The lack of systematic procedure for selecting equipment for a specific application or class of applications is believed to stem from the fact that we have not found a suitable way of formally characterizing either computers or computer applications.

The persistent feeling by the computer designer and the computer user that each has important information to impart to the other, but that neither is getting his message across.

In a short, informal article [74], T. B. Steel describes the problem this way: Too often automatic programming systems are being used as "a facility for the more rapid construction of ill-conceived programs. Rarely, if ever, is the more serious problem of selecting the appropriate procedures attacked." According to Steel, a theory of data processing is required which is *formal, consistent,* and *comprehensive.* A theory is formal in the sense that, given certain rules, the elements of the theory can be manipulated without a knowledge of their meaning (e.g., an algebraic expression can be manipulated without knowledge of the correspondence between its symbols and the entities for which these symbols stand). A theory is *consistent* as long as none of its developments or "constructs" contradicts its postulates or other constructs. Consistency is mandatory if results of the theory which cannot be readily verified experimentally are to be trusted. Finally, a theory is *comprehensive* if it can successfully predict the behavior of a wide range of phenomena. The Newtonian theory of mechanics was both formal and consistent but, as developments of the twentieth century proved, not comprehensive.

Efforts in the direction of a data processing theory have taken a number of forms. Some investigators have been concerned with ways of defining more precisely the flow of information through an organization, and have devised formal "systems" languages for this purpose. For example, Evans

[75] describes a method developed at Hunt Foods and Industries for systematically defining data handling procedures in terms of data elements, data sets (documents), data files, and data rules. The method of expression is primarily tabular and in particular the expression of data rules follows closely the principle of logic tables. A similar method was devised by Young and Kent [76], who used pseudo-algebraic expressions to specify the conditions under which output documents of a system are generated and the definition of individual items in the document. A characteristic of both of these efforts is the recognition that data of a given type may appear at many places in a system and it is better to treat their appearance as individual cases of a general occurrence rather than as unique events. This recognition has carried over into later work.

Other investigators have attempted to exploit the apparent analogy between classical mathematical operations and certain data processing operations. Kaplan [77], for example, points out the isomorphic relationship of sorting, searching, and insertions to division. Lombardi [48] suggests that files can be regarded as elements of a Boolean algebra and subjected to such operations as complementation, union (merging), and intersection (match-merging).

The principal current efforts toward a data processing theory are being carried out by the SHARE Committee on Theory of Information Handling (TIH) and the CODASYL Language Structure Group. The TIH Committee's work dates from 1959, when, under the chairmanship of W. Orchard-Hays, the committee published a definitive report [78] establishing certain basic data processing concepts. Principal among these were the concepts of *entity* (an object, person, or idea capable of being described for data processing purposes); *property* (characteristics in terms of which entities are described); and *measure* (values assigned to properties). A *datum*, the smallest unit of information, was defined as the triple (D, i, j) or Dij where D is a measure, i is the index of an entity, and j is the index of a property. From these concepts, the TIH report developed the notion of a *unit record* as being a one-dimensional array of datum triples, in which the index i is fixed and the index j ranges over all properties being represented; and the notion of a *file* as a two-dimensional array, with index j varying over all properties and index i varying over all entities. Analogies were then drawn between operations on a file and operations on arrays.

More recent work of the TIH Committee has been reported by Steel [79] and Smith [80]. This work introduces the notion of a *generalized array* whose elements have the general form of an "ordered pair" $\langle v, x \rangle$ in which v is a data value corresponding to an "argument" x. Arguments are expressed as a set of ordered pairs

$$\{\langle v_1, p_1 \rangle, \langle v_2, p_2 \rangle, \ldots \langle v_n, p_n \rangle\}$$

WILLIAM C. McGEE

in which p_i stands for the *name* of an array dimension and v_i is a value which the corresponding dimension can take. A two-dimensional generalized array in which one dimension is *property* and the second is *entity* is equivalent to the two-dimensional array of the earlier TIH work, with the data value v in an element corresponding to a datum Dij. Alternatively, if each dimension of a generalized array is associated with a different "dimension property," the equivalent of a rectangular array results, in which the data value v represents the value of one or more "array properties" (see section 4.2). The generalized array differs from conventional arrays in that it contains explicitly the definition of the data values being represented. Because of this, it is possible to postulate *formal* procedures for operating on generalized arrays, and thus obtain a general method of expressing various data processing operations.

The work of the CODASYL group has resulted in an "Information Algebra," reported originally by R. Bosak [81] and more recently in the ACM *Communications* [82]. This work, like that of the TIH Committee, is based on the "undefined concepts" of entity, property, and value (i.e., measure). Rather than representing files as arrays, however, the Information Algebra represents files as sets of points in an n-dimensional property space. This representation makes it possible to use the notation and constructs of set theory, and results in a tool of considerable generality and power. In this author's opinion, the Information Algebra will have considerable impact on the direction which developments in data processing theory will take in coming years, and it is therefore worthwhile to consider it here in some detail.

The essential feature of the Information Algebra is the manner in which the data involved in a process are represented. For each *property* in the process (property has the same meaning here as in the TIH work, and corresponds to "data element" in Evan's work and "information set" in the work of Young and Kent) a *property value set* is defined which contains all the possible values which the property can assume. For example, if *employee number* is a property, its value set might consist of the integers between 1 and 100,000. A *coordinate set* is then defined as the set of all properties involved in a process. For example, a coordinate set might consist of the properties *employee number, employee age,* and *employee sex*.

Finally, a *property space* is defined as the set of all points which can be found by taking one value from the value set of the first property, one value from the value set of the second property, and so forth, up to and including one value from the value set of the last property in the coordinate set. For the coordinate set (*employee number, employee age, sex*), such a point might be $p = (12345, 43, \text{м})$, where 12345, 43, and м are values from the value sets of employee number, employee age, and sex respectively.
40

One way of viewing a property space is as a geometric space of n dimensions, where n is the number of properties in the coordinate set and a different dimension is associated with each property. For $n \leq 3$, such a space can be depicted graphically, as in Fig. 3. For $n > 3$, however, this way of visualizing property space is of little use. For the sake of generality, the geometric view of property space should not be used excessively, but for gaining an insight into the method it probably does no harm.

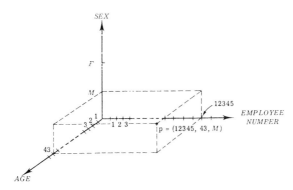

Fig. 3. Geometric interpretation of property space.

Obviously, in all but trivial processes there will be a very large number of points in the property space. In our example, if the property value sets for employee number, age, and sex contain 100,000, 100, and 2 values, respectively, the property space will in fact contain $(100,000)(100)(2) = 20$ million points. Equally obviously, not all of these points will be involved in a given processing, and one of the major contributions of the Information Algebra is to give us a way of referring to and manipulating *sets* of points in the property space.

Another way of viewing points in property space is as *representations of entities* (again used in the same sense as in the TIH work). Thus, the point (12345, 43, M) might "stand for" a particular employee of a company. By postulate, the Information Algebra assures that no entity will have more than one point in property space. However, there is a possibility that two or more entities may share the same point. If the coordinate set (age, sex) were used, for example, it is likely that a large number of entities(persons) would share the same points in property space. Coordinate sets and corresponding property spaces which assure that every entity will have a different point in property space are said to be *discriminatory*.

The method described above for representing data is quite abstract. It does not, for example, say anything about how data points would be stored in a computer memory, or on magnetic tape; or how they would be organized to take advantage of data redundancy or irrelevancy. It is this abstraction, in fact, which makes the Information Algebra a promising candidate for a machine-independent data processing language.

The principal function of data processing is to create output files from input files. In the Information Algebra, files are represented as sets of points of the property space known as *areas*. The creation of output files from input files is equivalent to transforming one or more given areas (i.e., the input files) into one or more new areas (the output files). Unlike actual data processing, however, this transformation does not in any way depend on the *sequence* of operations, and it is helpful, in fact, to visualize all transformations as occurring instantaneously.

To express these transformations, a number of operators or *functions* are provided. One such function is the *function of areas* (FOA), defined to be an operator which associates one and only one value with an area. For example, if an area A of the property space of the previous example has been established, then a function $f(A)$ of this area might be defined which sums the values of age for each point in the area and divides the sum by the total number of points in the area. In other words, the function computes the average age of the persons in the file represented by area A.

In addition to representing files, areas of property space can be used to represent groupings within a file. In the illustration, it might be desired to group the points in area A such that all points in one group have age values between 0 and 4, all points in another group age values between 5 and 9, and so forth. This facility is provided by a *glumping function* which partitions A into subsets of points called *elements* in such a way an element contains all points in A having identical values for the given glumping function. In the partition just referred to, the glumping function could be written

$$g = \left[\frac{\text{age}}{5} \right]$$

where the brackets signify "integral part of." Thus, for all points with ages 5, 6, 7, 8, and 9, g would be 1, and all such points would be members of the same element. The entire set of elements is called simply a *glump*, and is denoted

$$G(g, A)$$

where g is the glumping function and A is the area.

One of the purposes of glumping functions is to define areas (elements are areas) which can then be operated on with a function of areas to define new areas in the property space. The FOA used for this purpose is called a *function of a glump* (FOG). The FOG creates a new area by defining a point in property space (not necessarily a different one) for each element in a glump. This area is denoted

$$A' = H(g, A)$$

where A is the original area, g is the glumping function for that area, and H is the function of a glump which creates the new area. The points of the new area are defined by stating the values which each property in the coordinate set is to take on for each element in the glump. Since glump elements are areas, these values are stated as functions of areas. If there are k properties in the coordinate set $q_1, q_2, \ldots q_k$, the function of glump is written generally as

$$H = \begin{cases} q_1' = f_1 \\ q_2' = f_2 \\ \quad \cdot \\ \quad \cdot \\ \quad \cdot \\ q_k' = f_k \end{cases}$$

where the f's are functions of areas, and the notation

$$q_i' = f_i$$

means that property q_i is to take the value assigned by f_i.

To illustrate, suppose that we have a file of records each containing an employee number, his age, and his sex; and we wish to create from this file a new file of records each of which contains an age group code (such as 0 for ages 1 through 4, 1 for ages 5 through 9, etc.) and the *number of people* in the original file whose ages fall in the given age group. For this problem we require a coordinate set consisting of *employee number, age, sex, age group*, and *number* (i.e., a five-dimensional property space). The given file is an area, say A_1, of this space whose points have non-null values for *employee number, age*, and *sex;* and null values for *age group* and *number*. We wish to transform this area into a second area A_2 whose points have null values for *employee number, age*, and *sex;* and non-null values, derived in accordance with the above definition, for *age group* and *number*. We first partition A_1 with the glumping function $g = [\text{age}/5]$, as in the previous example. We then "map" each element of the resulting glump into area $A_2 = H(g, A_1)$ with the function of glumps H defined by

$$H = \begin{cases} \text{employee number} = \Omega \\ \text{age} = \Omega \\ \text{sex} = \Omega \\ \text{age group} = g \\ \text{number} = \Sigma 1 \end{cases}$$

In this definition, "Ω" denotes the FOA which associates the null value with an element; g is a FOA which associates the value $[\text{age}/5]$ with an element (a single value because of the way the elements were formed); and $\Sigma 1$ is a FOA which simply counts the points in an element. Thus, if the element with

43

$g = 2$ contained 204 points, the corresponding point in the new area would be $(\Omega, \Omega, \Omega, 2, 204)$.

The functions of glumps affords a way of defining a new file from a single file. In many applications, however, a new file is to be created by simultaneously considering the data in two or more files. For such situations, the Information Algebra introduces the *area set*, an ordered set of areas $(A_1, A_2, \ldots A_n)$. The areas in an area set need not be disjoint (i.e., non-overlapping), but usually are. With such a set of areas, one can envision a process which selects a point from area A_1, then selects a point from A_2 and so forth until a point has been selected from each area. The set of points selected by this process are referred to as a *line*, and the points in the line are *ordered* since the areas in the area set were ordered. Geometrically, one can envision a line as a curve which intersects each area in the set.

One can now envision this process being repeated, e.g., selecting the same points as before from A_1 through A_{n-1}, but a new point from A_n. This new set of points defines another line. Similarly, other lines may be defined, until all possibilities have been exhausted. If the areas contain $m_1, m_2, \ldots m_n$ points, respectively, a total of $m_1 \times m_2 \times \ldots \times m_n$ lines can be formed.

Out of the totality of lines intersecting an area set, one can now envision a selection process in which only those lines meeting a certain condition are selected. The set of lines so selected is called a *bundle*, and the condition for selection is expressed in a *bundling function*. The bundling function is a special case of a *function of lines* (FOL) which in general associates a single value with a line (in the same way that an FOA associates a single value with an area). The bundling function is called a *selection* FOL, because it can associate only two values with any line: *true* and *false*. The lines in a bundle are those lines for which the associated bundling function is *true*. All lines for which the bundling function is *false* are disregarded.

The purpose of the bundle is to associate points in different areas. If areas A_1 and A_2 represent a master file and a transaction file in a property space with $q_1 = $ *employee number*, then the bundling function

$$b = \big(q_1(1) = q_1(2)\big)$$

selects from all the lines intersecting A_1 and A_2 those lines which connect points in A_1 and A_2 having the same employee number. In other words, the bundling function b "matches" records from the master and transaction file. The "intersection" of a bundle B with an area A_i is denoted $I(B, A_i)$, and all points in A_i not intersected by B are denoted collectively as $I'(B, A_i)$. Thus $I'(B, A_1)$ would represent unmatched master records and $I'(B, A_2)$ would represent unmatched detail records.

In many processes it is desired to associate a single new record with each occurrence of matching records from two or more input files. In the

44

Information Algebra, this is accomplished with a *function of a bundle* (FOB). A FOB creates a new area by defining a point in property space for each *line* in a bundle. The area is denoted

$$A' = F(b, A_1, A_2 \ldots A_n)$$

where b is the bundling function, the A's are the area set over which b is defined, and F is the function of a bundle which creates a new area. The points in the new area are defined in a manner similar to the points in a function of a glump, except that the functions which assign values to the various properties of the coordinate set are now *functions of lines* instead of functions of areas:

$$F = \begin{cases} q_1' = f_1 \\ q_2' = f_2 \\ \cdot \\ \cdot \\ \cdot \\ \cdot \\ q_h' = f_k \end{cases}$$

To illustrate, start with the coordinate set (*employee number, hours worked today, hours worked this week*) and postulate three files (areas) as follows:

	Old Master File OM	Detail File DF	New Master File NM
q_1 = employee number	Relevant	Relevant	Relevant
q_2 = hours worked today	Not relevant	Relevant	Not relevant
q_3 = hours worked this week	Relevant	Not relevant	Relevant

We wish to create the NM file by matching detail records in DF with master records in OM, adding hours worked today in DF to hours worked this week in OM, and posting the updated hours to NM. Assuming that there is a single detail and a single master record for each employee, the new master file NM would be defined as a function of a bundle

$$\text{NM} = F(q_1(\text{OM}) = q_1(\text{DF}), \text{OM}, \text{DF})$$

in which the bundling function selects lines joining points on OM and DF having the same employee number; and the FOB is defined as

$$F = \begin{cases} \text{employee number} = \text{employee number (OM)} \\ \text{hours worked today} = \Omega \\ \text{hours worked this week} = \text{hours worked this week (OM)} \\ \qquad\qquad + \text{hours worked today (DF)} \end{cases}$$

45

For each line in the bundle, F will define a point in the new file according to the above rules.

As a final example of the Information Algebra, consider again the simultaneous merge-extract process used in Section 3.4 to illustrate the Algebraic Data System Language. In Section 3.4 we were not concerned with the content of the output records, just the conditions under which they were issued. Now, however, we must specify the content of the output records. In particular, assume that records in the new selected master file (NSM) and the new master file (NM) are exact copies of records selected from either the old selected master file (OSM) or the old master file (OM), except that each record of an output file contains a file code unique to that file. Further, assume that the records appearing in the error file (ER) are copies of records selected from the transaction file (T) except for an identifying file code and an *error code:* D for duplicate matched transactions, U for unmatched transactions. The coordinate set appropriate to this problem is given in the following table together with an indication of the relevance of each property in the various files (R stands for relevant, NR for not relevant):

	Input Files			Output Files		
	SM	OM	T	NSM	NM	ER
q_1 = file code	"SM"	"OM"	"T"	"NSM"	"NM"	"ER"
q_2 = key	R	R	R	R	R	R
q_3 = master data	R	R	NR	R	R	NR
q_4 = transaction data	NR	NR	R	NR	NR	R
q_5 = error code	NR	NR	NR	NR	NR	R

The expressions for the output files and, for ease of notation, certain intermediate areas are as follows:

MM (*Merged Masters*):

$$\text{MM} = \text{SM} \cup \text{OM}$$

This is an intermediate area which permits both SM and OM to be considered jointly for selection purposes.

CT (*Condensed Transaction*):

$$\text{CT} = H_1(q_2, \text{T})$$

$$H_1 = \begin{cases} q_1' = \Omega \\ q_2' = q_2 \\ q_3' = \Omega \\ q_4' = \min \{q_4\} \\ q_5' = \Omega \end{cases}$$

The transaction file T is glumped on key, and each element is mapped into CT such that a point in CT has the same key as the corresponding element in T and the *least* of the transaction data values in the corresponding element in T. This is an arbitrary way of singling out one of a number of transactions with identical keys. It is not required for selecting masters, but is required for placing duplicate transactions in the error file.

NSM (*New Selected Master*):

$$\text{NSM} = F_1(B_1)$$
$$B_1 = (q_2(\text{CT}) = q_2(\text{MM}), \text{CT}, \text{MM})$$

$$F_1 = \begin{cases} q_1' = \text{``NSM''} \\ q_2' = q_2(\text{MM}) \\ q_3' = q_3(\text{MM}) \\ q_4' = \Omega \\ q_5' = \Omega \end{cases}$$

The NSM is a function of the bundle B_1 formed by joining points in CT and MM having identical keys. For each line in the bundle, the function carries over the merged master key and merged master data into NSM.

NM (*New Master*):

$$\text{NM} = H_2(q_2, I'(B_1, \text{MM}))$$

$$H_2 = \begin{cases} q_1' = \text{``NM''} \\ q_2' = q_2 \\ q_3' = q_3 \\ q_4' = \Omega \\ q_5' = \Omega \end{cases}$$

The complement of the intersection of bundle B_1 with MM, denoted $I'(B_1, \text{MM})$, represents master records which are not to be selected, hence to be included in NM. To form NM, the area $I'(B_1, \text{MM})$ is glumped on key (by definition, there will be one point per element) and each element mapped into NM by copying the key and master data.

UCT (*Unmatched Condensed Transactions*):

$$\text{UCT} = I'(B_1, \text{CT})$$

This area is the complement of the intersection of bundle B_1 with CT, and represents transaction *keys* having no match in MM.

MCT (*Matched Condensed Transactions*):

$$\text{MCT} = I(B_1, \text{CT})$$

This area is the intersection of B_1 with CT, and represents transaction keys

47

which are matched by records in MM. The definition of UCT and MCT simplify the definition of the error file.

ER (*Error*):

$$ER = F_2(B_2) \cup F_3(B_3)$$
$$B_2 = (q_2(\text{T}) = q_2(\text{UCT}), \text{T}, \text{UCT})$$

$$F_2 = \begin{cases} q_1' =' \text{``ER''} \\ q_2' = q_2(\text{T}) \\ q_3' = \Omega \\ q_4' = q_4(\text{T}) \\ q_5' = \text{``U''} \end{cases}$$

$$B_3 = (q_2(\text{T}) = q_2(\text{MCT}) \text{ AND } q_4(\text{T}) \neq q_4(\text{MCT}), \text{T}, \text{MCT})$$

$$F_3 = \begin{cases} q_1' = \text{``ER''} \\ q_2' = q_2(\text{T}) \\ q_3' = \Omega \\ q_4' = q_4(\text{T}) \\ q_5' = \text{``D''} \end{cases}$$

The error file is the union of two areas: unmatched transaction records and duplicate transaction records. The first of these areas is expressed as a function of a bundle B_2 formed by joining points in T to points in UCT having the same key. Each line in the bundle represents an unmatched transaction record, and is mapped into ER by copying key and data from T, and by supplying "U" as error code.

The second area comprising ER is also a function of a bundle, B_3, formed by joining points in T and MCT which have identical key values *but* unequal data values. Recall that the condensed transaction area CT was so defined so that only *one* data value was supplied for each group of records with identical keys in T. Each line of the bundle B_3 therefore corresponds to the 2nd, 3rd, etc. record of a group with matching keys in MM. These lines are mapped into ER in the same way as the lines of B_2, except that "D" is supplied as the error code.

In developing the Information Algebra, the CODASYL Language Structures Group has attempted to provide a language which can serve as the basis for truly machine-independent programming systems. The notion of expressing computer processes in terms of sets of data produced by the process, rather than in terms of procedures by which these sets are produced, has been used extensively in the Information Algebra. To this extent, the Algebra could be classed as a non-procedural programming language. Unlike current nonprocedural languages, however, the Information Algebra is so general that the process of translating the algebraic statement of a problem into an equivalent machine program is far from obvious.

Hence, it is perhaps more appropriate to view the Algebra, for the time being at least, as a development in data processing theory. The extension of this theory into new areas of computer use, and the application of the theory to working programming systems will be major tasks. But they will perhaps be the most significant contributions that can be made to the field of data processing at this time.

ACKNOWLEDGMENTS

The author wishes to express his appreciation to the numerous individuals who supplied reports on which the present article is based. The help of Mr. Jesse Katz in developing the material included in Section 5, and of Mrs. Gene Beck in typing the manuscript is particularly appreciated.

REFERENCES

1. Gotlieb, C. C., General-purpose programming for business applications. *Advances in Computers* Vol. 1 (edited by F. L. Alt), Academic Press, New York, 1960.
2. Canning, R. G., *Electronic Data Processing for Business and Industry.* Wiley, New York, 1956.
3. Chapin, N., *Programming Computers for Business Applications.* McGraw-Hill, New York, 1961.
4. Gotlieb, C. C. and Hume, J. N. P., *High Speed Data Processing.* McGraw-Hill, New York, 1958.
5. Gregory, R. H. and Van Horn, R. L., *Automatic Data-Processing Systems.* Wadsworth, San Francisco, California, 1960.
6. Ledley, R. S., *Programming and Utilizing Digital Computers.* McGraw-Hill, New York, 1962.
7. Martin, E. W. Jr., *Electronic Data Processing.* Richard D. Irwin, Homewood, Illinois, 1961.
8. McCracken, D. D., Weiss, H., and Lee, T., *Programming Business Computers.* Wiley, New York, 1959.
9. Orchard-Hays, W., The evolution of programming systems. *Proc. IRE* **49**, 283–295 (1961).
10. Jenkins, L. J., Automatic programming for computers. *O & M Bull.* **15**, No. 6, 271–276 (1960).
11. UNIVAC FLOW-MATIC Programming System, U 1518, Sperry-Rand Corp., New York, 1958.
12. Hopper, G. M., Automatic programming for business applications. *Proceedings of the 4th Annual Computer Applications Symposium*, Armour Research Foundation, 45–50 (1957).
13. The AIMACO Compiling System-Preliminary Manual, Air Materiel Command, May 29, 1958.
14. Miller, E. R. and Jones, J. L., The Air Force breaks through communications barrier. *Univac Review*, Winter 1959, 8–12.
15. FACT—Fully Automatic Compiling Technique, Minneapolis-Honeywell Corp., DATAmatic Division, Wellesley Hills, Massachusetts, 1960.
16. General Information Manual—IBM Commercial Translator, F28-8043, Intern. Bus. Machines Corp., New York, 1960.

17. COBOL 1961—Revised Specifications for a Common Business Oriented Language, U.S. Government Printing Office, 1961.
18. Braunholtz, T. G. H., Fraser, A. G., and Hunt, P. M., NEBULA: a programming language for data processing. *Computer J.* **4**, 197–211 (1961).
19. Willey, E. L. *et al.*, *Some Commercial Autocodes*. Academic Press, London, 1961.
20. Bemer, R. W., COBOL—common language for computers. *Management and Business Automation*, March 1960, 22–24, 37–39.
21. Cunningham, J. F., Why COBOL? *Communs. Assoc. Computing Machinery* **5**, 236 (1962).
22. Sammet, J. E., Basic elements of COBOL 61, *Communs. Assoc. Computing Machinery* **5**, 237–253 (1962).
23. Berman, R., Sharp, J., and Sturges, L., Syntactical charts of COBOL 61. *Communs. Assoc. Computing Machinery* **5**, 260 (1962).
24. Ferguson, D. E., Input-output buffering and Fortran. *J. Assoc. Computing Machinery* **7**, 1–9 (1960).
25. Graham, J. W. and Sprott, D. A., Processing magnetic tape files with variable blocks. *Communs. Assoc. Computing Machinery* **4**, 555–557 (1961).
26. Mock, O. and Swift, C. J., The SHARE 709 System: Programmed input-output buffering. *J. Assoc. Computing Machinery* **6**, 145–151 (1959).
27. Roth, B., Channel analysis for the IBM 7090. *16th Nat. Meeting Assoc. Computing Machinery*. Los Angeles, paper 12C-3 (1961).
28. Bouman, C. A., An advanced input-output system for a COBOL compiler. *Communs. Assoc. Computing Machinery* **5**, 273–277 (1962).
29. Mullen, J. W., COBOL batching problems. *Communs. Assoc. Computing Machinery* **5**, 278–279 (1962).
30. Donally, W. L., A report writer for COBOL. *Communs. Assoc. Computing Machinery* **5**, 261 (1962).
31. Bromberg, H., What COBOL isn't. *Datamation* **7**, No. 9, 27–29 (1961).
32. Hughes, J. H., The trouble with commercial compilers. *Computers and Automation* **10**, No. 7, 13–14 (1961).
33. Humby, E., RAPIDWRITE—a new approach to COBOL readability. *Computer J.* **4**, 301–304 (1962).
34. Ellis, P. V., An evaluation of autocode readability. *Communs. Assoc. Computing Machinery* **5**, 156–159 (1962).
35. Longo, L. F., SURGE: A re-coding of the COBOL merchandise control algorithm. *Communs. Assoc. Computing Machinery* **5**, 98–100 (1962).
36. Mackinson, T. N., COBOL: A sample problem. *Communs. Assoc. Computing Machinery* **4**, 340–346 (1961).
37. Lippitt, A., COBOL and compatibility. *Communs. Assoc. Computing Machinery* **5**, 254–255 (1962).
38. Mullin, J. P., An introduction to a machine-independent data division. *Communs. Assoc. Computing Machinery* **5**, 277–278 (1962).
39. Bromberg, H., COBOL and compatibility. *Datamation* **7**, No. 2, 30–34 (1961).
40. A critical appraisal of COBOL. *Computer Bull.* **4**, 141–143 (1961).
41. A critical discussion of COBOL. *Automatic Programming Vol. 2* (edited by R. Goodman). Pergamon Press, Oxford, 1961.
42. Clippinger, R. F., FACT—a business compiler: description and comparison with COBOL and Commercial Translator. *Automatic Programming Vol. 2* (edited by R. Goodman). Pergamon Press, Oxford, 1961.
43. Bemer, R. W., A checklist of intelligence for programming systems. *Communs. Assoc. Computing Machinery* **2**, 8–13 (1959).
44. Choosing a language. *Data Processing Digest* **7**, No. 12, 21–23 (1961).

45. Cantrell, H. N., Where are compiler languages going? *Datamation* **8**, No. 8, 25–28 (1962).
46. Lombardi, L., Theory of files. *Proc. Eastern Joint Computer Conf., New York,* 137–141 (1960).
47. Lombardi, L., Non-procedural data system languages. *16th Nat. Meeting Assoc. Computing Machinery, Los Angeles,* paper 11-1 (1961).
48. Lombardi, L., Mathematical structures of non-arithmetic data processing procedures. *J. Assoc. Computing Machinery* **9**, 136–159 (1962).
49. McGee, W. C., Generalization: key to successful electronic data processing. *J. Assoc. Computing Machinery* **6**, 1–23 (1959).
50. McGee, W. C. and Tellier, H., A re-evaluation of generalization. *Datamation* **6**, No. 4, 25–29 (1960).
51. IBM 7090 Programming Systems: SHARE 7090 9PAC; Part 1, Introduction and General Principles (J28-6166); Part 2, The File Processor (J28-6167); Part 3, The Reports Generator (J28-6168), Intern. Bus. Machines Corp., New York, 1961.
52. Canning, R. G., How the four-tape sorter simplifies storage. *Control Engineering* **4**, No. 2, 95–97 (1957).
53. Kavanagh, T. F., TABSOL—a fundamental concept for systems-oriented languages. *Proc. Eastern Joint Computer Conf., New York,* 117–136 (1960).
54. Kavanagh, T. F., TABSOL—the language of decision making. *Computers and Automation* **10**, No. 9, 15, 18–22 (1961).
55. Cantrell, H. N., King, J., and King, F. E. H., Logic-structure tables. *Communs. Assoc. Computing Machinery* **4**, 272–275 (1961).
56. Klick, D. C., TABSOL: a decision table language for the GE 225. *16th Nat. Meeting Assoc. Computing Machinery, Los Angeles,* paper 10B-2 (1961).
57. Grad, B., Tabular form in decision logic. *Datamation* **7**, 22–26 (1961).
58. Proceedings of the Decision Tables Symposium, sponsored by CODASYL Systems Group and Joint Users Group of Assoc. Computing Machinery, New York, September 20–21, 1962.
59. DETAB-X: Preliminary Specifications for a Decision Table Structured Language, CODASYL Systems Group, September 1962.
60. Lombardi, L., On table operating algorithms, *Proc. of the IFIP Congress 62, Munich* (1962). (In preparation.)
61. McGee, W. C., The property classification method of file design and processing. *Communs. Assoc. Computing Machinery* **5**, 450–458 (1962).
62. Hoffman, S. A., Data structures that generalize rectangular arrays. *Proc. Spring Joint Computer Conf., San Francisco,* 325–333 (1962).
63. Glore, J. B., Sorting non-redundant files. *Communs. Assoc. Computing Machinery* **6**, 231–240 (1963).
64. Kosakoff, M. and Buswell, D. L., VIP—a variable information processing system for storage and retrieval of missile data. Tech. Memo. 64-474 (Uncl.), U.S. Naval Ordnance Laboratory, Corona, California, 25 April 1962.
65. Newell, A. (Ed.), *Information Processing Language—V Manual.* Prentice-Hall, Englewood Cliffs, New Jersey, 1961.
66. Colilla, R. A. and Sams, B. H., Information structures for processing and retrieving. *Communs. Assoc. Computing Machinery* **5**, 11–16 (1962).
67. Gower, J. C., The handling of multiway tables on computers. *Computer J.* **4**, 280–286 (1962).
68. Windley, P. F., Trees, forests, and rearranging. *Computer J.* **3**, 84–88 (1960).
69. Shera, J. H., Kent, A., and Perry, J. W., *Information System in Documentation.* Interscience Publishers, Inc., New York, 1957.

70. Robbins, D., Computer production of Peek-A-Boo sheets. *Communs. Assoc. Computing Machinery* **4**, 562–565 (1961).
71. Jonker's approach to information retrieval. *Management and Business Automation*, November 1960, 18–25.
72. Jonker, F., Total data processing. *Data Processing* **4**, No. 4, 43–46 (1962).
73. Fredkin, E., Trie memory. *Communs. Assoc. Computing Machinery* **3**, 490–499 (1960).
74. Steel, T. B. Jr., Toward a theory of data processing. *Data Processing* **4**, No. 2, 9–11 (1962).
75. Evans, O. Y., *Advanced Analysis Method for Integrated Electronic Data Processing.* General Information Manual F20-8047, Intern. Bus. Machines Corp., New York (undated).
76. Young, J. W. Jr. and Kent, H., Abstract formulation of data processing problems. *Journal of Industrial Engineering* **9**, 471–479 (1958).
77. Kaplan, S., The role of isomorphism in programming. *13th Nat. Meeting Assoc. Computing Machinery, New York*, 34–41 (1958).
78. General Data Files and Processing Operations, SHARE Committee on Theory of Information Handling, Report TIH-1, SSD-71, Item C-1663 (1959).
79. Steel, T. B. Jr., The foundations of a theory of data processing. *16th Nat. Meeting Assoc. Computing Machinery, Los Angeles*, paper 6B-2 (1961).
80. Smith, L. W., Information and transformations on general arrays. *16th Nat. Meeting Assoc. Computing Machinery, Los Angeles*, paper 6B-3 (1961).
81. Bosak, R., An information algebra. *16th Nat. Meeting Assoc. Computing Machinery, Los Angeles*, paper 6B-1 (1961).
82. An information algebra—Phase I report of the Language Structure Group of the CODASYL Development Committee, *Communs. Assoc. Computing Machinery* **5**, 190–204 (1962).

All-Magnetic Circuit Techniques

DAVID R. BENNION
HEWITT D. CRANE

Stanford Research Institute
Menlo Park, California

1. The Problem

1.1 Introduction

The great success of magnetic cores in computer memory systems in the early 1950's resulted in a strong desire to incorporate these reliable and inexpensive elements into logic circuits as well. Of special interest was the fact that the bulk of a typical magnetic memory system actually consisted of only the memory cores themselves and interconnecting wires. It was hoped that magnetic logic circuits could similarly be developed in which only cores and wire played the prominent role. There was strong doubt initially as to the possibility of achieving such systems, though, because of the more stringent demands of logic circuits as compared with memory circuits. However, this possibility has now been well exploited and the resulting circuits of this type are generally referred to as *core-wire* or *all-magnetic* circuits. It is the purpose of this section to review the status of this technology and, in particular, to emphasize the advantages and disadvantages of these techniques.

For memory, or storage, it is necessary only that the memory cores have proper remanence. For access to a particular bit of the stored data, we ask only that the selected core induce a suitable voltage in an output winding, whereas unselected cores should not be affected by this access, or selection, process. The output signal is usually then applied directly to voltage amplifiers and amplitude discriminators. In memory application, therefore, there is no special concern for output level as such, but rather only that the output signals for the stored binary *zero* and *one* states be sufficiently different that an unambiguous decision can be made.

For a logic system, however, still other requirements must be met. In particular, we require power gain in order to overcome inherent losses in the coupling circuits. Thus, in any logic system in which magnetic cores play a prominent role, some cores must be such that each one is capable of driving another core at least as large as itself. Although an isolated transfer from one core to another may be no special problem, we must be sure that the second core can in turn drive a third, the third can drive a fourth, and so on. In other words, it must be possible to transmit a signal stably (in this case a binary state) along an arbitrarily long chain of elements. Although the chain usually has many branches (fan-in and fan-out), let us consider here only the simpler case of a lineal chain, which will clearly indicate the nature of the problem.

With the more familiar active elements (such as transistors), we have an important isolation between output and input; signal gain is easily achieved along an arbitrarily long chain. Thus, in Fig. 1 we can obtain

54

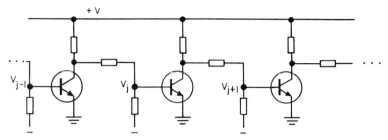

FIG. 1. A coupled chain of transistor circuits.

$\ldots \leq V_{j-1} \leq V_j \leq V_{j+1} \leq \ldots$ (We are concerned here only with the amplitude and not the polarity of the signal.) But similar gain conditions cannot be achieved in a simple chain of magnetic elements.

1.2 Use of Diodes with Cores to Achieve Gain

Consider a core with two windings, one considered as input and the other as output. In Fig. 2(a), the input and output windings are shown to have N_i and N_0 turns, respectively. A typical hysteresis curve of a "square-loop" core, useful in memory circuits, is indicated in Fig. 2(b). The major loop saturation flux levels are labeled as $-\phi_r$ and $+\phi_r$. The assumed positive direction of flux is indicated in Fig. 2(a) as counterclockwise. By the right-

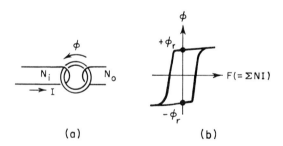

(a)   (b)

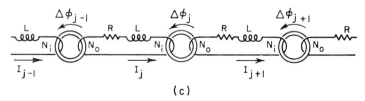

(c)

FIG. 2. Illustration for analysis of gain in a simple chain of cores. (a) A square-loop magnetic core with input turns N_i and output turns N_0. (b) Typical hysteresis loop. (c) A coupled chain of such cores.

hand rule, with the core initially in its $-\phi_r$ state, a sufficiently strong input current I will cause flux in the core to switch in the positive direction.

Let us now consider a chain of such cores, interconnected as in Fig. 2(c). Assume all cores are initially in negative saturation. An input current I_{j-1} will cause Core $j - 1$ to switch toward $+\phi_r$. As a result, an output current I_j will flow, tending to switch Core j, resulting in turn in a current I_{j+1}. And so on. Let us ask whether we can have flux gain along such a chain, i.e., $\ldots \le \Delta\phi_{j-1} \le \Delta\phi_j \le \Delta\phi_{j+1} \le \ldots$, where by $\Delta\phi$ we mean the magnitude of switched flux. (The answer is no.) To have any hope of flux gain, we can see first of all that the output turns N_0 must be larger than the input turns N_i. Consider the jth loop. At every instant,

$$N_0 \frac{d\phi_{j-1}}{dt} = RI_j + L \frac{dI_j}{dt} + N_i \frac{d\phi_j}{dt}, \tag{1.1}$$

where R and L are the resistance and air inductance of the loop. Assume the coupling loop current is zero at $t = 0$. Integration of (1.1) from $t = 0$ until switching is completed (say $t = \infty$) yields

$$N_0 \Delta\phi_{j-1} = R \int_0^\infty I_j \, dt + L\Delta I_j + N_i \Delta\phi_j. \tag{1.2}$$

The term $L\Delta I_j$ is equal to zero, since $I_j = 0$ at $t = 0$ and $t = \infty$. However, $\int I_j \, dt > 0$, and hence

$$N_i \Delta\phi_j < N_0 \Delta\phi_{j-1}. \tag{1.3}$$

Therefore, to have flux gain, i.e., $\Delta\phi_j \ge \Delta\phi_{j-1}$, we must have

$$N_0 > N_i. \tag{1.4}$$

But now consider again the chain of cores of Fig. 2(c). For the moment, assume that Core $j + 1$ is the last one in the chain. Certainly, it is required that

$$N_i I_{j+1} > T, \tag{1.5}$$

where T is the threshold mmf (magnetomotive force) of each core. For the previous element, we must have

$$N_i I_j - N_0 I_{j+1} > T \tag{1.6}$$

or

$$N_i I_j > \left(1 + \frac{N_0}{N_i}\right) T. \tag{1.7}$$

Now had we in (1.5) started instead with Core $j + 2$ as the last core in the chain, writing

$$N_i I_{j+2} > T, \tag{1.8}$$

then we would have found

$$N_i I_j > \left[1 + \frac{N_0}{N_i} + \left(\frac{N_0}{N_i}\right)^2 \right] T, \qquad (1.9)$$

or generalizing for an arbitrary number of additional cores added on,

$$N_i I_j > \left[1 + \frac{N_0}{N_i} + \left(\frac{N_0}{N_i}\right)^2 + \left(\frac{N_0}{N_i}\right)^3 + \ldots \right] T. \qquad (1.10)$$

In other words, since $N_0/N_i > 1$, any loop current (say I_j) must increase more and more, rather than less and less, as the chain is lengthened. Thus, for any given resistance value in the coupling loop, there is a maximum number of stages following any given stage before the loss in voltage in the coupling loop impedance in that loop is sufficiently large to overcome the potential flux gain from turns ratio $N_0/N_i > 1$.

One way to view the problem is that there is no decoupling between input and output at each core position. The output current, or output loading, affects the switching in a first-order manner. Compare this with the input-output isolation in the transistor chain, where variation in collector loading at any stage affects the input signal circuit in only a minor, second-order fashion. What is required in the magnetic chain, therefore, is a certain degree of input-output isolation. Let us consider the use of diodes for this purpose.

In the circuit of Fig. 3(a) a drive current I_{j-1} again switches Core $j - 1$, resulting in a current I_j, which tends to switch Core j. But now the diode in the output circuit of Core j prevents any current flow in the output loop. In this case we can easily achieve flux gain as long as N_0 is sufficiently more than N_i. But to continue moving the "signal" along the chain we

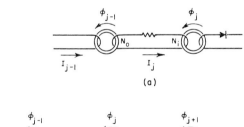

(a)

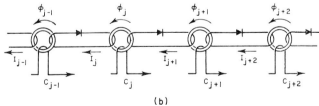

(b)

FIG. 3. Use of diodes to eliminate receiver loading. (a) Introduction of a diode in the output loop of a receiver. (b) A chain of decoupled core circuits, along which a flux level is moved by sequential application of clock pulses . . . , C_j, C_{j+1}, ...

must now explicitly drive Core j, as with current C_j in Fig. 3(b). (Assume again that all cores are initially in their $-\phi_r$ remanence state.) This will result in a current I_{j+1} to switch Core $j + 1$. Subsequently, current C_{j+1} drives Core $j + 1$ back to its negative saturation state, as a result of which flux in Core $j + 2$ is switched. Current C_{j+2} then drives Core $j + 2$, which results in flux switching in Core $j + 3$. And so on.

Note that exactly the same magnitude of flux is switched in a core (say Core $j - 1$) during its input phase (current I_{j-1}) as during its output phase (by drive current C_{j-1}), except that the polarity is reversed. During the output phase, current I_j tends to switch an amount of flux $\Delta\phi_j$ in Core j. (Output phase for Core $j - 1$ and input phase for Core j are simultaneous.) Hence, the signal can be kept "moving" along the line by sequentially driving each core in the chain, thus requiring a number of drivers equal to the number of cores in the chain, a clearly impractical method of achieving sequential flux transfer.

Let us concern ourselves now only with "binary" transfer along such a chain. By this we mean that the "signal" propagating along the chain takes only two forms, a high level of flux change or a low level of flux change. By convention, we will say in the first case that we are propagating a binary *one* state and in the latter case a binary *zero* state. To achieve such a mode of propagation, the amount of flux transferred in adjacent loops must be related as indicated in Fig. 4. (Assume again that all cores are

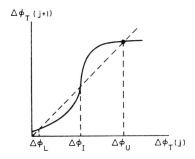

FIG. 4. Required form of the relation between the magnitudes of transmitted flux values from adjacent elements in order to achieve bistable, or binary, flux transmission.

initially in negative saturation, $-\phi_r$.) The flux transmitted from Core j is $\Delta\phi_T(j)$ and $\Delta\phi_T(j + 1)$ is the amount of flux subsequently transmitted from Core $j + 1$. Note that there are three unity gain points, i.e., levels for which $\Delta\phi_T(j + 1) = \Delta\phi_T(j)$. These levels are labeled $\Delta\phi_L$, $\Delta\phi_I$ and $\Delta\phi_U$ (subscripts L, I, and U for lower, intermediate, and upper). The levels $\Delta\phi_L$, $\Delta\phi_U$ represent stable points, and $\Delta\phi_I$ an unstable point. In other words, for any level of flux $\Delta\phi_T(j) > \Delta\phi_I$, the amount of flux subsequently trans-

58

mitted from Core $j + 1$ will be closer in magnitude to $\Delta\phi_U$. In fact, if all coupling loops are identical, during subsequent transfers the magnitude of transmitted flux will asymptotically approach $\Delta\phi_U$. Similarly, for transmitted flux $\Delta\phi_T(j) < \Delta\phi_I$, upon subsequent transfer the level will asymptotically approach $\Delta\phi_L$.

This required form of transfer curve applies to any binary transfer system, whether information is represented in terms of flux or any other quantity. Without going into great detail, let us consider how such a curve is achieved in the present case. Flux gain greater than unity can be achieved merely by arranging for $N_0 > N_i$ by an amount sufficient to overcome losses. The loss mechanism to ensure gain less than unity at low flux level is provided by the diode. The forward voltage drop in the diode can represent a significant loss at low level, whereas at high level of flux transfer (high voltages induced in the loop), the voltage drop is relatively insignificant. Thus, we can justifiably expect that the chain of Fig. 3(b) can be designed for proper bistable transfer.

Every core in the chain of Fig. 3(b) is driven independently and in sequence. However, this complete independence of drives is not necessary. The primary requirement is that adjacent cores should not be driven simultaneously; otherwise the receiver core could not switch at all. Actually, every other core of the chain can be driven simultaneously. Such an arrangement is indicated in Fig. 5. Only two clocks are used to drive the

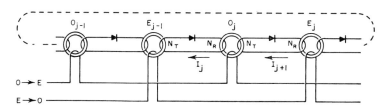

FIG. 5. A two-clock driving system obtained by interconnecting every other clock source indicated in Fig. 3(b).

chain, independent of the length of the chain. This is actually a workable arrangement, but we must be aware of a new complication, "back transfer," as described below. But first note the change in notation. According to usual practice, the core windings are relabeled N_T and N_R, for Transmitter and Receiver, and cores simultaneously driven are given the same type of label. In this case the cores are arbitrarily labeled O and E, for Odd and Even. The corresponding clock drivers are labeled $O \rightarrow E$ and $E \rightarrow O$.

Returning to Fig. 3(b), assume a certain amount of flux has been switched in the jth core during C_{j-1} drive. Then during the subsequent C_j drive, a current I_{j+1} will flow. But a current I_j will also flow in the previous loop tending to (re)switch Core $j - 1$, potentially causing "back transfer" of flux. In the circuit of Fig. 3(b), this would be of no consequence, since Core $j - 1$ is not used (driven) again. In the two-clock arrangement, though, *every* core is driven *every* clock cycle, and back transfer of flux may therefore be a problem. For example, suppose that Core O_j in Fig. 5 has received a high level of flux (*one* transfer). During the next $O \rightarrow E$ pulse, the following Core E_j will receive a correspondingly high level of flux. But if the preceding Core E_{j-1} is simultaneously caused to switch a sufficient level of flux, then during the following $E \rightarrow O$ transfer, the flux transferred from Core E_{j-1} may also tend to build up towards the upper state ϕ_U. In other words, back transfer is a potential problem because any flux transferred backward at one clock is transmitted forward at the following clock, and, if too large, will result in the build-up of a spurious *one*.

Since $N_R < N_T$, the amount of flux transmitted backward is less than that transmitted forward, so proper circuit operation may yet be achievable. In fact, with careful design, such a line can be successfully operated, although greatly improved versions are pointed out in this section.

Let us note two further properties of the line. The line can be closed upon itself, as suggested by the dashed line in the figure, so that a *one* state of flux can be continually and stably circulated around a closed ring. Second, more than one bit of information can be transferred simultaneously. All O cores may at some instant each independently be in the high (*one*) or low (*zero*) flux state. During the next $O \rightarrow E$ transfer, the binary state of each O core is transmitted to its neighboring right-hand E core. During the subsequent $E \rightarrow O$ transfer, the states are again transmitted to the O cores, but continually to the right. A lineal circuit such as this, which can stably shift a pattern along a closed ring, is called a shift register.

For later reference, let us suggest just two of a number of techniques for reducing the back transfer problem. The first scheme is indicated in Fig. 6,

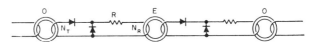

Fig. 6. Introduction of shunt diodes to reduce back transfer in the two-clock driver system of Fig. 5.

where an extra shunt diode is introduced into each coupling loop. The polarity of the diode is such that it does not interfere with the forward transfer. However, it is easy to verify that it short-circuits any back transfer, the resistor R being necessary in this case in order that the shunt diode not present a short circuit to the switching core itself. Two-core, four-diode-per-bit registers of this type perform very well and have been extensively marketed. Let us note a few properties of such a register.

(1) Although the initial motivation was to exploit the low cost and high reliability of magnetic cores, these circuits contain other components (particularly diodes) whose cost may be comparable to and reliability definitely lower than that of the cores themselves.

(2) The extra components in the coupling loops significantly increase the number of solder connections required. This again reflects on the over-all cost and reliability.

(3) The forward voltage drop in the diode is useful for providing relatively high loss for low level signals. So as not to present a high loss for the high level signals as well, however, we need a suitably high impedance transmission system, that is, a large number of turns in the transmitter and receiver windings so that the currents in the loops are relatively small. Thus, commercial registers of this type generally have several tens of turns on transmitter windings. The number of receiver turns in such registers is generally a half to a third the number of transmitter turns. These large numbers of turns are relatively costly to wind and also increase the possibility of intrawinding short circuits.

Finally, let us briefly note one other scheme for reducing back transfer. This is shown in Fig. 7, where it can be seen that the back-to-back diodes in

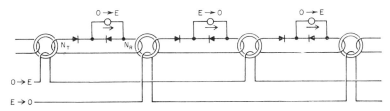

Fig. 7. An alternate technique for reducing back transfer. The back-to-back diodes in each loop prevent loop current unless one is forward biased.

each loop would prevent current from ever flowing except that one diode in each loop is forward biased (by a current source) during the time that particular loop is to be used for forward transfer. (Actually, more practical circuits of this type can be arranged so that only a single extra pair of diodes is required, rather than one extra diode per loop.)

1.3 Achieving Logic

To achieve general logic capability, there are more requirements than for only a shift register (e.g., the ability for one core to drive more than one receiver core, and the ability to mix signals according to different logical combinations). Nevertheless, the capability to build a shift register is a long step towards general logic capability, because it implies the very important ability to achieve bistable transfer, which in turn implies the ability to achieve signal gain greater than unity. Actually, a number of practical general logic schemes have been successfully developed using cores and diodes, these schemes generally being referred to as core-diode schemes. For further details the reader is referred to Meyerhoff [1] and Haynes [2].

Although core-diode logic circuits have been quite successfully applied, there has been a continuing desire to eliminate all components other than the cores themselves and the interconnecting wires, thus achieving core-wire or all-magnetic circuits. Though this effort was initially considered mainly as an intellectual challenge, the success to date warrants serious consideration of the techniques. All-magnetic circuit technology is presently such that, in many applications, circuits of this type are strongly competitive with the more conventional circuit techniques. In some applications, the advantages of this type of circuit cannot be matched by other techniques. The purposes of this article are to sketch the present status of logic realization with all-magnetic circuitry and to point out the special properties of such circuits.

2. Modes of Solution with All-Magnetic Circuits

Many different ways of building core-wire circuits are now known. However, in this brief article, we cannot hope to catalog them, or even to convey a complete picture of the possibilities. We can only hope to convey the nature of the possibilities.[1] To introduce the subject, we first consider in this section the transformation of core-diode circuits to core-wire circuits by replacement of diodes by cores. Then we consider a type of scheme that removes the need for diodes by replacement of the toroidal cores by more complex, multileg elements.

2.1 Replacing Diodes by Cores

Assume the core of Fig. 8(a) is in negative saturation, $-\phi_r$. A positive current I will then switch the core towards $+\phi_r$, with a resulting voltage drop across the winding. With the same initial flux state, however, a negative current, $-I$, will drive the core still further into saturation, with very small voltage drop. We thus have very different response to the two polarities of current flow and are, therefore, tempted to consider using a magnetic core to replace a physical diode, the corresponding orientations of the devices being as shown in Fig. 8(b). Let us refer to the direction of current in which the core is driven further into saturation as the "forward"

[1] This subject is treated much more comprehensively in the book *Digital Magnetics*, by D. R. Bennion, H. D. Crane, and D. Nitzan (tentative title; presently in preparation).

(low impedance) direction, in analogy to diode notation. The other direction will be referred to as the back direction.

Before replacing diodes with magnetic cores, however, we must note the following important similarities and differences. Some of the differences

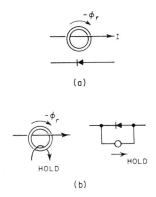

(a)

(b)

FIG. 8. Core, diode equivalence. (a) Analogous polarities. (b) Analogous use of a "hold" current to alter thresholds.

actually make the core more useful and others make the core less useful than the physical diode.

(1) The back impedance of a core is not constant: Even for a constant applied current, the switching voltage is not constant in time.

(2) A back impedance can be sustained only so long as the core is switching. Once the core becomes saturated in the opposite direction, the impedance is again essentially zero.

(3) Once the core has reached the opposite state of saturation, the magnetic "diode" has effectively been reversed, so that opposite polarity current will now cause the high impedance state. Although this is actually a useful property, we will consider here only schemes in which the "diode" core must be "restored" before it can be used again; that is, the core must be switched back to its $-\phi_r$ condition.

(4) If a current on a separate winding tends to "hold" the core in its $-\phi_r$ condition [Fig. 8(b)], then the core will exhibit a low impedance to either direction of current flow as long as the mmf in the normally reverse direction is less than the holding mmf. The same effect can be achieved by applying a forward-biasing current source across a diode, as indicated in the figure. In this case, a "backward current" equal to the holding current can flow before the diode circuit opens. (The normal threshold of a core can also be simulated by placing a current source across a diode, so that high impedance is obtained only after a certain "threshold" of current is reached.)

63

(5) Finally, we can generalize the two-winding notion of Fig. 8(b) by noting that the core can carry any number of windings, some of which may carry control currents (such as hold currents) whereas others may be parts of different circuit loops. The ability to obtain electrically isolated windings having different impedance levels (different numbers of turns) is very useful.

2.2 Register Circuit with a Series Diode and Shunt Diode per Loop

Let us apply these notions to try to replace the diodes of the circuit of Fig. 6 with cores. The resulting circuit is shown in Fig. 9(a), the diodes

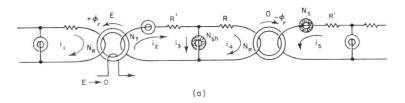

(a)

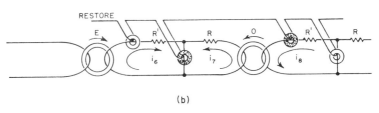

(b)

Fig. 9. Replacing the diodes of a register of Fig. 6 with cores to obtain a core-wire register. (a) Conditions during forward transfer, when the shaded cores are in their high-impedance condition. (b) Restoring the switched "diode cores" in preparation for the next advance pulse.

being replaced by cores with orientation as shown in Fig. 8(a). Let us trace the operation of this circuit in sufficient detail to see the requirements on these replacement cores.

Assume that the E core holds a *one*, i.e., it is nominally in its $+\phi_r$ state, and that the O element and all "diode" cores are in their clear condition, $-\phi_r$, i.e., their flux state is clockwise. These initial flux conditions are indicated in Fig. 9(a). Let us now consider the currents i_1 through i_5 that will flow as a result of driving core E back to its $-\phi_r$ state during the ensuing $E \rightarrow O$ pulse. From the previous discussion of the equivalent core-diode circuit, we know that during this transfer, the shunt diode in the $E \rightarrow O$ coupling loop is cut off as is the series diode in the following $O \rightarrow E$ loop. We have stated in Section 1 that the latter diode prevents loading of the receiver. In the all-core version, we therefore expect the

64

corresponding cores to exhibit their high impedance (switching) state. These two cores are shown shaded in the figure as a reminder that they switch during this $E \to O$ operation.

Current i_1 flows in the back loop through the forward direction of the shunt diode. "Back transfer" is therefore prevented by this low impedance shunt path. (The net effect of this current is merely to slow the rate of switching of the E core.)

Current i_2 must drive the receiver core by means of current i_4 and the shunt "diode" core by means of current i_3. During this switching, we see that at every instant

$$N_{sh}\dot{\phi}_{sh} = i_4 R + N_R \dot{\phi}_R, \qquad (2.1)$$

where N_{sh} and ϕ_{sh} are the number of turns and flux in the shunt core. Integrating, we find that the amount of flux switched in the shunt core, while the receiver is switched from $-\phi_r$ to $+\phi_r$, is

$$\Delta\phi_{sh} = \frac{R \int i_4 \, dt + N_R(2\phi_r)}{N_{sh}}. \qquad (2.2)$$

The shunt core must have a flux capacity equal to or greater than the amount given by (2.2) in order that the core will continue to exhibit a high impedance throughout the switching. With any smaller flux capacity, the shunt core would saturate before switching was complete and, by short-circuiting the receiver core, would prevent the receiver from completing its switching. [In circuit design, the value of R would ordinarily be chosen to make $R \int i_4 \, dt$ smaller than $N_R(2\phi_r)$.]

As a result of receiver switching, a current i_5 flows in the output circuit. But this current is relatively small because of the high impedance presented by the diode core as it switches. As above, it is simple to show that the flux capacity of this core must be at least

$$\Delta\phi_s = \frac{N_T(2\phi_r) - R' \int i_5 \, dt}{N_s}, \qquad (2.3)$$

where N_s and $\Delta\phi_s$ are the number of turns and the flux in the series cores.

If these "diode" cores have low drive requirements compared with the "storage" cores and, in addition, have flux capacity as noted above, then we can actually expect good flux transfer from this circuit. However, it must be noted that before the subsequent $O \to E$ pulse can be applied, these diode cores must be "restored" to their original flux state. This can be achieved by exciting the "restore" line of Fig. 9(b), which drives all diode cores toward their clear state, $-\phi_r$. Although the restore line drives all diode cores, in this case only the two shaded cores will actually switch, the other diode cores having been unaffected by the $E \to O$ transfer.

By the right-hand rule, it is simply determined that the currents i_6

through i_8 that result from switching back these diode cores have the polarities shown in the figure. Note that current i_6 tends to switch the E core away from its present cleared state, and that currents i_7 and i_8 both tend to clear the O core. Since we wish the E and O cores to be undisturbed during this restoring operation, the "diode" cores must be switched slowly, so that the currents resulting from the induced switching voltages remain sufficiently small. We can now see the need for the added resistor R'. If we write a voltage summation equation for the loop in which current i_6 flows, we find

$$R'i_6 = N_{sh}\dot{\phi}_{sh}. \qquad (2.4)$$

If the resistance in the loop were exactly zero, then $\dot{\phi}_{sh}$ would necessarily be zero. In other words, we could not restore the diode core (unless i_6 became so large as to switch the E core, but that cannot be allowed).

A suitable interpretation of the restoring operation is that the flux "stored" in the diode core during its backward (switching) phase is "dissipated" in resistance during the restore phase. But we can see now that this restoring process is necessarily slow, compared with the advance operation. For simplicity, assume i_6 is constant during the restore process. Integration of (2.4) results in

$$R'i_6\tau_1 = N_{sh}\Delta\phi_{sh} = \Delta\lambda_{sh}, \qquad (2.5)$$

where τ_1 is the restore time and $\Delta\lambda_{sh}$ represents the flux linkages "injected" into the loop when an amount of flux $\Delta\phi_{sh}$ is restored in the core. (Note that λ has the dimensions of voltage $\times$ time. Numerical values are often expressed in volt-μsec for λ or in volt-μsec per turn for ϕ.) For sufficiently small flux linkage loss in R during advance (which we will assume), then

$$N_{sh}\Delta\phi_{sh} = N_R\Delta\phi_R. \qquad (2.6)$$

From (2.5) and (2.6), we find the restore time τ_1 to be given approximately by

$$\tau_1 = \frac{N_R\Delta\phi_R}{R'i_6}. \qquad (2.7)$$

Let us now compare this with the amount of flux linkages $\Delta\lambda_{R'}$ "dissipated" in R' during the advance. In that case,

$$\Delta\lambda_{R'} = i_2R'\tau_2, \qquad (2.8)$$

where again (for simplicity) it is assumed that the current i_2 is constant during the switching time τ_2. Assuming further that the circuit is designed so that the flux linkages lost in R' during the advance is of the order of 10 percent of the flux linkages delivered to the receiver, i.e.,

$$\Delta\lambda_{R'} \approx \tfrac{1}{10} N_R\Delta\phi_R, \qquad (2.9)$$

then we can see from (2.7), (2.8), and (2.9) that

$$\tau_1 \approx 10\, \frac{\dot{i}_2}{\dot{i}_6}\, \tau_2. \tag{2.10}$$

Since current i_2 at advance time will be substantially larger than the current i_6 at restore time, we can see that in this case the restore time could easily be 20 to 30 times the advance time. Similar arguments can be applied to the other currents during the restore phase.

By symmetry, we should expect to excite the restore line after each $O \rightarrow E$ operation, as well as after each $E \rightarrow O$ operation. The over-all register circuit then operates on a four-clock cycle: . . . $E \rightarrow O$, Restore, $O \rightarrow E$, Restore, ... It should be noted that the restore line could actually be excited by a dc current (rather than by pulses), the only effect being that during advance, the currents i_3 and i_5 would be somewhat larger in order to overcome the holding tendency of the restore current. The resulting circuit operation would still have a basic four-clock rhythm, however, even though only two explicit clock pulses need be provided.

We will see shortly that core-wire circuits can be arranged in which resistances are not actually required in the coupling loops, and in which operation is correspondingly faster. In these "nonresistance" circuits, there is no equivalent restore operation. In fact, one can no longer identify equivalent diodes in the same way. Before introducing these circuits, however, we will pursue a bit further the replacement of physical diodes with cores in order to introduce some more new notions.

2.3 Register Circuit with Back-to-Back Diodes

If we replace the series diodes of Fig. 7 with magnetic "diodes," we obtain the circuit of Fig. 10. Since there are no basically new principles involved

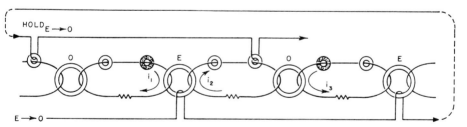

Fig. 10. Replacing the diodes of the register of Fig. 7 with cores to obtain a core-wire register. Conditions shown are for $E \rightarrow O$ transfer.

here, we only briefly consider the transfer of a *one* state during the $E \rightarrow O$ clock. As in the previous case, two diode cores switch during transfer, one to prevent receiver loading, and the other to prevent back transfer. The appropriate diodes are again shown shaded for emphasis.

As a result of E core switching during the $E \rightarrow O$ pulse, currents i_1, i_2, and i_3 flow as shown. Current i_1 is small in magnitude because of the low switching current required by the diode core. This current in the input circuit therefore represents very little loading on the E core during transfer. The main current i_2 would tend also to be small in magnitude because of the right-hand diode core, except that an explicit hold current prevents this diode from switching. (In the core-diode version the equivalent diode is forward biased by a current source.)

In this arrangement, the transmitter and receiver are coupled through a relatively low loss circuit during transfer. Receiver loading, represented by current i_3, is small, as in the series-shunt diode case previously considered.

The circuit is easily arranged so that the drive line and the hold line can be placed in series, as indicated by dashed lines in the figure. This results in the need for only a single power source for this phase of operation. An $O \rightarrow E$ line, which is symmetrically placed with respect to the $E \rightarrow O$ line, is omitted from the figure for purposes of clarity. A restore line linking all diode cores is also required, as before. The circuit has a four-clock beat, although again, the restore operation could be energized by a dc current, rather than by explicit pulses.

This core-wire scheme is essentially identical to one discussed by Briggs [3].

2.4 Register with Only One Shunt Diode per Loop

In Section 2.3, we made use of the ability to cancel, or overcome, the diode properties by holding. By extending this approach, we can develop a shift register arrangement in which there is only one shunt diode per loop. We will see that although the direct core-diode version of this circuit cannot actually work, the "magnetic diode" version can work well because of the ability to use multiple windings with different impedance levels.

Let us first develop the core-diode version and see why it cannot actually work. The basic concept is sketched in Fig. 11(a). The storage cores are simply lined up in series, with a shunt diode placed to ground between each pair of cores. Assume the E core holds a *one*. Upon application of the $E \rightarrow O$ advance pulse, the E core is switched back to $-\phi_r$. As a result, a current i tends to flow, as shown. Diode D_1 would present a low (forward) impedance to such a current flow. However, without special action, there could be no complete circuit, all diodes to the right being cut off. Since our main objective during this advance operation is to switch the neighboring right-hand O core, we wish the current i to link that O core, but go no further. This can be accomplished by turning on (forward biasing) Diode D_3, as shown. As long as the bias current is greater in magnitude than i,

68

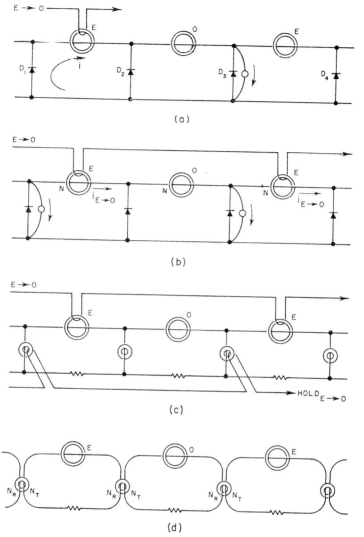

FIG. 11. Register with only a single shunt "diode" per loop. The scheme with an actual diode (a,b) is not workable, but the scheme with a "magnetic diode" (c,d) is workable, because of the possibility of using multiple windings to obtain a turns ratio $N_T/N_R > 1$, as indicated in (d).

Diode D_3 will present a low impedance to i. Hence, the E and O cores are directly coupled.

In order to transmit simultaneously, all E cores must be driven by the $E \rightarrow O$ drive, and every diode between an O and its right neighboring E core must be forward biased, as indicated in Fig. 11(b). During the alternate

$O \rightarrow E$ drive (not shown on the figure), the other set of diodes must similarly be forward biased. To this extent the circuit appears proper. But a turns ratio cannot be used in this circuit to achieve flux gain of more than unity. Therefore, because of inherent losses in coupling, the flux will necessarily deteriorate as a bit is propagated.

Simply replacing the diodes with cores (and resistors), as indicated in Fig. 11(c), offers no advantage regarding flux gain. However, by replacing the single winding on the diode cores by a separate pair of windings, of turns N_T and N_R, as shown in Fig. 11(d), we can quite easily obtain the required flux gain. For clarity in the figure, none of the drive windings are indicated although a pair of advance lines are required, as before. The required restore line again can be dc operated. Note also that each advance current must simultaneously be applied to the proper hold line as well.

The register of Fig. 11(d) can be made to operate quite well, although it again is relatively slow, the restore operation being long compared with the advance. This type of register, using one shunt diode per loop, has been discussed by Russell [4], and is referred to as Russell's Type II scheme. (Russell's Type I scheme is the analog of the one series diode per loop register of Fig. 5. Although both the core-diode and core-wire versions of the Type I circuit can work, the "back transfer" problem is such that they operate poorly, in the sense that there is little tolerance in circuit design and driver current magnitudes.)

Some aspects of the above technique of replacing diodes by cores, in addition to having been employed in [3, 4], have also been discussed by Stabler [5]. For additional discussion of circuits requiring resistance in the coupling loops, the reader is referred to Section 4.3 and to Gianola [6].

2.5 Nonresistance Schemes

In all of the above schemes, a core-diode circuit has been directly converted to a circuit containing cores, wire, and resistance. However, the magnitude of resistance required is often such that it is easily incorporated into the wire itself. Such circuits are therefore generally included in the category of all-magnetic or core-wire circuits, even though the wire must be chosen so as to provide proper resistance levels. Circuits of this type can generally be made to work very well, although they are relatively slow. The type of resistance circuit that presently appears to be most practical is discussed in Section 4.

It is of interest to consider whether resistance is a basic requirement for core-wire circuits. There is no objection to resistance as such, except that restoring the magnetic diodes (by flux "dissipation" in resistance) is a relatively slow process. If we could eliminate the need for resistance, we might then achieve faster operation.

Returning to the core-diode circuit of Fig. 6, we see that the circuit consists of two types of components, each of which provides certain crucial functions: The cores provide storage and the diodes provide the proper isolation between cores. To eliminate the diodes, we can feel rather certain that each toroidal core would have to be replaced with a more complex magnetic device, or at least with a network of such toroidal elements. We will see that both possibilities are realizable. In this section, we will indicate how such a register circuit can be developed using multiaperture cores (sometimes also referred to as multipath or multileg cores or multiaperture devices, or simply as Mads), as has been done by Crane [7]. In Section 3, we will indicate how multiaperture elements can in turn be replaced with networks of (simpler) toroidal cores. These core-wire circuits do not rely on the use of wire resistance in any first-order way, and are relatively fast because they do not require the relatively slow restore phase.

Recall that the series diode in the circuit of Fig. 6 was required to de-couple the output circuit of an element while it was switching as a receiver. But decoupling can be achieved in an alternate way. Assume that a small hole, or aperture, is centrally located in the wall of the core [see Fig. 12(a)],

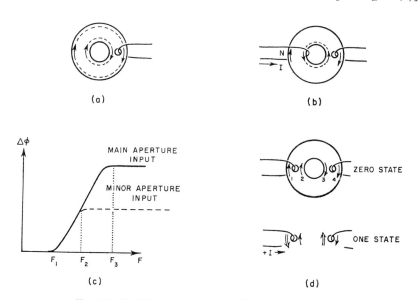

(a)

(b)

(c)

(d)

Fig. 12. Multileg cores and their "setting" properties.

so as to provide two essentially equal legs. The output winding then links only one of these legs (say the outer leg) of the core. The core is shown in the figure in its $-\phi_r$ state, i.e., clockwise flux. By having the output winding link only one half (i.e., one leg) of the core, flux can be switched in the other half (i.e., other leg) without inducing a voltage in the output winding, thus potentially eliminating the need for the series diode. Thus, in response to an "input" current I [Fig. 12(b)], up to half the flux capacity of the core can be switched without inducing an output signal. (Practically speaking, any tendency for the switching flux to "spread" into the outer leg would be resisted by current flow in the low resistance output circuit. The output circuit is therefore effectively decoupled; i.e., it does not significantly load the switching core.)

A typical relation between the amount of flux switched, or "set" about the main aperture and the magnitude of input current is shown in Fig. 12(c). For flux to switch at all, $F = NI$ must be greater than a threshold value F_1. For $F > F_3$ the flux in the core is completely reversed. (The magnitudes of F_1 and F_3 depend on the magnitudes of the inner and outer radii, respectively.) For some particular value F_2, exactly half the core flux is switched; this condition is sometimes referred to as the "maximally set" state. We will see in a moment that a register scheme can be devised in which a (binary) zero state is characterized by a low level (nominally zero) amount of set flux, and the (binary) one state by the maximally set condition. To represent a useful binary state, we would prefer the $\Delta\phi - F$ curve shown by the dashed line in Fig. 12(c), so that the core is maximally set for any mmf $F \geq F_2$. Such a relation can be obtained by having the input winding also link a separate small aperture in the core, as shown in Fig. 12(d). Now in response to an input mmf of value $F \geq F_2$, the core is set to the one state, as indicated below the figure. The double arrows symbolize flux changes that result from the input current. In this case, flux changes in Legs 1 and 3. (Note that although the path including Legs 1 and 2 is physically the shortest, no additional flux can switch in Leg 2 because it is already saturated in the switching direction. The path including Legs 1 and 3 is then the next shortest available switching path.)

We will now show how a diodeless system can be synthesized with these as our basic components. In Fig. 13(a), a pair of multileg cores is connected together with the output of one element connected directly to the input of the other. The intent is to transmit data from the left-hand to the right-hand element.

With the O element in its one state, as shown, application of an $O \rightarrow E$ current will cause flux to switch locally about the output aperture. This, in turn, results in a loop current $+i$ that sets the E element (to its one state). The flux changes during this transmission are indicated below the circuit.

If the O element is initially in the zero state, however, we desire that no flux switch upon application of the $O \rightarrow E$ pulse. (In this way, we can successfully "transmit" a zero, since the receiver element that is initially in the cleared state—nominally the same flux condition as a zero state—is not affected by the transfer operation.) To avoid flux switching in this case,

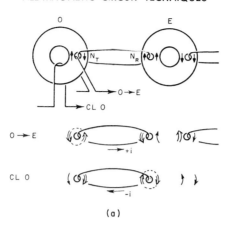

(a)

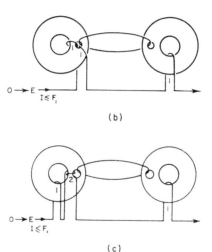

(b)

(c)

FIG. 13. Flux transfer between multileg cores. (a) A means for transferring flux from one multileg core to another. (b) An alternate method for applying drive current. (c) A winding arrangement equivalent to that shown in (b).

it is necessary that the $O \rightarrow E$ advance current be kept sufficiently small that flux cannot be caused to switch about the main aperture of the transmitter element. In other words, the drive strength in Fig. 13(a) must be limited to about one threshold. However, this would represent too weak a drive for successful *one* transmission.

A technique to increase the permitted drive strength is briefly noted in Fig. 13(b). In this configuration, the drive current links the transmitter output aperture with a one-turn figure-eight winding and also links the

73

main aperture of the receiver with a single turn winding. For $F = F_1$, the receiver is biased just short of threshold (so that a relatively small loop current is required for receiver switching), and the transmitter output aperture is driven relatively strongly with twice the threshold current. It can be simply verified that nominally zero flux will be switched during *zero* transfer with this drive arrangement. Of course, if the drive windings were increased from one to n turns and the advance current decreased by $1/n$, the drive ampere-turns (and hence the circuit operation) would be unaffected. Also note that the alternate drive winding arrangement of Fig. 13(c) is equivalent to that of Fig. 13(b), since the net ampere-turns through each aperture is the same in each case. An aid to visualization is to imagine pulling on the left end of the $O \rightarrow E$ line until the loop of wire slips through the main aperture of the core, leaving just the figure-eight winding shown in Fig. 13(b).

We have now indicated possibilities for successful binary transmission, but the picture is not complete. For one thing, note that during *one* transmission, the transmitter switches only locally about the output aperture. The transmission is therefore said to be "nondestructive." Although this property of nondestructive flux transfer is very useful, it implies here that before the O element can subsequently be used as a receiver it must be explicitly cleared, i.e., driven to its *zero* state. (In the core-diode register, the transmitter cores were automatically returned to their zero state as a part of the transmission process.)

Clearing of the transmitter can be achieved by energizing the Clear winding of Fig. 13(a). The result is that flux is again reversed in the output winding, and a current $-i$ therefore tends to flow in the output circuit. One might at first think that this is undesirable, since forward transmission has already occurred over this coupling loop. However, this negative loop current is precisely what is required to achieve successful operation. In particular, this negative current reverses the flux locally about the input aperture of the receiver, as indicated in Fig. 13(a). The significance of this is that the flux in the input leg is now back to its initial (cleared) direction, so that when the E core is subsequently cleared, there will be no back transfer. Hence the need for the shunt diode is also eliminated.

By symmetry, we see that the $E \rightarrow O$ and Clear E drivers are also needed, and the basic clock cycle for this register has a four beat rhythm, . . . , $O \rightarrow E$, Clear O, $E \rightarrow O$, Clear E, ... The basic circuit arrangement is indicated in Fig. 14. (For clarity, the simplified advance circuit of Fig. 13(a) is indicated.) The flux changes associated with transmission of a *one* is traced below the figure, one complete clock cycle being shown.

The type of shaping around output apertures shown in this figure (but not in previous figures) is generally desirable, in order that the major part of the core material can be saturated in the clear state. The magnetic

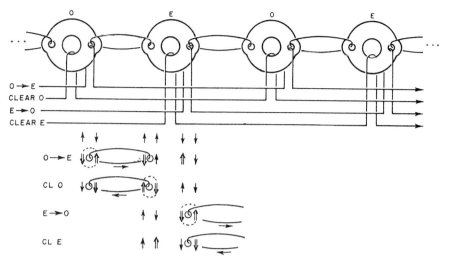

FIG. 14. Shift-register circuit and the sequence of flux reversals during a complete clock cycle, for transfer of a binary *one*.

properties of the unshaped multiaperture cores shown before are less square (e.g., threshold characteristics are more rounded), since a substantial amount of material around the periphery of the core can never be fully saturated. For more details on the effects of shaping and other phenomena occurring in connection with multiaperture cores, the reader is referred to Nitzan [8] and Hesterman [9].

One point needs emphasis here; this is the matter of flux gain. In the core-diode register it was implied that the diode could provide the relatively high flux loss required for low level (binary *zero*) flux transmission. But since we have eliminated the diodes, we must recheck the possibilities of achieving proper bistable gain conditions. Actually, there are a number of suitable flux loss mechanisms in the circuit of Fig. 13(a), and the circuit can be made to work well as it stands. [Discussion of these mechanisms is beyond the scope of this article but will be covered elsewhere (see Footnote 1).] For present purposes, however, let us introduce the use of a "clipper core," Fig. 15(a), as suggested by Engelbart [10]. By this means, it will be clearly seen that the proper gain curve can actually be achieved (if all other mechanisms should fail).

Assume for the moment that the clipper core is eliminated and that we have a zero impedance loop, with $N_T/N_R > 1$. In this case, the dashed curve of Fig. 15(b) would represent the relation between transmitted and received flux. The gain in this case would be greater than unity for all values of flux from zero to the maximally set level, and binary transfer would be impossible. Now introduce a clipper core, which has a very low

75

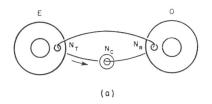

(a)

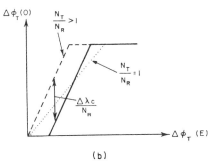

(b)

Fig. 15. Use of a "clipper" core and its effect on the flux transfer characteristic.

switching threshold and a capacity equal to $\Delta\lambda_c = N_c\Delta\phi_c$. Since no flux can be switched in the receiver until saturation of the clipper core (the switching of which limits loop current to a value below receiver threshold), to obtain the new flux transfer curve, it is merely necessary to subtract from the dashed curve a constant magnitude of "clipped" flux, $\Delta\lambda_c/N_R$ [unless $\Delta\phi_T(E) < \Delta\lambda_c/N_R$, in which case the flux absorbed by the clipper is just equal to $N_T\Delta\phi_T(E)$]. The clipper core should be cleared at the same time as the transmitter. By this means, excellent operation can be obtained.

In the following section, a number of basically different types of non-resistance core-wire circuits will be introduced.

3. Variation and Further Derivation of Core-Wire Transfer Schemes

3.1 Introduction

In the above material, core-wire transfer circuits were introduced by considering the functional properties held in common by cores and diodes. It was found that there are certain core-wire circuits in which some of the cores (or cores and wire resistance) play a role corresponding to the role of diodes in related core-diode circuits. We could, in fact, obtain still additional variety by similarly considering interchangeability of cores and wire resistance in coupling loops. The reason we can consider these various interchanges of cores, wire resistance, and diodes is because any emf $N\dot{\phi}$ injected into a coupling loop via an N-turn winding can (and must) be balanced by emf from other cores or by voltage drops through resistance or other electric elements in the loop. But similarly, note that at a physical junction of legs in a multiaperture core, a ϕ in one leg must be balanced by ϕ's in other legs common to the junction, suggesting, in turn, exchange of core junctions and coupling loops as still another example of a way to obtain circuit variety.

Besides exchanging circuit elements that play similar roles, we can also start with known circuits and eliminate nonessential elements or even add elements to obtain increased capability or improved operation. Or, we can change the mode of sequencing through a given set of elements. This leads to a large and confusing variety of possible circuits. Methods are needed for giving some system to the derivation of new and varied circuits and to the comparative evaluation of the circuits obtained.

There are several useful methods for graphical representation of core-wire transfer circuits and their modes of operation. One such method is the pictorial sketching of the circuits that has been used up to this point. Some of these methods are very useful for certain purposes, though no single one is ideal in all respects. One that is quite useful for effecting and studying circuit variations by means of eliminating, adding, or exchanging elements, or by changing the mode of sequencing is the magnetic-network representation to be described in this section.

[A preliminary look at Figs. 20(b) through 20(d) may be helpful in giving an idea of the power of the network method. By means of the common network representation of Fig. 20(c), the circuits of Figs. 20(b) and 20(d) will be seen to be functionally equivalent, a fact not readily apparent from simple comparison of the two circuits.]

3.2 Magnetic Networks

It is natural to consider the possibility of a network representation because of the well-known, well-proven usefulness of network theory in the study of linear electric circuits (and other types of systems as well). In fact, since a single-aperture core with n windings is merely an n-winding transformer in the electric domain, a core logic circuit in which each core has only a single aperture can readily be represented by an electric network, albeit a highly nonlinear one. The representation of multiaperture cores in the electric domain is possible; however, visualization is not simple because the configurations of the electric network and the corresponding magnetic core are topological duals. (That is, network nodes would correspond to core apertures and network loops to core junctions.)

An approach to a network representation that has proven to be generally (but not exclusively) more useful than the use of an electric network is to view single-aperture and multi-aperture cores as individual magnetic circuits and then to transform the electric coupling loops to the magnetic domain so as to be able to represent the whole circuit by a magnetic network. In viewing a core as a magnetic circuit, it is useful to consider the basic circuit variables to be mmf drop F ($= \int \mathbf{H} \cdot d\mathbf{l}$) and ϕ, corresponding to voltage drop V ($= \int \mathbf{E} \cdot d\mathbf{l}$) and current I, respectively, in electric circuits, where $\mathbf{H}$ and $\mathbf{E}$ are vector magnetic and electric fields, and where integration is along a specified circuit path. Note that with this view, the magnetic variables have interchanged dimensions relative to the corresponding electric circuit variables, suggesting the duality relationship mentioned above.

In illustration of how a circuit may be put into magnetic-network form, consider the example of Fig. 16(a). The numbers identify the various core legs. (The toroidal core may be viewed as a single-leg core.) The arrows on the cores indicate each core's reference state, which is generally taken to be the greatest negative residual state, $-\phi_r$.

Assuming no flux escapes from the core into the surroundings, the rule for flux continuity at a junction may be written

$$\sum_i \phi_i = 0, \tag{3.1}$$

which implies

$$\sum_i \dot{\phi}_i = 0, \tag{3.2}$$

where the ϕ_i's represent the values of flux leaving (or entering) the junction. Thus, in Fig. 16(a), for example, $\phi_1 - \phi_2 - \phi_3 = 0$.

For the moment, let us assume that there is no resistance or air inductance (i.e., inductance due to linking air flux) in the coupling loop. Then the algebraic sum of core emf's in the loop must equal zero. That is, $\sum N_j \dot{\phi}_j = 0$. For our purposes here, we need consider only the case of single-turn windings ($N_j = 1$ for all j) and hence can write

$$\sum_j \dot{\phi}_j = 0. \tag{3.3}$$

Integration of the terms in the above equation yields

$$\sum_j \phi_j = C, \tag{3.4}$$

where each ϕ_j represents the instantaneous value of core flux linking the loop, and where C is a constant equal to the total initial flux linking the loop. (For example, $\phi_3 - \phi_4 = C$.) Thus we see that such a coupling loop imposes exactly the same constraint on values of ϕ as does a core junction. The constraints on values of ϕ is also of the same form as for a core junction but weaker, since C in (3.4) need not (but may) equal zero, whereas for a core junction, the sum of ϕ values is necessarily equal to zero.

78

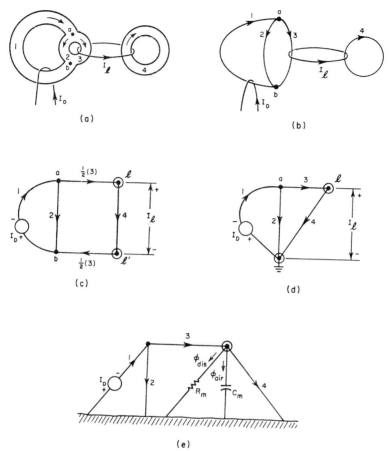

Fig. 16. Illustration of magnetic-network concepts. (a) A coupled pair of cores. (b) A schematic representation. (c,d) Two forms of the magnetic-network representation. (e) A form of the network including branches to account for coupling-loop resistance and inductance.

As an intermediate step in constructing a network, the circuit is represented in simplified form in Fig. 16(b), with magnetic network nodes and branches replacing core junctions and legs, respectively, but with electric circuitry still in place. Then, in Fig. 16(c), the coupling loop is represented by a pair of magnetic network nodes inserted into Branch 3, the loop current I_l as a node-pair mmf difference, and the drive current I_D as an mmf source in series with Leg 1. Note, by comparison with Fig. 16(a), that this model correctly represents the net mmf applied to the various core paths by the drive current I_D and the loading current I_l.

Figure 16(d) shows a reduced form in which the two branches represent-

79

ing Leg 3 have been combined and Nodes b and l' have been merged into a single reference node. In either case, the net mmf drop along a branch may now be interpreted as a magnetic potential difference between the nodes terminating the branch, since—with all mmf's due to linking currents replaced by branch mmf's—the mmf drop from one point to another is independent of the path. In other words, the network branch mmf's obey Kirchhoff's circuital law.

In order to distinguish between coupling-loop nodes for which flux values are constrained by (3.4), and core-junction nodes, which are subject to the stronger condition (3.1), we place a circle (suggestive of a coupling loop) around the former type, as shown in Figs. 16(c) and 16(d). The reference node will sometimes be expanded into a reference "plane" or "bus," as in Fig. 16(e), for convenience.

Thus far, we have assumed no electrical impedance in the coupling loop. But now suppose there are total resistance R_l and air inductance L_l in series in the loop, including or consisting of the parasitic distributed resistance and inductance of the wire itself. (Parasitic capacitance is, practically speaking, unimportant in these circuits.) Then, in place of $\dot\phi_3 - \dot\phi_4 = 0$, we have

$$\dot\phi_3 - \dot\phi_4 + \dot\phi_{\mathrm{air}} = -R_l I_l, \tag{3.5}$$

where $\dot\phi_{\mathrm{air}} = \dot\lambda_{\mathrm{air}} = L_l \dot I_l$ is the rate of change of the linking air flux and $R_l I_l$ is the resistive voltage drop in the loop. This equation can be put in the form of (3.3) by interpreting $R_l I_l$ as an equivalent $\dot\phi_{\mathrm{dis}} = \dot\lambda_{\mathrm{dis}} = R_l I_l$, for then we have

$$\dot\phi_3 - \dot\phi_4 + \dot\phi_{\mathrm{air}} + \dot\phi_{\mathrm{dis}} = 0, \tag{3.6}$$

where $\dot\phi_{\mathrm{dis}}$ represents the flux "dissipated" in the loop resistance. (Note that flux ϕ and flux linkage λ are identical here because of the assumption of single-turn windings.) This expression is in the form of (3.2), and hence we see that the coupling loop can still be represented by a magnetic network node, provided two branches are added for carrying the equivalent "magnetic-current" components $\dot\phi_{\mathrm{air}}$ and $\dot\phi_{\mathrm{dis}}$. These branches are shown as linear "magnetic capacitance" C_m ($= L_l$) and "magnetic resistance" R_m ($= 1/R_l$) in Fig. 16(e), since with I_l appearing as magnetic potential we have

$$\dot\phi_{\mathrm{air}} = L_l \dot I_l = C_m \dot I_l \tag{3.7}$$

$$\dot\phi_{\mathrm{dis}} = R_l I_l = (1/R_m) I_l. \tag{3.8}$$

This result is in agreement with the topological duality effect mentioned earlier, since the series R_l and L_l in the electric circuitry have transformed into parallel $R_m = 1/R_l$ (or conductance $G_m = R_l$) and capacitance $C_m = L_l$ in the magnetic domain. Similarly, a series capacitance C would transform into a shunt inductance. A series diode (nonlinear resistance R_D) would transform into a hypothetical shunt "magnetic diode" (of nonlinear conductance $G_{Dm} = R_D$).

With the magnetic network method in hand, let us now consider some of the alternate circuits that can be developed on the basis of the resistance and nonresistance types of transfer circuits introduced in Section 2. We will see that magnetic structure can be a useful basis for transfer scheme classification, even though there are often several distinct schemes having the identical network structure, variability in these cases being based on a particular clear state of the network, or the mode of sequencing through it. By "mode of sequencing," we mean the order and manner in which the various network branches are switched during one clock cycle as a *one* is propagated along the structure. Interchange of physical and coupling-loop node types in the network representation leads to further variations in physical realization of a network. All of these variations—structure, assignment of node type, choice of clear state, and mode of sequencing—will be illustrated in the material below.

Early work on some of the above network concepts was done by Engelbart [11] and Stabler [5]. For a more detailed treatment than that presented here, the reader is referred to Bennion [12].

3.3 Structural Variations, Nonresistance

The circuit of Fig. 13(c), with single-turn coupling loops, is shown in simplified schematic form in Fig. 17(a). The $E \rightarrow O$ and Clear E drive lines, not shown, would be symmetrically placed with respect to the two drive lines shown. For simplicity, it is assumed that Legs A through D are negligibly short compared to the sum of lengths of Legs E and F. Therefore, the major-aperture mmf threshold, T, which is just the F_1 of Fig. 12(c), is the sum of the thresholds of Legs E and F. The maximum value of $O \rightarrow E$ drive without spurious switching of cores during transfer is shown, i.e., T on each bias winding and $2T$ on the main drive winding.

Assuming negligible coupling-loop resistance and inductance, a magnetic network for this circuit is shown in Fig. 17(b). Legs E and F, which always switch together, have been lumped into one branch M, and a ground plane has been used to indicate reference. Note that branches representing Legs D_O and A_E appear in series in the network, which is reasonable since the (nominally zero impedance) coupling loop forces identical values of ϕ in each leg. The mmf potential of the associated coupling-loop node is, of course, equal to loop current I_b.

Let us now consider some of the circuit variations that can be realized by modifying the form of the network. Since series pairs of legs like D_O and A_E switch together, the coupling-loop nodes in Fig. 17(b) can be eliminated. We also wish to generalize the network diagram to allow for

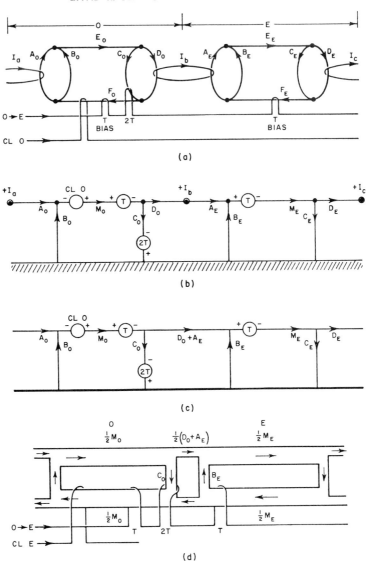

FIG. 17. Use of network methods. (a) Schematic form of the circuit of Fig. 13(c). (b) A network representation. (c) Elimination of the coupling-loop nodes. (d) A continuous magnetic-circuit realization.

interpretation of the remaining nodes as representing either core junctions or coupling loops. Therefore, in Fig. 17(c), nodes are shown without either dots or circles. (Reference or "ground" is now indicated by a heavy line.)

If we now interpret all the nodes remaining in the latter network as

82

representing core junctions (as originally), then this network may be realized by the magnetic circuit of Fig. 17(d). (Note that half of each of the horizontal branches has been placed along the bottom rail, since a magnetic "ground plane" of sufficiently low magnetic impedance cannot be realized physically.) With no coupling loops, there can obviously be no gain by means of turns ratio. However, this scheme should still be workable by virtue of the "soft threshold" type of gain mechanism discussed in Section 3.5.

Alternately, if we make the modification of reinterpreting the nodes in Fig. 17(c) to represent coupling loops, then the circuit of Fig. 18(a) (also described by Stabler [5]) is obtained. (We have shown the Clear E rather than the Clear O drive line in this case.) Note that there is no problem in establishing correct relative polarities for the coupling-loop windings in such a circuit. For example, given that clockwise saturation represents the clear state (as in this case), then it is only necessary that positive loop current link downward (or upward) through all cores corresponding to branches with clear-state arrows leaving (or entering) the node.

Corresponding to the Clear O drive shown in the preceding diagrams, only the Clear M winding should nominally be required in Fig. 18(a). In any practical circuit, however, the auxiliary Clear B winding is also necessary to ensure that Core B_E is cleared out thoroughly. (Otherwise, if we attempt to let Core B_E be cleared by loop current induced by the clearing of Core M_E after transfer of a *one*, Core B_E would be left in a partially set state due to flux loss in the resistance of the loop.) The additional auxiliary winding, labeled "Hold," is not necessary but provides a useful isolation function, which may best be explained after the next circuit is described.

The circuit just considered contains eight cores and four coupling loops per bit, as compared to two multiaperture cores and two loops per bit in the original circuit. The larger number of loops is an undesirable feature from the practical standpoint of more wiring and solder joints being required. The extra loops, together with the extra cores, also contribute to higher flux losses because of added resistance in the loops, and because of increased current in some loops, for switching the additional cores. Hence, although this circuit is operable, let us consider whether all of the cores and coupling loops in Fig. 18(a) [branches and nodes in Fig. 17(c)] are really necessary.

If we could eliminate alternate longitudinal or series branches and merge the flanking nodes, then the number of nodes (loops) per bit would be reduced by a factor of two. To see if this is possible, let us ask the following question: what functions can or must a series branch serve when realized as a coupling (i.e., double-linked) core? We have at least the following answers:

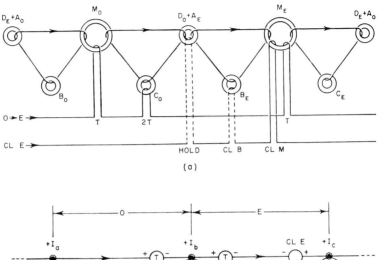

(a)

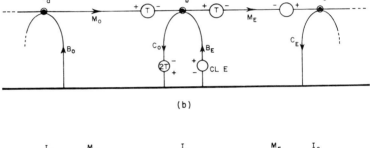

(b)

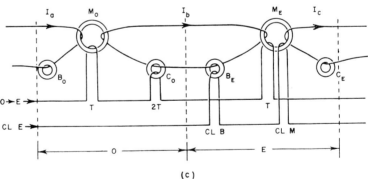

(c)

Fig. 18. Further use of network methods. (a) Realization of the network of Fig. 17(c) with an array of toroidal cores. (b) A network obtained by selective merging of nodes of Fig. 17(b). (c) A circuit realization of the network of (b).

(1) It provides a place for turns ratio for obtaining flux gain more than unity.

(2) It may have to retain a set flux state over one or more clock phases, which it can do by presenting a high threshold to loop currents induced by the switching of other cores during these phases.

84

(3) When not required to retain a set state, it can be held in its clear state in order to isolate data bits on either side of it.

In the circuit of Fig. 18(a), the first two of these functions can be realized with the series M elements, and the third function, although advantageous, is not essential in this case (as we will see). Therefore, let us eliminate the $(D_O + A_E)$ and $(D_E + A_O)$ branches in the network of Fig. 17(c) and merge the flanking pairs of nodes, thus obtaining the network of Fig. 18(b). This new network may be realized by the circuit of Fig. 18(c), which was originated by Engelbart [11] in much the same fashion as the derivation here. This circuit looks very simple as it contains only two coupling loops per bit, no more than the original circuit of Fig. 17(a), and six cores per bit. However, as implied above, this simplification has resulted in some loss of isolation. In particular, it is in this case somewhat of a problem to avoid back transfer, practically speaking, as will now be discussed.

Any unbalance in the switching rates of Cores B_E and M_E at Clear E time will produce a loop current tending to disturb the state of Core C_O, which may at this time be either *one* or *zero*, depending upon the succeeding data bit. Any spurious setting of C_O could be avoided by having the C_O threshold sufficiently high. However, this threshold should be as low as possible in order that C_O does not load Core M appreciably during input to the O section. Hence, compromise is necessary.

From the standpoint of obtaining the best possible balance in clearing rates in Core B_E and M_E, the former should be made more like the latter instead of being smaller as shown in Fig. 18(c). [Suitable biasing for this case is discussed in connection with Fig. 20(a).]

Further, the net mmf on these cores should be adjusted to be as nearly equal as possible at Clear E time, taking into consideration the fact that M_E is loaded but B_E is not. However, tolerance in core selection and differences in resistive losses during the setting of M_E and B_E will generally still result in some unbalance.

Now the isolating value of Core $(D_O + A_E)$ in Fig. 18(a) can be made apparent. During the clearing of cores M_E and B_E, the presence of this core prevents coupling back to core C_O if the induced loop current is in the clear direction of $(D_O + A_E)$; the Hold winding shown in Fig. 18(a) can be used to prevent coupling due to induced loop current in the other direction.

In summary, the circuit of Fig. 18(a) is seen to be better from the standpoint of isolation against back transfer, and the circuit of Fig. 18(c) is better with respect to the problem of losses during transfer. It is interesting to ask whether there could be some other transfer scheme with no more toroids and coupling loops per bit that has the advantage of both of these.

85

3.4 Sequencing and Clear-State Variations, Nonresistance

To attempt to answer the above question, we note that a series branch (such as M in Fig. 17) that is required to hold a set state during one or more phases cannot at the same time be used for isolation by holding, since the holding mmf would clear any set state. But the M branches are the *only* series branches in the network of Fig. 18(b), and we would like to be able to employ these for isolation. If this can be done at all, a change in sequencing (and perhaps a change in the clear state of the structure) will be required.

In seeking to derive a new scheme in which the M branches are used for isolation, let us attempt to vary the sequencing so as to clear each M branch immediately after it is set. Along with this, we will then have to rely on one or both of the shunt branches, B or C, for intermediate storage of data.

The network of Fig. 18(b) is redrawn in Fig. 19(a) in a modified form that is often useful for considering variations in sequencing. The branches are drawn with heavy lines of two different lengths to represent relatively long and short elements. Series (horizontal) branches are understood to be joined to each other and to adjacent shunt (vertical) branches. All shunt branches are understood to return to a common reference plane.

In Fig. 19(b), the previously assumed sequencing for the network and circuit of Figs. 18(b) and 18(c) is shown. The dashed lines show flux switching paths during the indicated clock phase. Note that two dashed lines must pass through each element, the first one in the sequence opposed to, and the second one in conjunction with the arrow showing the clear state. Closure paths through the reference plane are not shown.

Now we are prepared to consider an alternate scheme [Fig. 19(c)], that makes use of the series branches M for isolation and that uses a new mode of clock sequencing, although the network structure and clear state are actually unchanged. (Although this scheme works, we will see that a still better one can be derived by alteration of the clear state as well as the sequencing.) The $E \rightarrow O$ and $O \rightarrow E$ transfers occur in exactly the same paths as before. But now we clear the M elements (transferring into the B's) immediately after transferring through the M's. (Note the redefinition of the boundaries of the O and E sections.) After Clear E, both C_O and B_O contain the information state, and then M_E may be held clear during the $O \rightarrow E$ and Clear O phases if necessary. The M elements may therefore be physically short, since they are not required to retain a set state, and C and B must both be long since C_O must retain its set state during the setting of B_O, and B_O must retain its set state during the clearing of C_O (i.e., during the $O \rightarrow E$ drive).

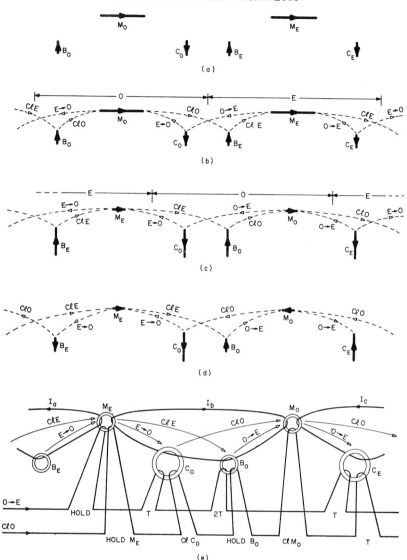

Fig. 19. Use of network manipulations to realize other core-wire schemes by means of sequencing and clear-state variations.

The toroid-wire realization of this skeletal network is identical to a circuit described by Russell [13]. There is no need to illustrate it here, since it has exactly the same coupling loops as the circuit of Fig. 18(c), although the drive windings would be different, as would the optimum

87

relative core sizes. (Actually, the toroid circuits we have been talking about may all be operable with all toroids physically identical, but probably with only very low drive-current tolerances.)

The scheme just considered has the disadvantage of requiring four high threshold (long) elements per bit as compared to only two per bit for the previous scheme, thus requiring more energy for operation at a given rate. However, if we could transfer out of B_O immediately after setting it, then this element could also be a physically short one. Hence, consider the still different scheme of Fig. 19(d). Here, by reversing the clear state of M_O, C_E, and B_E relative to M_E, C_O, and B_O, we make it possible (after a bit of information has been stored in C_O and then B_O), to transfer immediately from B_O to C_E. Hence, instead of C_O and B_O each having to hold information for one phase, as in the previous case, C_O now has to hold it for two phases but B_O during none; hence, only the C elements need have a relatively large threshold. This scheme has been described by Yochelson [14].

For comparison with previous circuits, the toroid realization of the last scheme is shown in Fig. 19(e), with drive windings for only two of the clock phases included. Isolation between bits, in particular against back transfer, is as good as in the circuit of Fig. 18(a). Yet the transfer loss problem is less severe in the present circuit than in that of Fig. 18(a) because transfer is from B_O to C_E through only two loops and one coupling core here, as compared to three loops (from C_O to C_E) and two coupling cores there. However, losses are still slightly more of a problem than in the circuit of Fig. 18(c), since two large loop currents (I_b and I_c) flow during transfer from B_O to C_E whereas only one large loop current (I_b) and one small one (I_c) flow during transfer from C_O to C_E, Fig. 18(c).

The question posed at the end of Section 3.3 has been substantially answered. We found not only one, but two, different schemes with the same network structure—and hence with no more toroids and coupling loops per bit—than the circuit of Fig. 18(c), yet both have isolation between adjacent bits on a par with the more complex circuit of Fig. 18(a). For both, transfer losses are less of a problem than for the circuit of Fig. 18(a), but slightly more so than for the circuit of Fig. 18(c). The first of the new schemes, Fig. 19(c), also has the disadvantage of requiring more of the larger cores per bit and hence more energy for operation.

(Although all of the schemes discussed here utilize a four-phase clock cycle, it is obvious that interesting schemes making use of five or more phases can be derived, as has been done by Hölken [15], for example. In fact, there are known practical schemes requiring only a three-phase cycle, as described by Haynes, et al. [16] and by Bennion and Engelbart [17].

3.5 Some Flux-Gain Mechanisms and a Flux-Doubling Scheme

For the schemes considered thus far, it has been assumed that turns ratios greater than unity in coupling loops would be utilized as needed to provide flux gain greater than unity [except for the circuit of Fig. 17(d), which contains no coupling loops]. What are some of the other possible flux-gain mechanisms?

One approach makes use of the feature of nondestructive readout noted in Section 2.5. It consists of transmitting a unit of flux from a minor aperture of a core in the manner described in Section 2.5, but then—instead of immediately clearing the core—restoring flux about the aperture to its prior state and transmitting a second unit of flux. The geometry and biasing of the receiving element can be so arranged that the successive amounts of flux transmitted are accumulated in the receiver. The transmitter can then be cleared or the process can be repeated any number of times. Flux gain per section up to an absolute limit of n:1, for n total transfer phases, can be achieved. This type of method is referred to as "flux pumping." Its use, of course, requires extra phases (subclocks) in the clock cycle. This technique will not be discussed further here, although a related method is used in the circuit of Fig. 26(e). In that circuit, subclocks are used to transfer out of a number of separate minor apertures sequentially before clearing out the transmitting core.

Another means for flux gain depends upon a material property known as "soft threshold," which a number of square-loop magnetic materials have to varying degrees. [This feature would be necessary for gain greater than unity in the circuit of Fig. 17(d).] A core with this property exhibits a lower (softened) switching threshold when in a partially set state reached by moderately rapid switching from the cleared (binary zero) state. In this case, an output drive current that would nominally be sub-threshold could actually cause switching of additional flux about the transmitter main aperture, after receipt of a one signal, but without causing additional switching after receipt of a zero signal (since the core would remain in its nominally clear state). Flux-gain factors of well over 2:1 have been achieved in this way, but drive current tolerances are generally quite low, since most materials do not have a large margin between the hard threshold and the soft threshold. For more details on soft-threshold considerations, the reader is referred to Bennion and Crane [18], Gianola [6], and Tancrell [19].

Now let us consider a means for flux gain known as "flux doubling." Whereas a variable amount of flux gain can be obtained by the methods previously described, doubling of flux is inherent in the transfer scheme to be described here. Each coupling-loop winding has the same number of turns, in particular a single turn only; no extra clock phases beyond the four discussed here are needed, and there is no dependence on the soft-threshold property.

The flux-doubling scheme could be arrived at by a more radical structural alteration of the network of Fig. 17(c) than any of the structural variations considered in Section 3.3. However, this particular scheme derivation is more readily visualized in terms of surgery on the toroid-wire circuit of Fig. 18(c).

As mentioned near the end of Section 3.3, equalization of the sizes of cores B and M in Fig. 18(c) would help minimize the problem of back transfer. Assuming that this is done, the circuit is redrawn with the solid-line coupling loops in Fig. 20(a). The turns N_4 and N_5 [the Cl M and Cl B windings of Fig. 18(c)] are adjusted so as to equalize as much as possible the net mmf's on Cores M_O and B_O at Clear O time.

Now note that input conditions for Cores M_E and B_E are very similar, M_E being set by a counterclockwise current at $O \rightarrow E$ drive time and B_E by a comparable magnitude of clockwise current at Clear O drive time. In order to prevent M_E from being cleared by the latter loop current, a positive bias winding has been added to the Clear O line on B_E.

Unlike input conditions for cores M_E and B_E, conditions are still very different as far as output is concerned. For any flux switched in M_E is coupled on ahead, whereas flux switched into B_E "dead ends" there, being used merely to balance the $\Delta\phi$ in M_E (when the latter is cleared out) so as to prevent back transfer. The question arises as to whether we can make B comparable to M relative to output in addition to input, i.e., make B a data coupling core also. This can in fact be done. All that is required is to thread the transmitting ends of the coupling loops through the B as well as the M cores, as indicated by the dashed lines in Fig. 20(a) and by the solid lines in Fig. 20(b), where the circuit is redrawn. Since loop current at $O \rightarrow E$ time negatively links B_O in addition to M_O, B_O (like M_O) is positively biased to oppose the tendency of loop current to clear these cores.

To verify that flux doubling actually occurs in the circuit of Fig. 20(b), let us review the sequence of flux transfers during a half cycle of operation during transfer of a *one*, assuming single-turn windings in the coupling loops. Let us suppose that we initially have one unit of set flux stored in each of the cores B_O and M_O and two units in Core C_O, and suppose that these quantities represent less than half the capacities for each of the cores. The $O \rightarrow E$ drive causes the two units of flux in C_O to be transferred to M_E. Then the Clear O drive causes the two units of flux stored in B_O and C_O together to be transferred to B_E. During both of these two phases, the flux switched in M_E and B_E is coupled additively into C_E via a small output-loop current, resulting in four units of flux being set into C_E. (Note

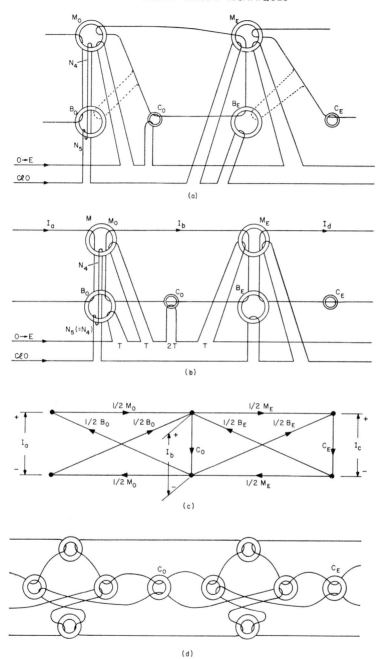

FIG. 20. A flux-doubling scheme. (a,b) Conversion of the circuit of Fig. 18(c) to a flux-doubling scheme. (c) A network form of the circuit. (d) An alternate physical realization of the network of (c). The circuits of parts (b) and (d) are operationally equivalent.

that the input and output windings of the M and B elements are oppositely joined.) Thus, after this half cycle of operation, we have the three E cores set comparably to the initial state of the corresponding three O cores, but with twice the original amount of flux.

As this flux state is transferred along the register, the level builds until saturation of either the C cores or the B and M cores causes limiting. The C cores do this limiting if the capacity of the B and M cores is more than half that of the C cores (as is generally chosen to be the case for operational reasons). For steady-state register operation, the limiting effect will ensure that over-all unity gain is achieved. But we start with gain of 2:1 before losses are counted, as compared to 1:1 for any of the previous schemes having only a single turn on each coupling loop winding.

This flux-doubling scheme has been described by Bennion, Engelbart, and Van De Riet [20]. This type of technique, which is one of the most interesting in the nonresistance realm, will receive further consideration in Section 4. To conclude the discussion here, it is of interest to note the nature of the magnetic-network representation, shown in Fig. 20(c) without drive sources indicated. The approach in constructing this network model was to represent the coupling loops by independent node pairs [each after the fashion of the pair of nodes l and l' of Fig. 16(c)], rather than by node pairs all with a common reference. Branches were then drawn in such a fashion that the net mmf potentials applied to branches representing a given core are exactly equal to the mmf's acting on that core in the circuit. Note that is was necessary to use a pair of branches to represent each M and B core (cores linked by two coupling loops) but only a single branch to represent each C core. Finally, note that the network structure, as an iterative chain, is nonplanar (three-dimensional) in nature. (The magnetic circuit realization of this network, obtained by treating all nodes as core-junction nodes, has been described by Van De Riet [21].)

In cases such as this, where some cores are each represented by more than one network branch, the network representation enables still another type of core-wire circuit realization. This alternate circuit realization arises from reinterpreting branches to represent toroidal cores on a one-to-one basis. There will then, in the present case, be ten cores per bit, and when these are linked with correct polarities by coupling loops representing each node on a one-to-one basis, the circuit of Fig. 20(d) is obtained. Assuming symmetrical application of drive, with no change in the sequencing, this circuit and the one shown in Fig. 20(b) are functionally equivalent. (More details on network equivalence, symmetry, and manipulations of the type indicated above are found in [12].)

92

3.6 A Resistance Scheme Using Multiaperture Cores

The schemes introduced in Sections 2.2 to 2.4 employed multiaperture cores in the nonresistance case and toroidal cores in the resistance case. In Sections 3.3 through 3.5, we have presented several nonresistance toroid circuits. We will now consider the remaining combination, multi-aperture cores with resistance-type coupling, in terms of a scheme sometimes known by the name "MAD-Resistance," or simply "MAD-R."

The circuit of Fig. 13(b) is redrawn in Fig. 21(a). [Note that the manner of linking the transmitter with the $O \rightarrow E$ line is a third wiring arrangement equivalent to the two shown in Figs. 13(b) and 13(c).] As we will see, alteration of this circuit to a resistance type of circuit results in a large increase in the allowed limits on the advance currents. In the nonresistance schemes, the advance currents must be great enough to cause transfer of

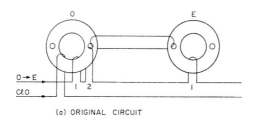

(a) ORIGINAL CIRCUIT

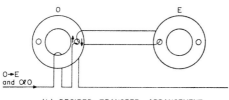

(b) DESIRED TRANSFER ARRANGEMENT

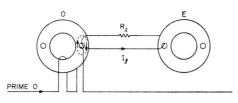

(c) PREPARATION FOR TRANSFER

Fig. 21. Conversion of a nonresistance scheme to a resistance scheme in order to achieve a higher allowed range on the advance pulse.

flux with unity gain; yet they are strictly "threshold-limited" at the upper end in order not to cause spurious setting of a transmitter in the *zero* state. If, however, we could advance flux from transmitter to receiver at the time of clearing a transmitter, then the "advance and clear" drive current would not be threshold limited, since a *zero* state flux in the transmitter could not be inelastically disturbed. To accomplish this, we must reverse the polarity of one end of the coupling loop, as shown in Fig. 21(b), where the desired transmitter flux state just prior to $O \rightarrow E$ transfer is shown. To achieve this transmitter state, after previous setting, flux must be reversed locally around the output aperture, as indicated in Fig. 21(c). The induced loop current during this operation is such that the receiver (E core) cannot switch, and hence the transmitter flux change during this phase must be dissipated in loop resistance R_l. Thus a resistance type scheme is indicated.

The operation indicated in Fig. 21(c) is commonly called a "priming" operation and the associated drive current is labeled "Prime O," since the effect is to prime (or "prepare") the core for the transfer operation. This phase of operation is completely on a par with the "restore" phase of Sections 2.2 to 2.4, so named there because of our thinking in terms of restoring a core (which was used in place of a diode) to its desired hard/easy sense. Here, the elements being restored and the elements that we must avoid disturbing in the process are legs of multiaperture cores. However, the remarks of Sections 2.2 through 2.4 relative to the necessity of performing this operation slowly apply here also. Whatever advantages are to be gained by this scheme, relative to the starting one of Fig. 21(a), must hence be at the expense of some loss in speed of operation.

To see that this scheme is readily workable, let us now consider the remaining features of the operation. The circuit with complete drive windings for a half cycle of operation is shown in Fig. 22(a). The initial state shows a *one* stored after the Advance $O \rightarrow E$ pulse. The E core is then primed. Finally, transfer to the next O core is accomplished. (The drive on the N_X winding is not actually necessary but is desirable for canceling the back mmf from the output loop.)

The priming mmf in this circuit is provided by the prime current through the N_p winding. The N_b winding is used to bias the main aperture of the core so as to increase the maximum allowable prime mmf about the output aperture. Since the main aperture mmf due to priming current is always below threshold, prime current could simultaneously be applied to the O elements during the Prime E phase, without disturbing their cleared states. In fact, the Prime current may even be left on during the actual transfers, as its effects are readily overcome by the much larger advance currents. Hence, priming may be achieved with a single dc current

94

CURRENT DIRECTIONS AT E→0 TIME

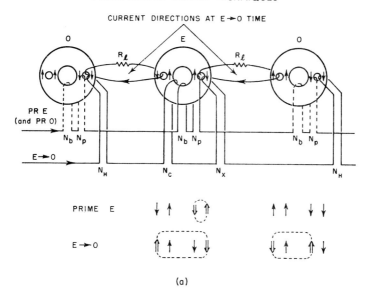

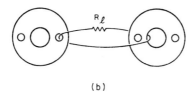

(a)

(b)

FIG. 22. Circuit diagrams for a resistance scheme based on the use of multileg cores. (a) Complete circuit diagram, including bias windings. (Priming occurs about the minor output apertures.) (b) Illustration of the possibility of having the input winding link the main aperture rather than a minor input aperture.

applied to all cores, as in the case of the "restore" currents of Sections 2.2 to 2.4. Pulsed driving is required, therefore, for only two of the four phases of operation.

An important point to note is that the flux switched in a core while it is being cleared links the input loop, inducing a back loop current in a direction to set (hence disturb a *zero* state) in the previous core. Thus, a Hold O winding of N_H turns, is placed on the output leg of this core in order to prevent this leg from switching. An example of a wiring arrangement for this type of circuit that has been used in practice is discussed in connection with Fig. 27. [Since the input aperture is not used for decoupling in this scheme, the input winding could alternately be wound through the main aperture, in which case the cores would need to be only two-aperture cores, as indicated in Fig. 22(b).]

Let us consider, in a qualitative way, whether we have gained something significant in drive current tolerances in exchange for the disadvantage in speed. Under certain simplifying assumptions, it has been shown by Bennion [22] that an absolute upper limit on speed for this circuit is one-fourth that for the nonresistance one of Fig. 21(a). We will consider only the priming drive in the present case and the advance drive in the former case, Fig. 21(a), since these are the currents that have strict upper limits (governed by the core threshold) to avoid spurious setting in the *zero* case or spuriously clearing in the *one* case. Under these constraints, the maximum mmf that can be applied to the output aperture is the same in both cases. Hence, the *upper* limit on mmf is the same in both cases. However, the *lower* limit on mmf can be much more favorable in the case of priming, for the following reason. The priming mmf need be only large enough to switch flux slowly around the output aperture but the advance mmf in the former case must switch flux at a minimum rate in order to induce enough additional current in the coupling loop to transfer flux to the receiver with unity gain.

It can be shown that with receiver bias supplied by the advance current [Fig. 13(b)], the absolute upper limit of maximum to minimum current in the former case is 3:1. [18] Practically speaking, a ratio of about 2:1 can be obtained. In the case of priming, an upper limit on maximum to minimum priming current is $2S_{min}/s_{max}$, where S_{min} and s_{max} are minimum main-aperture and maximum minor-aperture path lengths, respectively. Practically speaking, ratios in excess of 6:1 have been obtained. (It may seem that such a large ratio is not important, but it actually is very useful—for example, as an aid to obtaining operation over a wide temperature range, because of the shift of threshold with temperature.)

The relative advantages of high range of operation (in terms of drive currents or temperature) versus greater speed capability is a major distinction between resistance and nonresistance schemes in general, not only for the particular ones discussed here. Resistance schemes usually also have the advantage of requiring only two explicit pulsed clock phases, the other two phases of the four-phase cycle being supplied by a dc source.

3.7 A Correspondence Between Resistance and Nonresistance Schemes

The resistance scheme introduced above is a practically important one in the present state of the art, and it will receive further consideration in Section 4. For now, let us briefly return to the common language of the network representation to consider some corresponding resistance and nonresistance schemes. What we shall mean by "corresponding," in general,

is that the schemes have the same network structure *and* mode of sequencing, but that the nature of some of the network branches is different.
For nonresistance circuits, all branches represent square-loop magnetic
elements; for resistance circuits, some branches represent electrical resistance; for core-diode circuits, some branches represent electrical diodes.

Let us consider an example of correspondence. The network for a one-
bit length of the circuit of Fig. 11(d) (Russel Type II scheme) is shown in
Fig. 23(a). This is converted to skeletal form, with sequencing shown, in
Fig. 23(b). Now compare this diagram with that of Fig. 23(c), which shows

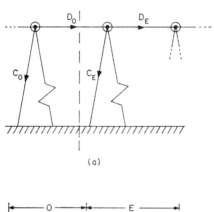

(a)

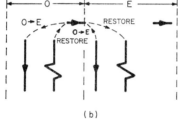

(b)

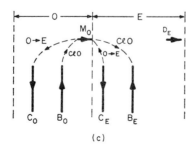

(c)

Fig. 23. Corresponding resistance and nonresistance schemes. (a,b) Resistance scheme
of Fig. 11(d). (c) Resistance scheme of Fig. 19(c).

a one-bit length extracted from the nonresistance scheme of Fig. 19(c). Except for interchange of the B elements with resistive branches, the structure and sequencing in the two schemes are identical. Hence the non-resistance scheme represented by Fig. 19(c) corresponds to the Russel Type II resistance scheme.

One might think the circuits of Figs. 21(a) and 22(a) to be corresponding schemes because of the similarity in their appearance, but actually they are far from it, since resistance, in the first network, appears only as a parasitic element and is not used as part of any of the sequencing paths. However, if we should replace the resistance element of Fig. 22(a) by a square-loop magnetic element, then we would obtain the corresponding nonresistance circuit, which would actually be workable with appropriate design.

3.8 Discussion of Core Function

It was seen in Section 2 how at the expense of an extra clock phase, a diode in a core-diode circuit can always be replaced by a toroidal core or at least such a core together with linear resistance. Furthermore, any corresponding pair of nonresistance and resistance schemes (such as those of Fig. 23) represents a case where a linear resistance may, in turn, be replaced by a magnetic element (toroidal core or leg of a complex core). A core that plays no role other than to replace a diode or resistance can never be a "data core" (i.e., one which is required to transmit an information state), since such a transmission could not have been achieved from the equivalent diode or resistance that is replaced. Rather, such a core can be viewed as being a "flux sink" that accepts flux during whatever auxiliary switching of data cores is required to guarantee the proper cycling of each core back to its cleared state, after a data bit has been transmitted through it.

It is apparent that the full functional capabilities of a core are not used when it simply replaces a diode or resistance. Often, when a flux-sink core appears in a nonresistance scheme, regardless of how the scheme was originally derived, it may be replaced by a resistance (yielding a corresponding resistance scheme) or by a diode.

However, we might expect that there may be some nonresistance circuits that contain no elements that can be replaced by resistance or diodes. For example, if the property of remanence is needed for all elements, there could be no corresponding resistance or core-diode circuits. Such a class of circuits does exist, and we already treated one example of it, namely the flux-doubling circuit of Fig. 20(b). In this circuit, each core stores flux that is later transmitted on to another core (i.e., each core is a data core), and diodes and resistances cannot simulate or replace these functions.

98

4. Currently Preferred Transfer Schemes and General Logic Capability

Network models and other abstract representations of circuits have been found very useful for obtaining variety, classification, and evaluation for the large classes of possible core-wire transfer schemes. But once some particular scheme has been selected for general digital logic use, abstract circuit representations are less necessary and also tend to become unwieldy due to the greater circuit complexity. Thus far, augmentation of a transfer scheme for general logic realization has seemed better done in terms of the usual pictorial sketching of the circuits. Once means for performing several basic logic functions have been achieved, then the usual abstractions in the realm of logic diagrams can be used in the portrayal of logic systems. The type of representation often appropriate for core-wire logic is a single two-phase logic diagram (one phase for O elements and one for E elements) in which there may be several subphases for each logical phase.

Let us now consider, very generally, some of the means for obtaining logic capability. Then we will see specifically how this is done for two of the schemes of most current practical interest (one resistance and one nonresistance in nature).

4.1 From Transfer Schemes to General Logic

Just as it was found in Section 2 that elimination of diodes from core-diode circuits requires additional complexity in either the coupling circuitry or the cores, so is further complexity needed, in one or the other of these aspects, for achieving logic. We could design a complex core structure such that insertion of variables $x, y, \ldots$ on different input legs would yield some logical function $f(x, y, \ldots)$ at an output aperture. Or we could interconnect two or more transmitting multiaperture cores of the type shown earlier (e.g., in Fig. 14) and perhaps toroids as well, into a coupling loop with one receiver and obtain some logic function via the wired coupling loop. One can easily deduce from the network concepts that both the complex-core logic and the wired logic would have the same effect in a network model, namely that of adding additional branches and nodes (of either the physical or coupling-loop type). Partly because of lack of sufficient development of fabrication techniques for complicated core shapes, complex-core logic has not as yet been widely applied and will not be considered further here. For information on methods of deriving and using complex cores for logic, the reader is referred to Crane [7], Gianola [6], and Cohler and Baker [23].

99

All of the useful techniques for achieving logic cannot be covered here, but let us briefly note a few of the currently important ones, as independently as possible of the resistance or nonresistance nature of the transfer scheme. This will be done in terms of multiaperture cores as the coupling cores, but the same considerations apply to circuits in which the multiaperture cores are replaced by arrays of toroids.

The circuits to be portrayed all consist of series or parallel combinations of output and input windings, with or without an auxiliary toroidal core in the coupling loop. The toroid may be used as an S core (which may be either a "flux source" or "flux sink") or a "data core" that receives flux at one clock time and then transmits it forward at a subsequent clock time. For simplicity, unshaped cores will be shown, but cores actually used should preferably be shaped according to the principle indicated in connection with Fig. 14. Values of turns ratios and coupling loop parameters must be adjusted to provide appropriate gain conditions through the loop. This matter is beyond the scope of this article.

An example of a circuit using an auxiliary core as an S core is shown in Fig. 24(a). (The use of an auxiliary toroid as a data core will be illustrated in Section 4.2 and Fig. 26.) Unlike a transmitter or receiver, an S core is not used to store information that is later to be shifted to a following stage. Rather, it may be unconditionally switched (i.e., driven) so as to act like a flux *source* injecting a quantity of flux linkage into the loop [as is the case in Fig. 24(a)]. Or, it may be undriven, in which case it acts as a (low threshold) *sink* for flux linkages, switching in response to a coupling loop current flowing in a direction to set it. In the latter case, the amount of flux linkages "absorbed" would depend on transmitter information. In either case, the S core must be "cleared" to a reference state at some other clock time. Note that a driven source is in effect cleared to a second reference state at the time of being driven, i.e., at $O \rightarrow E$ time in Fig. 24(a). (The toroidal core shown in Fig. 15 for clipping for gain control acts as a flux sink, but for a value of flux comparable to the normal *zero* level of flux, whereas the value of source or sink flux here, for logical control, is comparable to the *one* level of flux or larger.)

Plus and minus signs are used to show relative polarities of windings in the nonresistance case. [For the resistance case, the positively defined polarity of the receiver is reversed relative to the other cores; for example, compare Figs. 21(a) and 21(b).] When the algebraic signs for a particular transmitter and receiver agree, then transmission from that transmitter alone will be capable of setting the receiver. If the signs disagree, current induced by transmission from that transmitter will push in the clear direction of the receiver input leg and hence will tend to inhibit receiver setting. If signs on the two transmitters agree (or disagree), emf's induced in the output loop will be mutually aiding (or opposing).

100

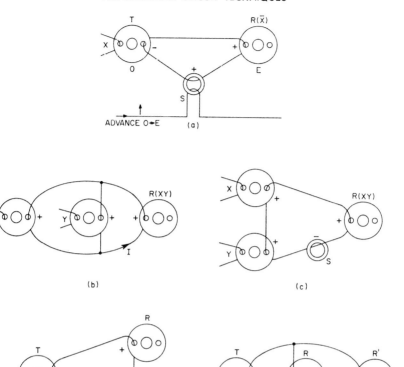

FIG. 24. Series and parallel combinations of transmitters, receivers, and S (source or sink) cores. (a) Negative transfer. (b,c) Transfer of AND function XY. (d,e) Fan-out from one transmitter to two receivers.

It is readily seen that the circuit of Fig. 24(a) provides the NOT function. The arrow pointing at transmitter T indicates the usual advance drive. If X is *one* (i.e., T has been previously set), then flux linkages from T and S cancel, and there is no loop current to set the receiver R. If X is *zero* (T is clear), then flux is transferred from S to R. Hence, R receives the function $\overline{X}$.

Two ways to obtain the AND function are suggested in Figs. 24(b) and 24(c). In the parallel connection shown first, current sufficient to set R to the *one* level cannot be established in the receiver branch of the coupling loop unless previous inputs X and Y have set *both* transmitters to the *one* level of flux. In the alternate AND circuit of Fig. 24(c), flux from either transmitter flux alone is canceled by the flux provided by S (which may be

101

either a source or a sink), so that only if both transmitters had been previously set can an appropriate amount of flux be transferred to R.

Additional two-input logic functions can be obtained with other combinations of windings on the transmitters and the S cores. For example, the circuit of Fig. 24(c), with no source core, and with the polarity on Y reversed, provides the function $X\bar{Y}$. The same principles may be extended for obtaining some logic functions of three inputs or more.

To conclude the general discussion on logic realization, let us consider means for obtaining "fan-out," i.e., advancing from one transmitter to more than one receiver. Two methods are shown in Figs. 24(d) and 24(e). In the first case, the turns N_T of the transmitter must be sufficiently large to provide the flux linkages required by both receivers. For the second method, the current provided by transmitter switching must be sufficiently large to supply the currents for the two receivers. The net effect of either of these requirements is to lower tolerances relative to the single receiver case. Thus it is sometimes desirable (especially when larger degrees of fan-out are required) to obtain fan-out by using subclocks to obtain some mode of flux pumping, or by read-out from separate apertures (Section 3.5).

Once a set of logical building blocks has been selected, and limits on their usage defined, design of systems can be done in terms of logic diagrams. To minimize diagram lettering, it has been sometimes found convenient to symbolize the two-phase nature of the logic by representing O and E cores (or modules) by circles and squares, respectively. In Fig. 25 are shown examples of the type of symbols used to represent logic connections. The same interconnection symbols, with circles and squares reversed, are used to show transfer from E to O cores.

The development of logic circuits as indicated above, with only simple

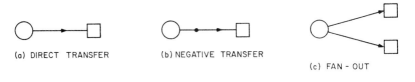

(a) DIRECT TRANSFER   (b) NEGATIVE TRANSFER

(c) FAN - OUT

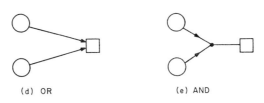

(d) OR   (e) AND

FIG. 25. Logic notation for various transfer configurations.

windings on each core, provide one means for obtaining general logic. One way to achieve still more logical flexibility is to employ more complex windings. For example, some schemes admit the use of figure-eight transmitter windings (providing either addition or subtraction of flux values in the two legs linked) or figure-eight receiver windings (enabling receiver setting by loop currents of either polarity).

4.2 Nonresistance Logic Employing Flux Doubling

As an alternative to the three-toroid array for each section of the flux doubling register of Fig. 20(b), we can use a pair of multiaperture cores, as shown in Fig. 26(a). In effect, Legs 3 and 3' replace the small diameter toroids of Fig. 20(b), and Legs 4 and 4' provide additional isolation between bits. Based on this flux-doubling scheme, we will now briefly outline the basic logic module used in the first all-magnetic (nonresistance) machine constructed, described by Crane and Van De Riet [24], and Crane [25] and discussed further in Appendix 5.

For performing logic, it is advantageous to use minor-aperture input as well as minor-aperture output. This is indicated in Fig. 26(b), along with a further modification in which the two transmitters directly connect to only a *single* receiver element, the two receiver elements being directly connected by a symmetric (i.e., unity turns ratio) coupling loop. With this arrangement, induced current in the cross-coupling loop at Clear O time will cause R' to be set to practically the same level previously received in R. An important feature here is that an input loop to only one receiver is sufficient for finally achieving the setting of both receivers. Let us now add an input loop to the free input leg on the other receiver and label the two inputs X and Y, as in Fig. 26(c). Now a *one* in either the X or Y input, or both, will result in both receivers being set after the $O \rightarrow E$, Clear O sequence. Thus we have the OR function along with flux doubling. (In the actual machine, the cross-coupling loop was energized separately from and just prior to the clear operation. This operation was then called "Set Slave," and the clock cycle sequencing was therefore . . . , Set Slave$_O$, Clear E, . . . , Set Slave$_E$, Clear O, ... The reader is referred to [21] and [22] for the specific reasoning leading to this mode of operation.)

To achieve negative transfer, i.e., $\overline{(X + Y)}$, the technique of Fig. 24(a) could be directly applied, although a different scheme, shown in Fig. 26(d), was actually employed. (The details of the choice are too involved for our purposes here, and the interested reader is again directed to the references.) In this scheme, a data core D_E is used in the loop, the core being initially cleared in the usual clockwise sense. If we then apply a separate transfer pulse, labeled $(A_E B_E) \rightarrow D_E$, just prior to the Advance $E \rightarrow O$ pulse, loop current will saturate D_E counterclockwise if either A_E or B_E, or both, contain *one* states. but not if both contain *zero* states. If

103

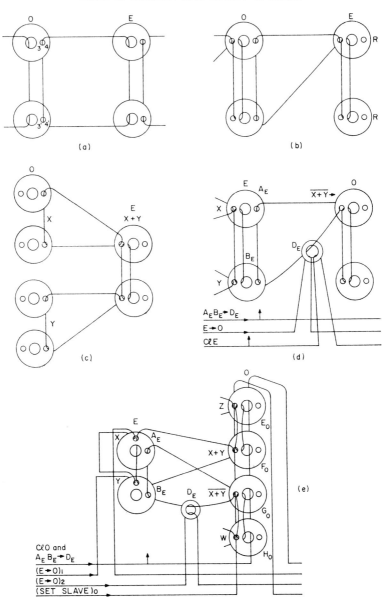

FIG. 26. Conversion of the basic flux-doubling circuit of Fig. 20 to a flux-doubling, OR circuit, with multiple positive and negative output.

(and only if) the latter is true will the subsequent $E \rightarrow O$ pulse be able to switch D_E (counterclockwise), inducing thereby a loop current that will set the upper O core. Hence, the function $(\overline{X + Y})$ will be transferred. Thus we have a logic module that can be wired for transmitting either the OR or NOR function of X and Y.

We could use the flux doubling feature together with coupling loop turns ratio to provide enough flux gain for fan-out and to cover losses. However, it was found convenient, in the case of this first system, (1) to retain *single-turn windings*, exclusively, in the minor apertures; (2) to let flux doubling take care of loop losses; and (3) to provide fan-out by using subclocks to sequentially transfer from separate apertures [Fig. 26(e)]. (For simplicity, the drive-current lines are shown without bias windings.) In this circuit, the OR function $(X + Y)$ is shown as being provided by one set of output apertures, and the NOR function $(\overline{X + Y})$ by another set (in conjunction with the core D_E), to yield a fan-out of one-to-two. The transfer labeled $(A_E B_E) \rightarrow D_E$ is accomplished at the same time as the Clear O operation.

To recapitulate the operation of this circuit, the $(A_E B_E) \rightarrow D_E$ drive causes D_E to be set to the sum of the levels held by A_E and B_E (less some small loop losses). Then transfer to F_O and G_O is done in sequence by the subclocks $(O \rightarrow E)_1$ and $(O \rightarrow E)_2$ (at which time the greater part of the loop losses occur). Hence, F_O is set only if the E cores had been set, and G_O only if they had not. The other inputs to the pair of receiver "modules" are available for other variables, Z and W. The (Set Slave)$_O$ pulse then brings E_O and F_O to the same state, resulting in the OR function $(X + Y) + Z$ being stored in E_O and F_O. Similarly, the G_O, H_O pair takes on the function $(\overline{X + Y}) + W$. (Although one positive and one negative transfer has been discussed here, it should be clear that each transfer could independently be positive or negative.)

This module consisting of a pair of cross-linked multiaperture elements, and augmented to provide three instead of two independent OR or NOR outputs, is basically the one that was used for construction of the machine previously referred to [24, 25]. Although this system was built several years ago, flux doubling is still the most attractive type of transfer scheme as a basis for a nonresistance core-wire system.

(As a final note, although the physical wiring of a system involving many modules, interconnected as in Fig. 26(e), might at first appear "impossible," it was in fact far simpler than originally guessed. Techniques of wiring are discussed in the referenced papers.)

4.3 Mad-Resistance Techniques

Mad-Resistance (Mad-r) logic techniques, based on the transfer scheme described in Section 3.6, presently provide the mainstay for applications of core-wire circuits. Three main reasons for the current popularity of this system are (1) wide driver and temperature tolerances, (2) simplicity, and (3) practical realization of logical flexibility.

The basis for achieving wide current and temperature tolerances was outlined in the derivation of the MAD-R scheme in Section 3.6.

Let us consider the point of simplicity by reviewing the basic transfer scheme of Fig. 22 in terms of a specific wiring arrangement, Fig. 27, that

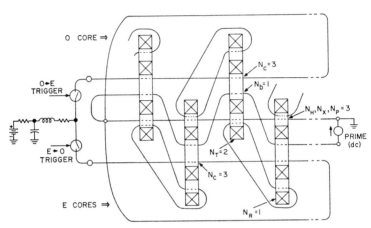

FIG. 27. A wiring configuration for the MAD-R register of Fig. 22. The numerals on straight-through windings indicate the number of passes of the wire through the line of elements. For example, $N_C = 3$ implies that the winding makes three complete straight-through passes.

has sometimes been used in practice. Typical numbers of turns are indicated on each winding, in particular $N_C = 3$, $N_b = 1$, $N_H = N_X = N_P = 3$. The clear windings are each wired straight through the main apertures of each bank of cores. Because N_H, N_X, and N_P are equal, they are realized by a single common drive winding wired straight through the output apertures of all the cores. (The dc source need not have a very large source resistance at dc, but should be well isolated from the pulse sources, as can easily be done with an rf choke. For applications in which zero standby power is desired, it is possible to arrange the wiring such that the current that recharges the driver capacitor simultaneously effects priming.)

Only two phases of clock pulse currents are required, $(O \rightarrow E$ and $E \rightarrow O)$, and these may be provided by two triggered switches (e.g., four-layer diodes, silicon-controlled rectifiers, transistors, thyratrons) discharging damped half-sinusoidal pulses from a common charging circuit as indicated. If an ac in addition to a dc power source is available, then Melville drivers consisting only of capacitors and saturable inductors may be used, although a pair of diodes may also be required, depending

106

upon the details of the application; this is discussed further in Appendix 4 and by Baer and Heckler [26].

Let us finally comment on the point of logical flexibility. By alternate choices of polarities and flux source values in circuits of the type shown in Fig. 24(c), we can obtain all nontrivial logic functions of two variables. For some of these functions realized straightforwardly in this way, prime-current tolerances are somewhat lower than for a simple register coupling loop. However, modifications can be made such that general logic can be achieved with current tolerances substantially as good as for registers, but with somewhat lowered speed capability. (The design details of such circuits are beyond the scope of this present article.)

Fan-out of 1:3 per section (half a bit length) can be achieved quite easily without use of subclocks. Furthermore, many three-variable logic functions can readily be obtained if another transmitter is added to the loop. With fan-in of 3:1 and fan-out of 1:3 per section (during half a clock cycle), we can obtain fan-in of 9:1 and fan-out of 1:9 per clock cycle.

5. Application Notes

5.1 Introduction

The early work on all-magnetic logic circuits was justified primarily on the basis of reliability. Since ferrite cores have essentially unlimited life, it would seem that all-magnetic systems should be infinitely reliable! Experience gained from operating systems has permitted somewhat more meaningful evaluation of these techniques. Other important points (besides reliability) pertinent to useful application of these techniques are environmental effects, operational properties, power supply requirements, economics, and compatibility (with other devices in hybrid logic systems, as well as with peripheral equipment). Actually, the same multiaperture cores used for logic can serve nicely as the key devices for some peripheral equipment of the output type (e.g., for control of power or analog signal devices). As a result, the applicability of the basic core-wire logic techniques is actually enhanced in certain cases by virtue of the compatibility consideration.

5.2 Reliability and Environmental Properties

Insufficient data has been accumulated to give data in terms of "mean time to failure" and similar standard measures, so we must resort to mere mention of those properties that seem important to over-all reliability.

In an all-magnetic system, the primary sources of trouble are (1) short circuits between different windings (insulation problems), (2) poor connections between wires (e.g., solder connections), (3) power supplies

107

(i.e., drivers), and (4) other components that may have been added (for example, power handling devices in output circuits).

With respect to short circuits, we can only note that one advantage of a core-wire system in comparison with a core-diode system is that far fewer turns are required in the coupling loop circuits. This significantly reduces the possibility of intrawinding short circuits.

With respect to poor connections, limited experience to date has shown that for applications in which these techniques are well suited, there is often a very significant reduction in the number of solder connections required, compared with a comparable transistor realization. (For an example, refer to Appendix 5.) The reason that only a relatively low number of solder connections is needed stems from the fact that a magnetic element is controlled by electric currents rather than by voltages. These currents "link" or "thread" the elements rather than terminate on them, as in the case of voltage controlled devices. A core itself, therefore, has no connection terminals. Hence, in wiring a system, one tends to line up a large group of cores that are to be simultaneously driven and to pass the drive winding straight through the array line (as suggested in Fig. 27). Thus, a drive line can link a relatively large number of elements at the cost of perhaps two solder connections, one at each end of the line. Of course, each coupling loop requires connections, but generally no more than one or two, depending upon the specific circuit technique.

The magnetic components themselves are extremely reliable because they are composed of polycrystalline materials and because they operate on bulk rather than surface properties. They are insensitive to physical vibration and are chemically inert. In fact, because of their chemical inertness (and because the circuits are of very low impedance), systems of this type could actually be immersed in different types of solutions without problems of protecting the magnetic devices proper. (The only concern would be that the conductivity of the solution should not be so high that the liquid surrounding the core would act as a significant short-circuiting turn for the element.)

The fact that these magnetic elements are polycrystalline and depend on bulk properties should suit them well to nuclear environments. Evidence that this is actually the case has been collected from experiments in which isolated components have been placed in atomic reactors with relatively little effect. However, to the authors' knowledge, no operating systems have as yet been subjected to such an environment. Such tests are likely to be made soon; we will have to await the outcome of these tests to see just how resistant core-wire circuits are to nuclear radiation.

With the ferrite materials presently used, these systems are somewhat limited in temperature range. To meet typical satellite and upper MIL temperature specifications, e.g., from $-55°C$ to $+85°C$, it is generally desirable, or even necessary, to arrange the drivers to "track" the ambient temperature, i.e., to vary the magnitude of the drive current in accordance with the temperature variation. This is primarily because of the change in coercivity of the material with temperature. But this type of tracking is relatively simple. For less stringent specifications, however (e.g., −35°C to 60°C), even this tracking is generally not necessary. Presently, the main limit to temperature range is the rather low Curie temperature of the materials used. Adaptation of the higher Curie temperature materials for use in these systems would offer considerable advantage.

5.3 Operational and Compatibility Properties

The primary limitation of all-magnetic systems is speed. Although nonresistance type shift registers have operated at close to megacycle bit rates, such speeds would presently be difficult to achieve in a large system. At the present state of nonresistance circuit techniques, it would probably be difficult to design a system with bit rates of over 50 to 100 kc. For resistance techniques, a comfortable speed range is even lower, as previously discussed. Systems operating with clock rates in the 50 kc range could probably be designed, but at present the 5 to 20 kc range is far easier, in consideration of over-all cost, designability, and wide tolerances in operation.

There are two types of limitation on speed: One is the maximum rate at which cores can be switched in the circuit; the second is core heating due to internal dissipation (which results in a shift in core properties, particularly threshold). Without special means for carrying the heat away, the heating limitation is usually reached first in nonresistance type circuits, but the switching limitation is usually predominant for the resistance circuits.

It is quite clear that these techniques are not suited for general purpose high-speed computers, but rather for the design of special systems in which properties other than high speed are to be emphasized. There seems to be a very large class of such applications. It is in these cases that all-magnetic circuit techniques have been particularly useful. The following are some of the important points in this regard:

(1) *Easy Input-Output Communication*—Data or control can easily be applied to such a system via ordinary selection means—such as switches, relays, etc. It is merely necessary to generate a current that links the appropriate elements so as to properly set or reset them. There are generally no special limits on the rise time of these control currents, nor on their duration. In fact, such currents could be left on so as to affect control over an extended period. With respect to output, relatively high-power output devices can be

109

directly controlled from these elements in a nondestructive read-out mode (see Appendix 1). This permits continuous read-out during processing. Furthermore, there is the very convenient capability of controlling analog signals with these elements as well (see Appendix 2). The main point is that these circuits are generally compatible with more conventional components, so that hybrid arrangements, where advantageous, are relatively easy to design.

(2) *Relatively Low Component Count*—This feature can often result in small physical volume, compared even with transistor circuits. A shift register, for example, generally has only two magnetic cores per bit, compared with a transistor version which would typically contain the circuitry for a complete flip-flop, plus the coupling and gating circuitry. Sequence detectors, discussed in Appendix 3, provide another striking example of component savings. The shift register and sequence detector are used here merely to illustrate the possibilities for low-component-count circuits. Experience to date on larger systems has shown that utilization of all-magnetic circuits can often result in a significant reduction in total component count over a transistor counterpart, e.g., see Fig. 33. Needless to say, we are referring here to applications adapted to these techniques. These can probably be characterized as those in which there is a great deal of repetition of basic circuit types (such as counters, in addition to the registers and sequencers already noted) and relatively small logic interconnectivity. At least, it is with operating systems of this type that there is experience on which to base observations.

(3) *Low Cost*—This is especially so in systems in which there is high repetition of basic types. There is a potential cost advantage due primarily to the low component cost and relatively low wiring complexity.

(4) *Reliability*—The advantage of high reliability is clear in both short-life circuits (perhaps a short orbital task) as well as long-life circuits (e.g., a control system). In either case, high reliability minimizes the possibility of catastrophic failure. In the latter case, it can also result in significant reduction in maintenance procedures.

(5) *Dissipationless Storage*—By this it is meant that zero power is dissipated between clock pulses. Cores maintain their (flux) state without expenditure of energy. Thus clocks can be shut off and restarted at any later time, without loss of information and without dissipation of power. This has important consequences for those systems in which power is at a premium, e.g., in satellite systems. The same consideration of dissipationless storage provides an advantage for low rates of continuous operation, since the average power required for switching increases in direct proportion to the

frequency of operation. For example, for one type of core (AMP Incorporated #395813-1), power that must be delivered by the drive lines to the core circuits, as a function of frequency f, is about $2 \times 10^{-6} f$ watts (e.g., 2 mw/core for 1 kc operation).

(6) *Insensitivity to Noisy Electrical Environments and to High Nuclear Radiation Fields*—High external magnetic fields can cause malfunctioning, but these can be quite easily shielded out.

(7) *Pulse Driver Considerations*—One of the earlier difficulties in applying these techniques was the need for relatively high-power current sources. Although in experimental systems this power was generally supplied from conventional laboratory vacuum-tube drivers, it was not especially attractive to consider using such driver techniques in real applications. (Although we might note that in the case of high nuclear radiation fields, where semiconductors may not be operational, vacuum-tube drivers might actually be quite useful.) The commercial development of the high-powered four-layer diode type of devices has greatly improved the driver picture. Relatively small and inexpensive drivers of this type can be arranged to drive relatively large systems. The Melville driver (discussed in Appendix 4) used to drive the MAVERIC machine (Appendix 5) has interesting possibilities, although it has not yet been applied to other systems. We might finally note in passing that even mechanical drivers, commutators or relays, may be quite interesting for driving relatively large, low-speed systems.

6. Annotated Bibliography on All-Magnetic Logic Schemes

This bibliography, in semichronological form, includes all presently known literature pertaining to the development of all-magnetic (core-wire) logic schemes. It amounts to a revised and up-dated version of the annotated bibliography previously published by Bennion, Crane, and Engelbart [31].

6.1 Bibliography on Resistance Schemes

1. Wang, A., Investigation for design of digital calculating machinery, Harvard Computation Laboratory Progress Report 2, Section IV, pp. 6-18, September 1948.

Controlled nonlinear inductances are used in coupling loops in order to prevent both receiver loading and back transfer. Bistable operation of a closed-loop one-bit shift register was obtained; it is therefore apparent that receiver loading was prevented. But with the scheme as given, it does not appear likely that back transfer as well as receiver loading could be reduced enough to result in a workable multibit register.

2. Rey, T. J., Registers such as are employed in digital computing apparatus, U.S. Patent No. 2,683,819, July 13, 1954 (filed May 28, 1952).

The diodes in a one-diode-per-loop shift register are replaced by biased saturable inductors. It is not clear that the method as given could simultaneously prevent back transfer and receiver loading sufficiently to make a workable scheme.

3. Briggs, G. R., A magnetic core gate and its application in a stepping register, Digital Computer Laboratory Engineering Note E-475, Mass. Inst. Technol., Cambridge, Massachusetts, October, 1952.

Two square-loop core, A and B, are wired into each coupling loop between coupling cores. When transfer is occurring through a given loop, the two cores are held in a saturated state by an auxiliary current. Receiver loading and back transfer are inhibited, respectively, by the switching of Core A in the succeeding loop and of Core B in the preceding loop. The result is a workable scheme requiring six cores per bit.

4. Minnick, R. C., Magnetic switching circuits, *J. Appl. Phys.* **25**, 479–485, 1954. (This material is also found in the author's doctoral thesis: The use of magnetic cores as switching devices, Harvard University, April 1953.)

A means for performing logic in diodeless coupling loops is presented. However, no means is given for stringing logic stages together without the use of diodes in alternate coupling loops. Hence the scheme is not an all-magnetic one (although it does appear to require a much lower ratio of diodes to cores than previous core-diode schemes).

5. Saunders, N. B., Magnetic memory circuits employing biased magnetic binary cores, U.S. Patent No. 2,781,503, February 12, 1957 (filed April 29, 1953).

A single biased core is used in each coupling to prevent back transfer, but it does not appear as though the method could do this and also avoid receiver loading. The idea of a bi-directional register using a turns ratio of unity is presented, but the scheme provides no means for achieving sufficient gain in this case.

6. Russell, L. A., Diodeless magnetic core logical circuits, *IRE National Convention Record*, Part 4, pp. 106–114, 1957.

Two different schemes employing four cores per bit are described. The "Type-I" scheme has been made to operate despite the fact that it has a back-transfer problem. The "Type-II" scheme interchanges the roles of the cores in a way that solves the back-transfer problem while still preventing receiver loading, resulting in an improved four-core-per-bit scheme.

7. Haynes, M. K., Russell, L. A., Coughlin, J. J., Crapo, W. A., Kauffman, J. A., Lockhard, N. F., Rutz, R. F., Tomasulo, R. M., and Cole, J. N., Improvement program for magnetic logical circuits physical research effort, Terminal Report, June 1, 1956 to May 15, 1957, IBM Research Laboratory, Poughkeepsie, New York (no date of issue).

   Additional details are given on the schemes described in the previous item. (See also Ref. 30.)

8. Briggs, G. R., Lo, A. W., Magnetic systems, U.S. Patent No. 2,968,795, January 17, 1961 (filed May 1, 1957).

   The concept of a resistance scheme using multipath cores is introduced. Flux is "primed" around a minor aperture in order to avoid back transfer and to aid the achievement of transfer without receiver loading.

9. Onyshkevych, L. S., Analysis of circuits with multiple-hole magnetic cores, Technical Report 329, Research Laboratory of Electronics, Mass. Inst. Technol., Cambridge, Massachusetts, July 9, 1957.

   Additional material on resistance schemes using multipath cores is presented. The treatment is brief but includes several ideas common to schemes developed independently at a later date.

10. Broadbent, K. D., Magnetic device, U.S. Patent Nos. 2,993,197, July 18, 1961 and 3,046,532, July 24, 1962 (both filed August 2, 1957).

   The transfer scheme described is essentially the same as one of those presented in 8.

11. International Business Machines Corporation, Magnetic logic improvement program, Final Report, Contract AF 30(635)-3130, Kingston, New York, January 1, 1958.

   Diagrams of some resistance schemes are shown, but the principles of operation are not described.

12. Engelbart, D. C., High speed components for digital computers, Quarterly Report 3—Part A, April 1959, and Quarterly Report 4—Part A, Contract AF 33(616)-5804, Stanford Research Institute, Menlo Park, California, August 1959.

13. Proebster, W. E., Methfessel, S., and Kinberg, C. O., Thin magnetic films, a paper presented at the International Conference on Information Processing, Paris, June 1959.

14. Green, M. W., High speed components for digital computers, Final Engineering Report—Part A, Contract AF 33(616)-5804, Stanford Research Institute, Menlo Park, California, December 1959.

113

15. Proebster, W. E., Oguey, H. J., Thin magnetic films for logic and memory, Digest of Technical Papers, 1960 Solid-State Circuits Conference, Philadelphia, pp. 22–23, February 10–12, 1960.

In the above four items, resistance schemes making use of the coherent rotational switching properties of thin films are suggested.

16. International Business Machines Corporation. Federal Systems Division, Final report on the development and use of multiaperture-core flux logic devices to perform logical functions in digital data processing, Vol. II, Appendix A, Contract AF 33(600)-31315, Owego, New York, December 1959.

17. Gianola, U. F., Integrated magnetic circuits for synchronous sequential logic machines, *Bell System Tech. J.* **39**, 295–332, March 1960.

18. Zeiger, H. P., Diodeless magnetic-core logic circuits, Master of Science Thesis, Mass. Inst. Technol., Cambridge, Massachusetts, June 1960.

19. Tancrell, R. H., Inertial selection for magnetic core logic, Report 52G-0014, Contract AF 19(604)-7400, Lincoln Laboratory, Mass. Inst. Technol., Lexington, Massachusetts, October 11, 1960.

20. Bennion, D. R., MAD-resistance type magnetic shift registers, *Proc. 1960 Nonlinear Magnetics and Magnetic Amplifiers Conf.*, Am. Inst. Elec. Engrs., Philadelphia, Pennsylvania, pp. 96–112, October 1960.

21. Nitzan, D., Analysis of MAD-R shift register and driver, *Proc. 1960 Nonlinear Magnetics and Magnetic Amplifiers Conf.*, Am. Inst. Elec. Engrs., Philadelphia, Pennsylvania, pp. 113–133, October 1960.

22. AMP Incorporated, Bulletins #610A, Harrisburg, Pennsylvania, 1960.

23. Gianola, U. F., The possibilities of all-magnetic logic circuitry, *J. Appl. Phys.* **32**, suppl., 27S–34S, March 1961.

Items 16–18 and 20–23 provide many details on resistance schemes employing multipath cores. Most of this material is concerned with a scheme employing a "holding" mmf to prevent back transfer.

24. Tancrell, R. H., Impulse selection for core logic, *J. Appl. Phys.* **32**, suppl., 40S–41S, March 1961.

In 19 and 24, a scheme is described whereby, during transfer, coupling-loop current (in a single-turn loop) is employed to reduce the dc threshold of the receiver rather than to transfer flux with unity gain. A drive current of amplitude lower than the normal dc threshold can subsequently switch the receiver, resulting in sufficient overall flux gain (only possible with certain materials). This result has been achieved with a register configuration for which sufficient gain by means of coupling-loop turns ratio only would be prevented by receiver loading. The gain mechanism used is similar to the ϕ^* flux gain reported in items 31, 32, and 34, but the author reports obtaining a temporary reduction of threshold as well (on the order of one microsecond in duration).

25. Harper, P. T., Magnetic logic elements using a single MAD device and wire interconnections only, *Proc. Special Technical Conference on Nonlinear Magnetics and Magnetic Amplifiers*, Am. Inst. Elec. Engrs., Los Angeles, California, pp. 169–200, November 1961.

NOR logic is realized by means of augmenting the type of scheme described in 16–18 and 20–23 with an additional pulsed clock phase, making a total of five phases (three pulsed and two dc priming) per cycle.

26. Englebart, D. C., Bi-Polar Magnetic Core Circuit (patent pending).

A bipolar scheme related to the unipolar scheme discussed in 16–18 and 20–23 is described.

27. Norde, L., Integrated magnetic logic, Motorola, Inc., Solid State Systems Division, Phoenix, Arizona (no date).

A scheme for all-magnetic logic employing multiaperture cores is referred to. Details are not given, but it has been indicated in private communication that this is a resistance scheme of a bipolar type (transmission of a negative rather than zero flux change to represent a binary *zero*).

6.2 Bibliography on Nonresistance Schemes

28. Russell, L. A., Magnetic core transfer circuit, U.S. Patent No. 2,907,987, September 15, 1959 (filed December 3, 1956).

A workable scheme employing arrays of toroids is described. This scheme is similar to the Russell Type-II scheme of 6, but with the resistive elements replaced by cores.

29. Crane, H. D., Multi-aperture magnetic devices for computer systems, Special Report to Burroughs Corporation, Paoli, Pa., Stanford Research Institute, Menlo Park, California, February 1957.

30. Haynes, M. K. *et al.*, *op. cit.* (Ref. 7) Section 1, pp. 1–6.

The "high speed diodeless transfer circuit" described in this report employs a three-phase clock cycle and three coupling loops per bit, and it requires six single-path cores per bit. During propagation of a *one*, a single "relief" core in a given loop (1) sets to prevent receiver loading during transfer through the preceding loop, (2) stays set (with the help of a positive bias) during transfer through the given loop, and (3) is reset to prevent back transfer during transfer through the succeeding loop.

31. Bennion, D. R., Crane, H. D., Heinzman, F., Multi-aperture magnetic devices for computer systems, Technical Report 2 to Burroughs

Corporation, Paoli, Pa., Stanford Research Institute, Menlo Park, California, October, 1957.

32. Bennion, D. R., Crane, H. D., Heinzman, F., Multi-aperture magnetic devices for computer systems, Final Report to Burroughs Corporation, Paoli, Pa., Stanford Research Institute, Menlo Park, California, January 1958.

33. Bennion, D. R. and Engelbart, D. C., Multiple-setting magnetic core circuits, U.S. Patent No. 2,936,445, May 10, 1960 (filed June 12, 1958).
   A three-phase scheme similar to that of 30, but using multi-aperture cores, is described.

34. Crane, H. D., A high speed logic system using magnetic elements and connecting wire only, *Proc. 1958 Conference on Nonlinear Magnetics and Magnetic Amplifiers*, Am. Inst. Elec. Engrs., Los Angeles, California, pp. 465–482, August 1958. (Also published in revised form in *Proc. Inst. Radio Engrs.* **47**, 63–73, January 1959.
   In 29, 31, 32, and 34 a workable scheme employing multipath cores (multi-aperture devices, or MADS) is described. (This scheme is also touched on in 16.) The minor-aperture properties of the cores are used to prevent back transfer and receiver loading. Methods for achieving general logic are also indicated.
   In 31, 32, and 34 operable registers with unity-turns-ratio coupling loops are described. Because complete symmetry of wiring is possible, these registers can be bidirectional. Internal gain is achieved by the so-called ϕ^* flux-gain mechanism.

35. Prywes, N. S., Diodeless magnetic shift registers utilizing transfluxors, *Inst. Radio Engrs., Trans. on Electronic Computers* **EC-7**, pp. 316–324, December 1958.
   Registers are described that employ the same basic scheme of transfer underlying the work reported in 29, 31, 32, and 34. The idea of eliminating coupling loops to obtain a continuous magnetically coupled register is expressed, but no means is given for solving the gain problem. (Another scheme that leaves the gain problem unsolved is found in 17.)

36. Stabler, E. P., Square-loop magnetic logic circuits, General Electric, Electronics Laboratory, Technical Information Series, R59 ELS8, January 16, 1959. (Also published in *Proc. Western Joint Computer Conference, Inst. Radio Engrs.*, pp. 47–53, San Francisco, California, March 3–5, 1959.)

37. Engelbart, D. C., A new all-magnetic logic system using simple cores, Digest of Technical Papers, 1959 Solid-State Circuits Conference, Philadelphia, pp. 66–67, February 1959.

38. Engelbart, D. C., High speed components for digital computers, Quarterly Report 2, Contract AF 33(616)-5804, Stanford Research Institute, Menlo Park, California, February 1959.

In the above three items, it is shown how multipath cores used in previous schemes can be replaced by arrays of single-path cores.

In 36, there is also some suggestion of means for eliminating coupling loops in circuits to yield continuous magnetically coupled circuits, but no solution is given for the gain problem.

39. Bennion, D. R. and Crane, H. D., Design and analysis of MAD transfer circuitry, Proc. Western Joint Computer Conference, Inst. Radio Engrs., San Francisco, California, pp. 21–36, March 3–5, 1959.

Additional details and variations are given on the transfer circuitry for the techniques described in 29, 31, 32, 34, and 35.

40. Engelbart, D. C., Research on the philosophy of logic realization, Quarterly Progress Report 1, Contract AF 33(616)-6303, Stanford Research Institute, Menlo Park, California, August 1959.

It is shown, in magnetic-network terms, how a scheme of the type described in 34 may be realized with multiaperture cores having input and output minor apertures side by side as opposed to being in different locations around the periphery of the core.

41. Engelbart, D. C., Combined synthetic and multiaperture magnetic core systems (patent pending).

Means are described for using single-path and multipath cores together in a "hybrid" circuit in order to obtain some of the advantages of both.

42. Crane, H. D., Research on general digital logic system utilizing magnetic elements and wire only, Quarterly Status Report 1, Contract AF 19(604)-5909, Air Force Cambridge Research Center, Bedford, Massachusetts, September 30, 1959.

43. Van De Riet, E. K. and Heckler, Jr., C. H., Research on general digital logic systems utilizing magnetic elements and wire only, Final Engineering Report, Contract AF 19(604)-5909, Air Force Cambridge Research Center, Bedford, Massachusetts, October 1960.

44. Crane, H. D. and Van De Riet, E. K., Design of an all-magnetic computing system: Part I—circuit design, Inst. Radio Engrs. Trans. on Electronic Computers EC-10, pp. 207–220, June 1961.

45. Crane, H. D., Design of an all-magnetic computing system: Part II—logical design, Inst. Radio Engrs. Trans. on Electronic Computers EC-10, pp. 221–232, June 1961.

In the above four items, the design, construction, and operation of an all-magnetic decimal arithmetic unit based on the use of the techniques of 33 and 41, with elaborations, is described.

117

46. Crane, H. D., Magnetic core logic element, U.S. Patent No. 2,935,622, May 3, 1960 (filed June 12, 1958).
47. Bennion, D. R., A new multiaperture magnetic logic element, *J. Appl. Phys.* **31**, suppl., 129S–130S, May 1960.
48. Bennion, D. R., Research on multiaperture magnetic logic devices, Technical Report 1, Contract Nonr 2712(00), Stanford Research Institute, Menlo Park, California, May 1960.

In the above three items, a class of multipath cores that can be wired for either logical positive or logical negative transfer is described.

49. Engelbart, D. C. and Haynes, J. L., Research on the philosophy of logic realization, Final Report, Contract AF 33(616)-6303, Stanford Research Institute, Menlo Park, California, May 1960.

The subject matter of 40 is given further treatment here. In addition, general consideration is given to logic scheme derivation and analysis (including, but not limited to, all-magnetic schemes).

50. Bennion, D. R., Engelbart, D. C., and Van De Riet, E. K., Flux-doubling in magnetic cores, U.S. Patent No. 3,009,136, November 14, 1961 (filed June 8, 1960).

A toroidal-core scheme is described whereby the flux level is basically doubled (prior to subtraction of losses) during each stage of transfer.

51. Crane, H. D., Sequence detection using all-magnetic circuits, *Inst. Radio Engrs., Trans. on Electronic Computers* **EC-9**, pp. 155–160, June 1960.

A particularly simple application of all-magnetic arrays to sequence detection is described.

52. Yochelson, S. B., Diodeless core logic circuits, *Inst. Radio Engrs., 1960 WESCON Convention Record*, Part 4, Los Angeles, California, pp. 82–95, August 23–26, 1960.
53. Bennion, D. R., Review of "Diodeless core logic circuits," by S. B. Yochelson (above item) *Inst. Radio Engrs. Trans. on Electronic Computers* **EC-10**, p. 114, March 1960.

The above two items deal with a scheme that employs a four-phase clock cycle and single-path cores, but which uses a different mode of transfer than the schemes described in 36–38.

54. Stabler, E. P., Methods of magnetic logic, Ph.D. Thesis, Electrical Engineering Dept., Princeton University, Princeton, New Jersey, March 1961.

By consideration of schemes in magnetic network terms, a toroidal-core scheme similar to that of 37, but with two extra cores per bit for additional isolation, is described.

55. Hölken, U., Möglichkeiten zur Realisieruns logischer (Boolescher)

Funktionen mit rechteck magnetischen Netzurg, *Archiv der Elektrischen Übertragung* **15**, 482–494, 1961.

Logic is considered in terms of continuous magnetically coupled structures ("rectangular-magnetic networks" in his terms). Schemes for transferring are given but, as with the previous literature on this type of structure, no experimental verification of operability is given.

56. Hölken, U., Ferrite core logic in all-magnetic technique, Preprint of the Proceedings of the IFIP Congress 1962, International Federation for Information Processing, Munich, August 1962. (The paper by the same title actually delivered at the conference provides a revised but less complete treatment.)

The author derives a three-phase circuit (the same as is introduced in 30), then shows means for obtaining greater coupling-loop currents by successively adding a pair of additional cores per stage and an additional phase per clock cycle. The resultant four-phase circuit is similar to the one shown in 52. An original, five-phase circuit is obtained from the second step. (The circuits described in the revised paper presented at the conference are the one introduced in 28 and a modified form of the one indicated in 54.)

57. Van De Riet, E. K., Improved Flux-Doubling Structure (patent pending).

Means are given for realizing the scheme of 50 in terms of a continuous magnetically coupled structure.

58. Engelbart, D. C., Orthogonal magnetic systems and a new example of all-magnetic logic. *Proc. International Conference on Nonlinear Magnetics*, Washington, D.C., April 1963.

A type of core-wire circuit is described for which different modes of flux switching remain independent until some core saturates. A scheme based entirely on such orthogonal modes and comprising eight uniform toroidal cores per bit is described, and means are given for achieving general logic.

59. Bobeck, A. H. and Fischer, R. F., Reversible, diodeless, twistor shift register, 1958 Conference on Magnetism and Magnetic Materials, *J. Appl. Phys.* **30**, suppl. 43S–44S, April 1959.

60. Moore, D. W., Magnetic domain switching in evaporated magnetic films, *Proc. 1959 Electronic Components Conference*, pp. 11–14, May 1959.

61. Broadbent, K. D. and McClung, F. J., Thin magnetic films for logic and memory, Digest of Technical papers, 1960 International Solid-State Circuits Conference, Philadelphia, Pennsylvania, pp. 24–25, February 1960.

62. Broadbent, K. D., A thin magnetic film shift register, *Inst. Radio Engrs., Trans. on Electronic Computers* **EC-9,** pp. 321–323, September 1960.

The above four items describe magnetically coupled schemes of the type involving moving domains in thin continuous strips of metallic magnetic materials. (This type of scheme is also discussed in 17 and 23.)

63. Smith, D. O., Proposal for magnetic domain-wall storage and logic, *Inst. Radio Engrs., Trans. on Electronic Computers* **EC-10,** 708–711, December 1961. (Also published as Report 53G-0059, Lincoln Laboratory, Mass. Inst. Technol., Lexington, Massachusetts, May 31, 1961.)

64. Ballantyne, J. M., Demonstration of magnetic domain-wall storage and logic, *J. Appl. Phys.* **33,** suppl., 1067–1068, March 1962.

In the above two items, a scheme is described which involves moving domain walls, but for which the sense of rotation of a domain wall, rather than the direction of magnetization, is used as the data-carrying means.

The following items were found after the time of mailing the manuscript to the publisher. Such new material was added to the bibliography in the order received within the time allowed by printing requirements.

65. Dick, G. W. and D. W. Doughty, "A full binary adder using cylindrical, thin-film logic elements, Digest of Technical Papers, 1963 International Solid-State Circuits Conference, Philadelphia, Pennsylvania, pp. 86–87, February 1963.

The unit described is based on a transfer scheme involving electrical wiring in a lattice configuration for each stage. A cylindrical thin-film element is deposited on each arm of the lattice. Means for achieving general logic are indicated.

66. Newhall, E. E., and J. R. Perucca, "Energy gain and directivity achieved using balanced magnetic circuits," Digest of Technical Papers, 1963 International Solid State Circuits Conference, Philadelphia, Pennsylvania, pp. 74–75, February 1963.

67. Newhall, E. E., "The use of balanced magnetic circuits to construct digital controllers," Proceedings of International Conference on Nonlinear Magnetics, Washington, D.C., April 1963.

In the above two items, the authors describe a multiaperture core that may be used in such a way that part of the core acts as a flux source; flux from this source is forced into two balanced paths (in the same core) linked in opposite sense by each connected coupling loop. A bipolar input loop current unbalances the switching in one way or the other, resulting in a bipolar output current. A three-phase transfer scheme is described (like the scheme shown in 30 but with each toroidal core replaced by a core of the type described). In 67, it is shown how general logic circuits may be realized with cores of this type.

7. Appendices

In the following five appendices, attention is focused on a number of items having particular bearing on the application of these techniques. The authors refer to work only from their own laboratory, because the interesting system developments presently under way in a number of other laboratories are not yet public information.

7.1 Appendix 1: Nondestructive Readout

The ability to read the state of a multipath magnetic element non-destructively is extremely useful. To understand the principle, consider the element of Fig. 28, which is shown as having three minor apertures;

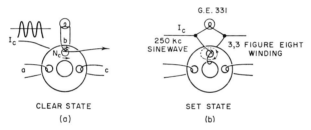

CLEAR STATE   SET STATE
(a)   (b)

FIG. 28. Nondestructive readout. (a) Lamp is not energized with element in CLEAR state. (b) Lamp is continuously energized with element in SET state. (After Crane and Van De Riet [24]).

apertures a and c are used perhaps in connection with some digital system and aperture b is available for readout. We are not here concerned with the details of the system to which apertures a and c connect, except to note that at the time of readout the element may be in its binary *zero* (Clear) state, or its binary *one* (Set) state, Figs. 28(a, b), respectively.

Consider now the readout. To "test" the state of the element, a carrier signal is applied to the output aperture, its amplitude being limited so that the peak value of mmf $N_c I_c$ is less than that necessary to switch flux about the major aperture. Hence, no flux switches in the Clear state. In the Set state, though, flux is relatively easily switched, the flux being reversed about the minor aperture each half cycle of the carrier. Thus, in the Set state, a significant carrier frequency voltage is induced in the secondary winding.

121

Any load (e.g., an incandescent lamp) connected to the secondary therefore experiences a relatively high or low steady excitation, depending upon whether the element is Set or Cleared, respectively. In this way, the binary state of an element can be read out continuously, the read-out process being nondestructive to the state of the remainder of the core because flux is switching only locally about the output aperture. Commercially available 50 to 100 mw incandescent bulbs are easily driven directly in this manner without the need for intervening coupling elements. A specific example of such a read-out circuit is shown in Fig. 28(b), which is copied from Fig. 15 of [24]. Note in this case that the same winding is used for excitation and for coupling to the indicator, in order to minimize the number of turns through the minor aperture. A figure-eight winding is used because, with the same magnitude of carrier current, the local drive about the minor aperture is doubled without any increase in the net drive about the major aperture.

An incandescent lamp is an example of a device that can be directly excited from a high frequency signal. In the case of output devices requiring a dc component of excitation, the output aperture signal can, of course, be rectified. In this way, for example, heavy duty commercial relays have been excited directly from an output aperture via a single coupling diode [27].

In summary, small loads can be driven directly from the output aperture circuit. For large loads, power gain elements, such as relays, or breakdown devices, such as four-layer diodes, can very easily be incorporated between the output aperture and load.

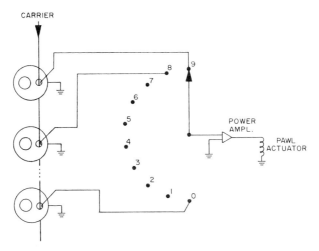

Fig. 29. Direct print wheel control from a one-out-of-ten code register. Commutator rotates until it finds a signal to actuate the pawl mechanism, which in turn stops the print wheel.

An important point is that it is not necessary to remove the carrier signal during digital processing involving the other apertures. This is especially true in MAD-R systems, where the tolerance on driver currents is so large that the carrier signal has relatively small effect on performance. This property is important in many applications because it eliminates the need for special circuits to turn the carrier generator on and off.

In a system presently being built at Stanford Research Institute, the carrier output signal is used directly for printer control. Each printer wheel has a separate commutator and pawl arrangement. As the wheel rotates, the commutator "searches" for a signal at each position. When a signal is detected, a pawl is actuated, which stops the wheel at that point, Fig. 29. In the figure, it is suggested that one decimal digit is represented in a one-out-of-ten code in the 10 core register and that the commutator segments are driven directly from the minor-aperture output windings. The very low impedance of these minor-aperture output windings results in very stable operation, in spite of the noisy electrical environment.

7.2 Appendix 2: Signal Switching

Although the nondestructive read-out technique discussed in Appendix 1 is extremely useful in many applications, the capability can be employed in even more powerful ways. In particular, it has been interesting to consider the possibility of switching audio (or more generally, analog) signals in this way. In other words, the MAD element is used as a switch: Cleared, signals are blocked; Set, the channel is open. Techniques for achieving such switching capability have been studied and the results are presented by Crane and English [28]. Following is a portion of the abstract of that paper; reference is also made to Fig. 30:

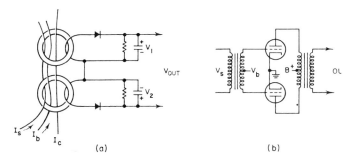

(a)   (b)

FIG. 30. Signal switching with magnetic elements. (a) Cores represent a pair of apertures in a MAD. When the MAD is CLEAR, $V_{out} = 0$; when SET, V_{out} is proportional to input signal I_s. (b) Analogous push-pull vacuum tube arrangement; V_s, V_b, B^+ correspond to I_s, I_b, I_c, where the latter is a carrier frequency current. (After Crane and English [28].)

123

"An analog signal (audio, for example) applied to the small aperture of a multipath element can be switched to an output winding or not, depending on the binary flux state of the element. In particular, by using a pair of small apertures, a push-pull operation is achieved in which a signal current, a carrier current, and a dc bias current play the respective roles of signal voltage, dc supply, and dc gain-control voltage in conventional push-pull systems. With such an arrangement, one obtains "noiseless" switching, gain-control, frequency response from dc to well beyond the audio range, high linearity (less than one percent total distortion), high on-off ratios (better than 70 decibels), and output levels of 5 mw with multipath elements presently in use in logic systems. The principles of these types of circuits are discussed. Various applications are also indicated: e.g., a magnetic cross-bar system and a time-multiplexing system based on a scanning all-magnetic shift register."

The primary reason for using a carrier signal in these switching circuits is to alleviate two problems. The first problem is that when the element is Set, we desire a linear transfer function between the input and output. But because we are primarily concerned with elements uniformly composed of square loop materials, the coupling between input and output on an audio basis would be highly nonlinear. The second problem is that the energy transferred to the secondary would be very small at low (audio) input frequencies because of the very small magnitudes of flux (volt-time integral) involved. Both of these difficulties can be effectively eliminated by incorporating a carrier signal in addition to the input audio signal.

Assume first that the carrier applied to the read-out aperture is amplitude modulated by the audio signal. Suppose further that the amplitude of the unmodulated carrier is adjusted to several times the small aperture threshold, and that the carrier frequency is increased until roughly one-half of the flux switchable (or Set) about the read-out aperture is actually switched each half cycle. In other words, although the drive is relatively strong, it is also relatively short. In this case it is clear that as the amplitude of the carrier is increased (or decreased), then the amount of flux switched per half cycle will similarly increase (or decrease). Now it is easy to show that the average output voltage is proportional to the amount of flux switched per half cycle. Hence, the amplitude of the rectified output voltage tends to follow the envelope of the modulated carrier, and good performance can actually be achieved with such an amplitude modulated drive—the output signal being essentially zero when the element is Clear and a good replica of the carrier envelope when it is Set.

Such an arrangement is not interesting from a practical point of view, however, because it requires the use of separate modulators, apart from

124

the magnetic switch elements. Of special interest, therefore, is the observation that the core itself has the right properties to perform the modulation function, as well as to control the switching. In other words, if a carrier current *plus* audio current signal is applied, then the voltage drop across the carrier winding (both windings for that matter, since they experience the same ϕ) will be amplitude modulated. This is the basis for the circuit of Fig. 30(a) in which a carrier current and audio current, along with a bias current, are added in the pair of core apertures. Space limits discussion of the details of this switching operation, and the reader is referred to [28].

7.3 Appendix 3: Sequence Detector

The "sequence detector" is an example of a "subsystem" that has a very simple core-wire form of realization, compared, for example, with a standard transistor realization. This topic is discussed by Crane [29]; the discussion below serves merely to introduce the nature of the technique.

The idea is to use a shift-register type of structure to detect if a particular (previously specified) sequence of pulses should ever appear at the network of input lines. Thus, in Fig. 31 (which is copied from Fig. 3 of

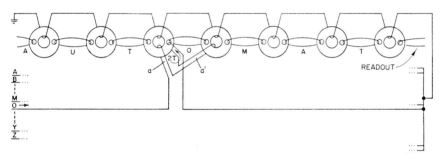

FIG. 31. Sequence detector. Only if the inputs are excited in the exact sequence AUTOMAT will a *one* state propagate to the end of the register. (After Crane [29].)

[29]), it is desired that the correct sequence of inputs (in this case AUTOMAT) and only that sequence of inputs will result in the propagation of a binary *one* completely down the chain. (In this arrangement, the input currents themselves serve as the advance pulses.)

Suppose the register is initially cleared. Receipt of an "A" will result in setting of the first element. Receipt of a "U" will cause a *one* state to be shifted to the second element. Suppose now that "AUT" has already been received, so that the third element is Set. Let us see how receipt of "o" will cause still another shift, whereas receipt of any other letter will cause the register to clear out (much as in a mechanical combination lock).

Note that all input lines return to ground through a common clear winding on the register. Thus, whenever any input current flows, all elements tend to be cleared. Suppose though that with the third element Set, the "o" line carries a current. In this case, the current through the clear winding of the third and fourth element is exactly bucked by the same current through the windings labeled (a, a'). Thus, the transfer in this loop is completely unaffected by the current in the clear winding. Current on any other line, however, would result in the clearing of the third element without any transfer. The only exception is if current is carried on the line representing the previous letter, in this case "T". In other words, the circuit would respond equally well to AUTTTT . . . as to AUT. . . . This is because the very first application of the "T" current will complete the local switching, and additional application of the same current immediately after can have no additional effect. This means that the circuit is "bounce insensitive," but also that it could not distinguish between words that differ only in adjacent letter repeats, e.g., loose and lose. However, special provisions can be made for detecting repeated characters, as described in [29] and as indicated by example in Appendix 5.

As explained in the references, detectors of this type can be arranged in many different forms; for example, they can be arranged to detect sequences of words (or phrases), or sequences within sequences, or they can be arranged to detect sequences with certain types of "error neglect" (in other words, a detector can be arranged to detect a sequence with any single error, or any two errors, and so on).

7.4 Appendix 4: Melville Driver

In the search for techniques for using as few nonmagnetic components as possible, even in the power supplies, the following interesting scheme was evolved, by means of which it is possible to drive an all-magnetic system almost directly from an ac power source. The basic idea is to develop a compression circuit so that the energy supplied per cycle is compressed in time, and then released at the output during a short pulse. The basic Melville principle (which is fairly old and has been used extensively in connection with radar modulators) is very briefly noted here in connection with Fig. 32, which is copied from Fig. 5 of Baer and Heckler [26].

Cores P_1, P_2, . . . , P_n are square-loop cores. Assume that they are initially saturated so that current from left to right is in a direction to cause switching. The resonant frequency of L and C_1 is essentially the same as the frequency of the generator voltage. Assume the generator voltage is initially zero and that it starts to go positive in a sinusoidal manner. Capacitor voltage C_1 will rise as shown in the figure and a small current will switch flux in Core P_1 simultaneously. When the volt-time product

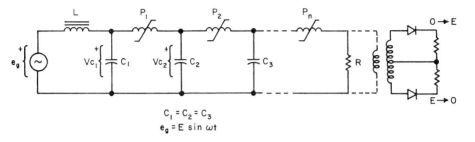

$$C_1 = C_2 = C_3$$
$$e_g = E \sin \omega t$$

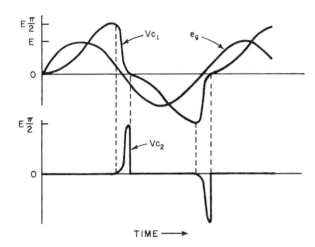

FIG. 32. Melville driver. The basic principle is that the energy supplied from the input (sine wave) source is compressed in time and then released in short pulses. (After Baer and Heckler [26].)

across the capacitor C_1 equals the flux-linkage capacity of core P_1, then P_1 becomes saturated. This is designed to occur at (or near) the time when the input voltage again goes to zero. The core P_1, then, has switched flux from one remanent state to the other saturation region during this half cycle of the input voltage.

Capacitor C_1 now tries to discharge. This discharge takes place primarily through P_1, the inductance of P_1 when saturated being much smaller than that of the coil L. Thus, practically all of the charge can leave the capacitor through P_1 before the amount through L has time to build up to any appreciable value. Likewise the generator voltage will have not had time to change appreciably. During this discharge of C_1 through P_1, P_2 is in a high impedance condition; i.e., it is switching from one remanent state toward the other, so the discharge current flows mainly into the capacitor C_2.

127

We have now traced the operation of the input section for one-half cycle of the input voltage. Let us now consider the next section of the network. When C_1 is discharging into C_2, the current waveform is essentially a half sine wave. After C_2 is charged, it tries to discharge through P_1 and through P_2. However, current to the left through P_1 is now in a direction to cause it to switch, while current through P_2 flows in a direction which would cause it to be driven further into the saturation region. Hence, the current is steered almost completely into P_2 and C_3, and after discharge the peak voltage value is essentially the same on both C_1 and C_2.

This transfer of charge from one capacitor to the next continues to progress in the circuit from left to right, the pulse narrowing at each stage, until the output stage is reached. Since the transfer of charge down the line takes place in a short time interval, the generator voltage does not have time to increase negatively to any appreciable extent. As an approximation, then, we can consider the negative half-cycle of operation to begin with no currents in the circuit, except that which is an immediate consequence of the generator voltage. The cores are all in the opposite remanent state from that which they were in at the beginning of the positive half-cycle, so the operation proceeds as before, except for polarities.

This circuit is then characterized by two output pulses per input cycle, one positive pulse and one negative pulse. A circuit such as this could be used to drive a two clock MAD-R system by "separating" the positive and negative pulses, as indicated by the dashed circuitry that substitutes for the load resistor. In this arrangement, the alternate positive and negative pulses generated are used as $E \rightarrow O$ and $O \rightarrow E$ drive pulses. (A scheme such as this was actually used in the MAVERIC system, briefly described in Appendix 5. The exact circuitry of the power supply is shown in [26]. The unit is designed to develop four-ampere pulses of 1.7 μsec rise time with a 450-volt drop across the load, supply frequency being 400 cps.)

The circuit described above is said to operate in a bi-cycle mode. We might finally note here that a "uni-cycle mode" of operation can also be arranged in which only a single pulse is obtained each cycle (with a small current of opposite polarity occurring during the interpulse period). With ·a pair of such circuits, synchronously phased, each could be used to directly drive one advance line, so that in this case even the diode "separators" would not be required as in the bi-cycle mode. For further details of this type of driver, the reader is referred again to [26].

7.5 Appendix 5: Specific Applications

From the annotated bibliography of Section 6, it can be seen that extensive work in this field, measured in terms of the output of technical papers, did not begin until the late 1950's. It is not surprising, therefore, that there is not as yet an extensive literature on operating systems, although there is considerable work in progress in the design of such special systems. The only papers on working systems are [24], [25], and [30], the first two of which refer to the design of a "feasibility study model" intended strictly for laboratory study, and the third to a system built as a laboratory "instrument" for studying the design of error-correcting codes. Brief comment is made below on special points of these two systems.

AFCRL System—This system, so-called because of having been built under sponsorship of Air Force Cambridge Research Laboratories, is briefly described in the abstracts of the two papers [24], [25]. From Part I,

"This paper describes the circuits used in a decimal arithmetic unit which utilizes ferrite magnetic elements and copper conductors only. The arithmetic operations of addition, subtraction, and multiplication are performed with a product and sum capacity of three decimal digits. The sole logical block of this system is a two-input inclusive-OR module with a fan-out capability of three with any desired logical positive and negative combination. The system involves the use of some 325 modules, each of which contains two magnetic multiaperture devices (MADS). This paper gives a complete description of the circuit and physical arrangement of the machine. The system is controlled from a manual keyboard, and read-out from the machine is via incandescent lamps controlled directly from the MAD elements, no intermediate elements being required.

"The 'worst case' drive-pulse amplitude range for the completed machine, varying all clock pulses simultaneously, is ±10 percent."

From Part II,

"A logical design technique is developed for use with the particular module developed for this system. . . . Some comparisons are noted between this particular all-magnetic logic scheme and conventional core-diode schemes. Comparisons are also made between magnetic logic schemes in general and some other realization schemes, such as ac operated parametrons and conventional transistor systems."

This system was built primarily to demonstrate the feasibility of constructing all-magnetic systems larger than small shift-register arrays, counters, and so forth, to which roles all-magnetic logic circuits had been limited at that time. The basic circuit module used is that outlined in Section 4.2 in connection with Fig. 26. It is based on a flux-doubling scheme, in which all coupling loop windings through minor apertures are single turn. A triple subclock system is used for fan-out, and negation is achieved as shown in Fig. 26(d). Wiring of the machine was greatly simplified by stacking relatively large numbers of cores in three dimensions, so that the drive windings could be achieved simply by pushing them straight through a long chain of elements at once.

Perhaps the only other point worth noting is that in spite of two cross-continental trips for demonstration purposes, there has not been a single component failure to date.

MAVERIC—(*Magnetic Versatile Information Corrector*)—This system is a highly versatile encoder-decoder for studying cyclic-error detecting and error-correcting codes. By a mode-selector switch it can be operated as an encoder or as an error correcting decoder. In other words, it can perform both as a transmitter station and receiver station. By relatively slight modification this machine could be adapted to on-line use. (The theory of such coding and description of the machine is covered in detail by Elspas [30].)

For our purposes here, there are three points worth noting with regard to this system (which is based on a MAD-R logic): (1) the component count, (2) the driver system, and (3) "prime drivers."

Shown in Table I is the component count for the system as built, and a rough, but realistic, component count that would have resulted from a "standard" transistor realization [30]. (By "standard," we mean off-the-

TABLE I. COMPARISON OF COMPONENT COUNTS FOR MAGNETIC AND TRANSISTOR
REALIZATIONS OF A SYSTEM FOR THE ENCODING AND DECODING
OF ERROR-CORRECTING CODES.

	MAVERIC	EQUIVALENT TRANSISTOR MACHINE
TRANSISTORS AND SCR"S	17	220
DIODES	4	458
RESISTORS	49	848
CAPACITORS	20	384
MADs	587	—
TOROIDS	40	—
SOLDER JOINTS	2400	4300

NOTE: Indicator circuits and DC power supply included. Solder joints at patch board and front panel not included.

shelf circuitry; a clever designer could undoubtedly reduce the count somewhat.) The savings in the total number of parts is due to the fact that the major part of this system relies on shift registers (including a large one of the feedback type) to generate certain sequences for coding purposes, and on an array of sequence detectors for monitoring the received data for decoding purposes. We have already noted how efficient, with regard to component count, circuits of this type can be.

This system was driven from a Melville driver of the type described in Appendix 4, the exact circuit diagram of which is given in [26]. In order to be able to start and stop the clock pulses on command, the "ac power" to the Melville system was derived from a 400-cycle core-transistor square-wave generator. This accounts for a number of the semiconductor elements noted in the chart. The square-wave generator and Melville drivers occupied a total volume of somewhat less than 75 in.

Four of the semiconductor elements were used in circuits called "prime drivers." As already noted, a large part of the system was concerned with searching for patterns (sequences) in binary data. In terms of the sequence detection scheme of Fig. 31, this implies an input "alphabet" of only two symbols, *zero*, and *one* (let us call these inputs A and B), and provision for detecting repeated characters. To drive this relatively large array, the technique sketched in Fig. 33 was very convenient. In this scheme, the

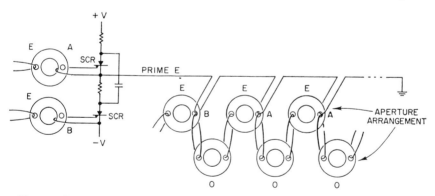

Fig. 33. Sequence detector for a two-symbol input alphabet. Control is effected by alternating the polarity of the Prime E current in accordance with the incoming sequence of characters (A, B).

polarity of the Prime E current alternates in accordance with the data being scanned. If an A (or B) symbol is received at a certain $O \rightarrow E$ clock then the subsequent Prime E current for the detector array will be positive (or negative). By selecting the polarity of the prime winding at each E core, a sequence sensitive circuit is easily achieved. Hence, the circuit shown in Fig. 33 will respond only to the data pattern . . . BAA . . . (note

131

that only a negative prime current through the first E core of the figure, and a positive prime current through the last two E cores, can actually result in priming, due to the selected winding polarity). This prime line drives approximately 200 MAD's in series. By utilizing silicon-controlled rectifiers for the actual driving, a significant reduction in the number of magnetic elements was achieved, especially since a large number of patch-board connections were involved in these circuits. (Although coupling-loop circuits were not permitted to pass through patch-board connections in this system, for another MAD-R system presently being considered, the coupling loop circuits themselves will actually be switched in patchboards.)

REFERENCES

(Note: Items indicated with asterisks are also listed with annotations in Sec. 6.)

1. Meyerhoff, A. J., *Digital Applications of Magnetic Devices*, Wiley, New York, 1960.
2. Haynes, J. L., Logic circuits using square-loop magnetic devices: A survey, *IRE Trans. on Electronic Computers* **EC-10,** pp. 191–203 (June 1961).
*3. Briggs, G. R., A Magnetic Core Gate and its Application in a Stepping Register, Engrs. Note E-475, Digital Computer Lab., Mass. Inst. Technol., Cambridge, Massachusetts, October 1952.
*4. Russell, L. A., Diodeless Magnetic Core Logical Circuits, *IRE National Convention Record*, Pt. 4, pp. 106–114 (1957).
*5. Stabler, E. P., *Methods of Magnetic Logic*, Ph.D. thesis. Princeton University, Princeton, New Jersey, 1961.
*6. Gianola, U. F., Possibilities of All-Magnetic Logic, *J. Appl. Phys.*, **32** suppl., 27S–34S (March 1961).
*7. Crane, H. D., A High-Speed Logic System Using Magnetic Elements and Connecting Wire Only, *Proc. IRE* **47,** 63–73 (January 1959).
8. Nitzan, D., Flux Switching in Multipath Cores, Report 1, Contract 950095 under NASw-6, Jet Propulsion Laboratory, Pasadena, California, Stanford Research Institute, Menlo Park, California, November 1961.
9. Hesterman, V. S., Evaluation of Flux-Switching Models for Magnetic Devices, Tech. Rept. 2, Contract Nonr 2712(00), ONR, Information Systems Branch, Washington, D.C., Stanford Research Institute, Menlo Park, California, September 1961.
10. Engelbart, D. C., Improvemeet in Magnetic Flux Transfer Systems (patent pending).
*11. Engelbart, D. C., High-Speed Components for Digital Computers, Quarterly Report 2, Contract AF 33(616)-5804. Stanford Research Institute, Menlo Park, California, February 1959.
12. Bennion, D. R., Network Models for Magnetic-Core Logic Circuits, Technical Report 3, Contract Nonr 2712(00), ONR, Information Systems Branch, Washington, D.C., Stanford Research Institute, Menlo Park, California, July 1962.
*13. Russell, L. A., Magnetic Core Transfer Circuit, U.S. Patent No. 2,907,987, September 15, 1959.
*14. Yochelson, S. B., Diodeless Core Logic Circuits, *IRE WESCON Convention Record*, Pt. 4, pp. 83–95 (1960).

ALL-MAGNETIC CIRCUIT TECHNIQUES

*15. Hölken, U., Ferrite Core Logic in All-Magnetic Technique, Preprint of *Proc. IFIP Congress*, Munich, August 1962.

*16. Haynes, M. K., Russell, L. A., Coughlin, J. J., Crapo, W. A., Kauffmann, J. A., Lockhart, N. F., Rutz, R. F., Tomasulo, R. M., and Cole, J. N., Improvement Program for Magnetic Logical Circuits, Physical Research Effort, IBM Corp., Research Laboratory, Poughkeepsie, New York, 1957.

*17. Bennion, D. R. and Engelbart, D. C., Multiple-Setting Magnetic Core Circuits, U.S. Patent No. 2,936,445, May 10, 1960.

*18. Bennion, D. R. and Crane, H. D., Design and Analysis of MAD Transfer Circuitry, *Proc. Western Joint Computer Conf.*, San Francisco, California, pp. 21–36 (March 3–5, 1959).

*19. Tancrell, R. H., Impulse Selection for Core Logic, *J. Appl. Phys.*, **32**, suppl., 40S–41S (March 1961).

*20. Bennion, D. R., Engelbart, D. C., and Van De Riet, E. K., Flux-Doubling in Magnetic Cores, U.S. Patent No. 3,009,136, November 14, 1961.

*21. Van De Riet, E. K., Improved Flux-Doubling Structure (patent pending).

22. Bennion, D. R., A Note on Magnetic Shift Registers, *IRE Trans. on Electronic Computers* **EC-9**, p. 262 (June 1960).

23. Cohler, E. U. and Baker, T. E., Geometric Factors in Multiaperture Ferrite Devices, *Proc. Special Technical Conference on Nonlinear Magnetics*, Los Angeles, California, November 6–8, 1961, AIEE, New York, pp. 215–249, 1961.

*24. Crane, H. D. and Van De Riet, E. K., Design of an All-Magnetic Computing System: Part I—Circuit Design, *IRE Trans. on Electronic Computers* **EC-10**, pp. 207–220 (June 1961).

*25. Crane, H. D, Design of an All-Magnetic Computing System: Part II—Logical Design, *IRE Trans. on Electronic Computers* **EC-10**, pp. 221–232 (June 1961).

26. Baer, J. A. and Heckler, C. H., Research on Reliable and Radiation Insensitive Pulse-Drive Sources for All-Magnetic Logic Systems, Final Report, Contract 950104 under NASw-6, Jet Propulsion Laboratory, Pasadena, California, Stanford Research Institute, Menlo Park, California, June 1962.

27. Sweeney, J. P., AMP Incorporated, Personal communication (1962).

28. Crane, H. D. and English, W. K., Signal Switching With Magnetic Elements, *Proc. International Conference on Nonlinear Magnetics*, Washington, D.C., April 1963.

*29. Crane, H. D., Sequence Detection Using All-Magnetic Circuits, *IRE Trans. on Electronic Computers* **EC-9**, pp. 115–160 (June 1960).

30. Flspas, B., Design and Instrumentation of Error-Correcting Codes, Final Report (RADC-TDR-62-511), Contract AF 30(602)-2327. Stanford Research Institute, Menlo Park, California, October 1962.

31. Bennion, D. R., Crane, H. D., and Engelbart, D. C., A Bibliographical Sketch of All-Magnetic Logic Schemes, *IRE Trans. on Electronic Computers*, **EC-10**, pp. 203–206 (June 1961).

Computer Education

HOWARD E. TOMPKINS*

National Institutes of Health
U.S. Department of Health, Education and Welfare
Bethesda 14, Maryland

1. Introduction

"Thereupon those [blind men] who had been presented with the head answered, 'Sire, an elephant is like a pot.' And those who had observed an ear only replied, 'An elephant is like a winnowing-basket.' . . . Then they began to quarrel."

. . . Udana, Section V, Chapter IV [1]

A digital computer is a bit like the elephant as seen by the blind men in the Buddhist fable—very different from different points of view, but definitely large and important. One may approach a computer as an ex-

* Currently at the Department of Electrical Engineering, University of Maryland, College Park, Maryland.

ecutive interested in its effect on profits, as a user with a specific job to be done, as a programmer with a job to do, as a maintenance man required to keep the equipment running (hopefully a lazier and lazier man from lack of work), as an engineer hired to design better circuits, as a logician hoping to design better systems, or as a layman who is "just interested." The last mentioned class is important, for many of its members will be back next month, or next year, with a problem for the computer to solve, and it is well that they know something of what the computer can and cannot do, and what it demands of the user.

The foregoing classification is certainly not exhaustive, and admits of extension. Substantial variety exists among each class of person mentioned. Users may have problems from the business world, or from science, engineering, mathematics, medicine, linguistics, or literature, to name but a few. If the matter is cut down to its fundamentals or essentials, four subjects or disciplines can be discerned that encompass most approaches to computers:

Mathematics
Programming
Logic
Engineering and Technology

Each of these aspects of computers is in practice taught to many differing age groups, from elementary school through graduate school, and out in industry and government. Much of the teaching is in regular academic settings, but some is in industry, and some is personal learning at home.

Furthermore, the title of this article, Computer Education, does not restrict us to discussing the education of computer specialists. Computers as a factor in business education and engineering education are most important. Computers as tools in the educational process, semi-independently of the subject matter, are also worthy of consideration.

Then, too, what about the education of computers? How can computers ever learn to think if we do not bother to educate them? This topic, reluctantly, must be ruled outside the scope of this survey. Computers *are* becoming more educated, and more sophistocated, and are being constructed and programmed so that they *learn*, in a real if restricted sense, and do in their own way things that are called *thinking* when humans do them—but that is another story.

Furthermore, we must arbitrarily but reluctantly exclude analog computers from consideration. There is much evidence that hybrid systems with analog computing elements under digital control will find wide application in the future, particularly in science and engineering, and in fields such as medicine. That, too, is another story.

136

Finally, before getting down to the subject, the author's large debt to the many people who helped him with this article should be acknowledged. In particular, George G. Heller was most helpful in providing detailed references on many topics and Professor Donald L. Katz generously provided information from the Final Report of the Ford Foundation Project at Michigan. Many other correspondents were very cooperative in supplying data.

2. Computer Education in Industry

The digital computer industry has a substantial and essential stake in computer education. This is particularly true if we include in our concept "education" that which some educators call "training." The task of recruiting and training computer operators, installers, and maintenance personnel, not to mention sales representatives, is large, expensive, and necessarily done by the manufacturer of the particular machine being considered. As an indication of some of the nontechnical aspects of the problem, the following definition of an ideal computer technician is offered [2]:

"The ideal computer technician has several degrees in electrical engineering and related disciplines; he has been in the computer field for twenty years and has ten years of experience on his present machine. He gets along well with the programming and operating staffs and clears up their little problems for them. He is an inspiring teacher. He likes to see how small an inventory of spare parts he really needs. Last year, when the company offered to buy him a new oscilloscope, he declined because he found that by working a few weekends he could modify the old 1933 model so it would do the job. He also has repeatedly refused offers of pay raises since he considers his present modest salary completely adequate for his needs. His present income is even sufficient to defray the costs of the courses in computer technology that he takes at night. He displays fanatical loyalty to the company, and will not speak with recruiters from other organizations."

Computer manufacturers also have a large responsibility for programming education. (Here the line between training and education is slightly blurred, and we choose to call it all education.) When a new machine is delivered it must, in today's market, be accompanied by a substantial softwear (automatic programming) package. To prepare the programming system for a new machine requires dozens to hundreds of man months, depending on the size of the machine and how much could be adapted from its predecessor machines. The manufacturer must either have a staff to do this job, or must contract out the job to someone who does have the staff. In either case, educated systems programmers are needed. As it stands today, almost all systems programmers have learned their art on the job. Many of them brought to the job a formal education in established related disciplines such as mathematics, statistics, physics, or engineering. Many, however, are liberal arts graduates. In this field as in few others the mark of success is success itself, for a suitable formal educational discipline has not existed.

A major corollary problem has been the lack of effective methods for evaluation of the performance of programmers. Industry is still struggling with this problem, and so will the universities [3].

The computer manufacturer's responsibility for training has in most cases extended beyond his walls to include a certain amount of customer education, for education is a necessary (but not sufficient) condition for long-term customer happiness. The major computer companies have responded to this need with vigor. For many, such as IBM, Remington Rand, Burroughs, and NCR this represented simply an extension of their practices of many years standing in the business machines field.

IBM makes an extensive array of educational opportunities available to its customers. About 140,000 customer personnel participated in their Customer Education program during 1962. Most of these attended one-day to five-day courses given in one of 22 District Education Centers, but some participated through correspondence. Much of the instruction in this program is aimed at specific machines (e.g., 407 wiring), but some is general (e.g., critical path scheduling, simulation concepts, numerical methods). A separate series called the Customer Executive Program is aimed at the manager who wants the bigger picture, but will not operate the equipment himself. In addition, specialized symposia are organized and sponsored on special topics such as Medical Research, Agriculture, etc., to highlight the possible uses of computers in those areas.

Within the company, aside from the normal employee educational benefits that are characteristic of most large companies, IBM embarked in 1960 on the ambitious enterprise of sustaining a graduate-level school of its own, the Systems Research Institute, under John McPherson, a corporate Vice President. Located in New York City, near the United Nations building, it is organized into six departments, Systems, Applications, Programming Languages and Techniques, Machine Organization and Logic, Mathematics and Statistics, and Operations Research. About 80 students (all IBM employees) are in residence each quarter, and usually spend one quarter at the school. A permanent staff, supplemented by visiting instructors from other IBM installations, and an occasional university fellow, carries out the teaching and related research.

138

Other companies, on a smaller scale, have conducted employee educational programs of similar nature. Are these programs a reflection of inadequacy on the part of conventional educational institutions? We do not believe that a clear-cut "yes" or "no" is possible on this question. Certainly the objectives of industry training programs overlap the objectives of university education, but the two do not coincide. Instruction specific to a manufacturer's equipment is in general not acceptable, for its own sake, in a university setting. On the other hand, if the universities did not lag so far behind industry in their ability to teach new concepts and methods that have arisen from industrial research and development, the universities could shoulder a larger share of the load. How can this be brought about? In part, further use of the technique of using the professor in industry both during his summers and during the school year would be desirable. There are many detailed problems connected with such action, both financial and technical, but solutions should be attempted.

Furthermore, there should be use, where possible, of sabbatical semesters or years, with senior people from industry visiting the universities for a suitably extended period, and professors spending comparable periods in the industrial setting. Such a program can be made to work only if neither organization fears that the other's setting is too superior, and only if financial problems can be coped with. Difficult or not, it should be done.

3. University and College Computer Education

3.1 University Computer Equipment and Its Administration

Conjunction (logical OR) of three recent surveys of university computer installations indicates that about 187 United States universities or colleges have digital computers on campus [4, 5, 6]. These computers range in capability from the little Burroughs E-102 to the large IBM 7094. A few, like SWAC at UCLA and ILLIAC at Illinois, are real old-timers, hand made on the spot a decade ago. The most popular computer is the modern IBM 1620, with the older Royal-McBee LGP-30 still widely used. A number of larger schools are getting installations of the IBM 7070 or 7090 class.

Of the 168 United States schools granting engineering degrees in curricula accredited by the Engineers' Council for Professional Development (E.C.P.D.), 140, or 83.3%, have computers available on campus [7]. An additional 47 schools not having engineering curricula nonetheless have computers, which are used in conjunction with their mathematics, physics, or other relevant curricula.

The total of 187 schools reported as having computers is still far less than the 1014 schools reported by Dr. Lindquist [5] as offering mathe-

139

matics majors, but most of the noncomputer schools are small, and so
enroll a smaller proportion of the total mathematics and science student
body. In engineering, for example, the 16.7% of the schools that do not
have a computer enroll only 7.2% of the 197,450 engineering undergraduates and only 2.8% of the 36,155 engineering graduate students
enrolled in E.C.P.D. schools in the fall of 1962 [7].

Administration of the computer on campus varies widely, indicating
either the widespread applicability of computers in different areas, or the
variety of responses possible in the administrative organism of the university, or both. Data by Dr. Keenan [6] indicate the following distribution of supervision over the faculty or staff man directly responsible
for the computer:

Supervision point	Number of schools
Vice president or director of research	20
Academic vice president or dean, or provost	17
President or chancellor	14
Dean of the graduate school	13
Dean or director of engineering	12
Head or chairman of the mathematics department	11
Dean of the faculty or college	8
Assorted department heads	8
University computer committee	7
Assorted specialized deans	3
Administrative vice president or dean	3
Registrar, comptroller, or business manager	3
Total	119

It can be seen that in most schools an attempt has been made to have
the computer responsive to the needs of the administration or university
at large, rather than just to a single department or school. This has been
very desirable, and will continue to be so for the principal computer
facility on campus. During the coming era there will be increasing occasion
to consider the desirability of having specialized computer installations
serve special needs. There are no clear-cut answers to this problem. It can
be hoped that the central computer facility will be effectively managed
and sufficiently self-effacing to make possible a decision in each case on
the technical merits of the situation, rather than on the basis of personal
prerogatives and internal budget distribution. Certainly on-line computation in specialized areas such as medical research will be made easier and
more effective with specialized systems designed with the needs of that
service in mind.

COMPUTER EDUCATION

3.2 Curriculum Types

The status of computer curricula in most universities today can be described as "experimental" or "in transition." There is little consensus yet as to the desirable scope or content of these curricula, but there is much activity.

3.2.1 Engineering Design of Computers

Electrical design of computers does not appear as such in most engineering curricula, but the subjects underlying computer design—pulse circuits, electronics, transmission lines, electric and magnetic fields—usually do. All is not well, however. The electrical technology of computers of today and tomorrow is based firmly upon solid-state devices, such as transistors, semiconductor diodes, magnetic cores, magnetic thin films, and superconductors. The degree of emphasis that these devices receive in many undergraduate engineering curricula today is insufficient, when compared to the emphasis still placed on the vacuum tube. The development of large computer systems and introduction of solid-state devices has reached into the roots of engineering, and shaken some of the fundamentals into different focus. Distinctly nonlinear, but piecewise linear, circuits have assumed greater importance. There is increased use of statistical techniques, both for reliability studies and noise studies. The emergence of nanosecond computer circuits has placed new emphasis on the transmission line approach, and the distributed circuit concept.

Some engineering schools have not yet been able to translate these trends in effective curriculum changes. In part this has been caused by the natural lag between the progress of engineering and the emergence of good textbooks, which approximates five to seven years, on the average. In part also the delay has been caused by a lack of familiarity with these new developments on the part of faculty members. Much has been done, in many schools, and the rest are following as fast as circumstances permit.

Graduate programs have in some cases provided adequate study of electronic computer technology, but often the electronic aspects are assumed to have been covered elsewhere, and graduate computer courses emphasize the logic and systems design aspects rather than the circuit engineering. In view of the trend toward universal availability of predesigned and prepackaged circuit building blocks, this approach meets the needs of many engineers. However, someone must design the building blocks, and they in turn are moving rapidly toward "integrated" circuits fabricated using "molecular electronics" techniques. Accordingly, methods and processes that were formerly the province of the physicist are becoming widely used in engineering, and should become part of the education of

141

the computer oriented engineer. Here is a further challenge for engineering education.

Detailed logic design, in the computer context, should ideally be built upon a dual foundation of logic and switching theory on one hand, and the properties of available switching components on the other. The two points of view, logical and electrical, should be coordinated into a meaningful whole. This is difficult to achieve in practice, and more often than not switching theory is presented without reference to practical devices, and the student is left to make his own synthesis between it and the electronics. This may not hurt him, if he is able, and there are some arguments that this synthesis is best realized in industry, in a practical situation.

A number of the available textbooks in the field of computer engineering, logic, and systems design are commented on in the bibliography [8–21].

3.2.2 Utilization of Computers

Courses and curricula aimed at the education of computer users are quite diverse in their structure and content, their principal common denominator being that they involve some actual programming of a real computer whenever possible. In the undergraduate domain, the main trends that can be observed from catalogs, private discussions, and Keenan's report [6] include:

(1) The use of informal noncredit programming instruction followed by use of the computer for solving problems assigned in regular engineering courses.

(2) The presentation of isolated credit courses in computer programming to students in a particular discipline such as civil engineering, electrical engineering, statistics, or business administration, by the particular department; usually in the junior or senior year.

(3) The offering of a general introductory programming course to a wider audience by the mathematics department or computer center staff, followed by optional advanced courses in numerical methods and advanced programming (compiler languages, etc.).

(4) The offering only of mixed graduate-undergraduate computer courses in computers that include some programming, and some logic and systems design.

(5) The presentation of full curricula with a major in engineering mathematics, or applied mathematics, or some such title.

Whatever the technique of course organization used, the courses appear to meet a need, for they tend to be popular when they are optional. In many schools they are required in certain curricula. For example, the Ford Foundation Project at Michigan (to be discussed in Section 3.5) estimates that at least one computer course is required for over half of today's engineering undergraduates.

142

In the graduate area, almost every university lists at least one or two computer courses, either in mathematics or electrical engineering. The three major patterns observed are:

(1) Scattered courses in different departments, such as Numerical Analysis in Mathematics, Symbolic Logic either in Mathematics or Philosophy, EDP Methods in Business Administration, Switching Theory, Digital Computer Logic Design, and Analog Computation in Electrical Engineering, with no special degree programs in computing offered.

(2) Full graduate majors leading to master's or doctoral degrees in Computer and Information Sciences, or Communications Science, or some such title, with a choice of subspecialties within the field. Such programs are usually supervised by some established department, or by an interdepartmental committee.

(3) Specialized graduate degree programs aimed at a relatively narrow segment of the field, such as Information Storage and Retrieval.

3.3 Curricula at Selected Universities

A few selected programs will now be described; the basis for selection is largely the author's personal acquaintance, and omission of discussion of a particular program does *not* imply a judgment of quality.

The Massachusetts Institute of Technology (M.I.T.) offers four undergraduate courses (the equivalent of twelve normal semester credits) in the electrical engineering curriculum in programming, logic, and computer applications. Single courses appear in the civil engineering and industrial engineering curricula. No less than twelve graduate courses in various departments cover closely related topics from switching circuits through symbolic processes, industrial dynamics, numerical weather prediction, to numerical analysis. A "Center for Communication Sciences" exists in the Research Laboratory of Electronics, and is a focus for graduate student and faculty research in information processing in both living and man-made systems [22]. The work in this program extends into many aspects of biophysics and neuro-physiology, and much special-purpose computing equipment has been developed at M.I.T. An individual graduate student's program is tailored to his own needs by a faculty advisor; the successful student receives a degree in an established discipline such as electrical engineering [23].

The University of Michigan offers the undergraduate an option; there is a "crash" noncredit course on digital computer programming that meets for three weeks or so in evenings at the beginning of each term, and provides each attending student with the opportunity to have one problem that he has programmed run on the central computer, an IBM 7090. The mathematics department offers a two-hour-per-week one credit course in computer programming taught by Bruce Arden [24] and countless assistants, who cope with 450 to 500 students each semester. In this course each student programs and submits to the computer three to four problems during the term. In both courses the computer language used is MAD, the "Michigan Algorithmic Decoder," which was designed at the Michigan computer center by Bernard Galler, Bruce Arden, and Robert Graham [24–27]. The MAD compiling processor was designed for rapid compilation, at the expense of final object program efficiency, to minimize the total "compile-and-run" time on student problems, which typically are short problems that are run only once. Good basic diagnostics were included in the MAD processor, to help the student find his errors. In contrast, a production compiler such as FORTRAN will logically sacrifice speed of compilation for a faster more efficient object program. MAD is available to other installations using 704, 709, or 7090 machines.

The University of Michigan also offers five other regular undergraduate computer courses in electrical engineering or mathematics, plus seven courses of mixed level, for undergraduates or graduates, and six courses restricted to graduates [28–30]. A "Communication Sciences" program to the doctorate is offered, and combines studies in logic, mathematics, linguistics, and computer technology. Michigan has been the location of the Ford Foundation Project described in Section 3.5.

The University of Illinois has a required sophomore computer course for mathematics majors, and several related graduate courses in mathematics, including logical design. An extensive computer research and development program has existed on campus for over ten years, and it produced the venerable ILLIAC, one of the first fully parallel asynchronous logic computers. It is still operating. ILLIAC II, its large ultraspeed descendant, went into service this year. Across campus at the Coordinated Sciences Laboratory the CSX-1, an interesting small multi-accumulator machine, designed for rapid handling of small (16-bit) words, was developed.

Harvard University, through its Division of Engineering Sciences and Applied Mathematics, offers one undergraduate course and eight or nine graduate courses (half-courses, in their terminology), including numerical analysis, switching theory, information retrieval, computer languages, logic, computability, and inferential analysis. Extensive research on mechanical translation of natural languages is being carried on at the Computation Laboratory.

The University of Pennsylvania, largely through the Moore School of Electrical Engineering (source of ENIAC, the first electronic digital computer), offers an extensive graduate program in Computer and Information Sciences, leading to an M.S. or Ph.D. degree. A total of seventeen two-credit courses in this field is offered in the electrical engineering school. These are supplemented in the program by courses in the linguistics, logic,

144

and mathematics departments. Research in logic and machine organization supplements the course work. There is relatively little emphasis on utilization of a computer in this program. Engineering undergraduate instruction in programming is noncredit, but the Moore School's RPC-4000 is used extensively by undergraduates in their work in other engineering courses. Two of the graduate courses are available to qualified seniors [31].

In Purdue University the undergraduates also do not get credit for programming instruction, which is very informal. Then, in their regular courses, they are assigned some problems involving extensive calculations, for which subroutines are available on the local computer—for example, a least-squares curve fitting problem. Use of the computer is optional, but is practically universal! Clever people, these Hoosiers [32].

New York University offers an extensive graduate program, with twelve courses ranging from analog computation through automata theory in subject matter. The Computation Center includes CDC 1604 and 160A computers, the latter intended for application in medical research.

At the University of Oklahoma an engineering undergraduate may follow a curriculum in computer science, including about eighteen credits specifically in computer courses, and culminating in a B.S. in General Engineering degree. Three or four closely related mathematics courses are available, as is graduate work.

The University of Arizona is unique in having a separate academic department for computer studies, the Systems Engineering Department, in the School of Engineering. The degrees of B.S. in Engineering Mathematics and M.S. in Systems Engineering are offered, to supplement the more conventional B.S., M.S., and Ph.D. degrees. Some nineteen courses are offered at various levels, many jointly with the mathematics department or other engineering departments.

Carnegie Institute of Technology, through its Department of Mathematics and Computer Center, directed by Al Perlis, offers a few mathematics majors the opportunity to go rather deeply into the art of programming languages while still in undergraduate study.

Georgia Institute of Technology is instituting a graduate program focused on documentation, that is, information storage and retrieval [33].

Case Institute of Technology has as its graduate specialty systems engineering, with extensive research in progress. A substantial number of related mathematics courses supports the program.

American University, in Washington, D.C., devotes its computer curriculum entirely to graduate students in the schools of Government and Public Administration and of Business Administration. Documentation is a featured area in the program.

Other universities with extensive programs include Arizona State, Arkansas, Brown, Buffalo, California (at Berkeley and at Los Angeles) [34], Chicago, Columbia, Florida, Iowa State (at Ames), Kansas State, Minnesota, North Carolina State, Northwestern, Polytechnic Institute of Brooklyn, Princeton [35], Rensselaer Polytechnic Institute [36], Rochester, Stanford [37, 38], Syracuse [39, 40], Tennessee, Washington State [41], Washington University (St. Louis), Wayne State, and Wisconsin.

The foregoing list is undoubtedly not complete, but represents all the universities whose programs are known to the author either through acquaintance, catalogs, or reference in Keenan [6]. Many other universities are developing curricula or course sequences, including the author's own University of Maryland, where Dr. Werner Rheinboldt heads the new Computer Science Center.

To conclude, we list in the bibliography a number of texts in the general area of programming and machine utilization for scientific or general use [42–52]. Business oriented books are considered later. Of particular interest is Iverson's book [47], which represents a substantial step toward a machine-independent language for describing processes, and hence for describing the behavior of machines themselves.

3.4 Faculty Training

On the day-to-day level it is the faculty who makes or does not make progress toward adequate computer education. Faculty training is an evident necessity, for the majority of present engineering, mathematics, and business administration faculty completed their formal education before the computer appeared prominently on the scene.

In mathematics it might be argued that only a few faculty members need knowledge of computer mathematics, for that is but one narrow and not very prestigious corner of the rich domain of mathematics. In engineering, however, the optimum educational payoff is obtained if the computer is used not just in "computer courses" but in problem work in many other engineering courses as well. This will not be possible unless a large percentage of the engineering faculty is familiar with computer usage in their own fields of specialization.

To meet the general problem of faculty training there have been several sets of workshops, short courses, and special programs, many of them supported by NSF. For example, the summer institutes at the University of Oklahoma under Dr. Richard Andree, Chairman of the Mathematics Department.

3.5 The Ford Foundation Project at Michigan

By far the largest effort to cope with the faculty training problem and related problems has been the Ford Foundation Project on the Use of

Computers in Engineering Education, at the University of Michigan, under Professor Donald L. Katz, Chairman of the Department of Chemical and Metallurgical Engineering. Beginning in the fall of 1959 and extending to the summer of 1963, the project sponsored workshops, summer terms, full-semester visiting professorships, lectures on campus, surveys, and the preparation and dissemination of literature on computer education. A total of 217 faculty members from 65 United States and Canadian universities participated in the workshops, or summer or full-semester programs. Of these, 161 were faculty from other universities than Michigan, seventeen of whom spent a full semester at Michigan, and sixty of whom spent a two-month summer term there [53].

All of the training programs were problem oriented, and detailed accounts of many of the problems conceived and programmed are included in the project progress reports, which are available at most engineering schools, through the Dean of Engineering.

The Final Report of the project [53] contains an illuminating tabulation of responses to a questionnaire sent to all faculty who had participated in the program. The major factors tending to delay widespread utilization of computers in engineering curricula was alleged to be lack of faculty know-how, with lack of an adequate computer stated as the second major deterrent. The need for better literature and textbooks was also mentioned frequently.

The Final Report also contains a detailed discussion of the introductory programming courses at Michigan, and is valuable reading for the aspiring professor anxious to avoid unexpected pitfalls. For example, instructing the students in keypunching and routine handling of punch cards was found to be consuming an exorbitant amount of faculty time. Hence it was found expedient to use two "lecture machines," each consisting of a tape recorder with associated controlled slide projector, to dispense prerecorded instructions. The "teaching machines" proved highly successful. Other judgments rendered in the Final Report are:

(1) That there should be ready computer accessibility, with minimum red tape and no charge to the student. Computer operation is, of course, in professional hands when a large machine such as a 7090 is used.

(2) That programming should be on an open-shop basis, with advisers on duty at suitable hours to help students (or faculty!) to find their way out of serious difficulties.

(3) That a good problem-oriented language such as MAD, having a processor of high compiling speed, should be used, supplemented by a good assembly language.

(4) That a good executive routine is needed, so that minimum stress is put onto new programmers having simple input-output needs, and so that minimum turnaround time is achievable.

(5) That funds for computer operation on academic problems should come from a central budget (analogous to a library budget), and *not* be provided pro rata by each department that has students using the machine.

(6) That a central computer facility works well provided there are card punches spread around campus in convenient locations, with transportation service for card decks and results provided.

(7) That a large machine is less expensive than several small machines, for equivalent computing accomplished, the cost of a student problem ranging from $2.50 to $19.00 on a composite large machine, and from $3.20 to $80.00 for the same problems on a composite small machine.

(8) That console button pushing is of little educational value.

These points are discussed in more detail in the Final Report of the Ford Foundation Project. We find the arguments and data convincing, but disagree with point (8). For many students in engineering, and in particular for those who are going on to work in the field of computer systems design, there is definite educational benefit in following the course of a simple problem at the console, observing the registers. Once done, however, there seems little reason to make a regular practice of it. A good program, then, would provide a small machine for introducing the students to computers, and for special work, and a large machine for carrying out most of the students' routine problem work. If one machine is a variable field decimal computer, and the other is fixed-word-length binary, so much the better.

Several of the publications sponsored by the Ford Foundation Project are listed in the Bibliography [24–26, 54–59].

3.6 Issues in University Computer Education

Of many issues that are live today, we shall comment on only a few. Many others are discussed in bibliography items already listed, in connection with Section 3.3 [22–41].

On the issue of computing in undergraduate mathematics programs, the point of view of some mathematicians is that occasional casual mention of "computational implications" in conventional mathematics courses is sufficient [60]. When such opinions form the basis for the mathematics program in a university, the engineering faculty must necessarily fill the gap, if today's student is not to be short-changed.

3.6.1 The Credit vs. No-credit Issue

The decision as to whether a first course in computer programming should be offered for credit or not has been a difficult one. In favor of the noncredit approach are the following arguments, which apply most forcefully in science and engineering curricula.

(1) The computer is just a big costly slide rule, and the straightforward

148

techniques for its use can be acquired most efficiently by the student on his own, under the pressure of needing the computer's help on some of his regular course work.

(2) The intellectual-theoretical content of computer programming is too slight for a credit course. "Why, the subject is even taught in high school!"

(3) There is no spare room in the engineering curriculum anyway, so programming will have to be acquired by the (engineering) student on his own time.

The arguments favoring credit status for the introductory programming course are as follows:

(1) The student learning programming should acquire more than just the ability to solve the little problem he has today. The influence of the computer is sufficiently pervasive that the student should get a perspective on its utilization, abilities, and limitations that he will not get in skimpy, on-his-own learning to meet today's problem.

(2) There is more than enough intellectual content in the subject of computer programming and computer languages, if a general point of view is adopted, and proper examples are employed. The algorithmic process itself becomes the proper subject of the course, with a particular language on a particular computer as a laboratory example. (Programming is an example of a subject that can be approached on many different intellectual levels; English is another; languages are also of this nature; all may be taught in high school, or in college.)

(3) Credit should be given for work accomplished, if the work is of college level, and if it is not of college level, it shouldn't need even an informal course.

(4) No curriculum is too crowded for inclusion of material of fundamental importance; objective weighing of course content can be hard on tradition, and hard on professors.

We see no reason to deny credits where mental effort has been expended to achieve goals of intellectual value, for example, in a course that offers substance beyond the coding for a specific machine, or beyond the details of a particular programming language. In the algorithmic method, its formal properties and modes of expression, its limitations, the ways in which it has been mechanized, and the scope of its application to date, there is ample intellectual nourishment. A good course along these lines deals in a fundamental way with the basic aspects of the logical organization of almost all types of intellectual effort. It is a study of certain aspects of the intellectual process itself. Such a course does not suffer in comparison with introductory courses in other fields of science or nonscience.

On the other hand, it seems desirable to have a noncredit short course available to assist those students whose computing needs are immediate,

149

and who cannot at the time take the full course. They should be encouraged to take the credit course subsequently, and should find much additional material of value in it.

A related problem that has often been faced in the past is whether to teach a programming language such as FORTRAN or the machine coding of the particular small machine available. The problem today, with larger machines available, may take the form, "Shall we teach the assembly language or the compiler language?" In the light of the philosophy previously stated, the answer is "Neither, until the algorithmic process is well in hand." At the present time, flow charts are the most widely used representation of a process. They are perhaps the best representation to use in introducing the subject, at this time, but the development of suitable algebraic methods may take place, in time. Subsequently, there should be consideration of the different levels of language, English, flow charts, problem-oriented (compiler) language, assembly language, and machine code. Finally, the particular language *for laboratory use*, i.e., for student use in their problems for the computer, should be chosen on the basis of local conditions, to get the most efficient and least time consuming utilization of the available human and machine resources. With this approach, the teacher can be secure in the knowledge that the able student will be able to make the transition to other languages for his future computer work, as the need arises.

If the student specializes in computers, he will of course have to know examples of languages of various levels, and the basis of their structure, and their relationship to the systems logic and hardware.

At this writing, suitable texts for courses such as we suggest are still lacking.

3.6.2 Decision Machines, a Cultural Course for Nonscientists

One educational need that is not, as far as we know, being met today is a need for a knowledge of the capabilities and limitations of computing and data processing machines on the part of students of political science, sociology, economics, and "liberal studies" generally. We suggest that an appreciation of the scope and properties of "decision machines" will be a necessary part of the cultural experience of a well educated person of the 1970's . . . certainly before 1984. The impact of the computer sciences on modern society and its economic and political foundations will be sufficiently intense and widespread to have made an indelible impression by then.

The economic effects of automation in the factory are already being felt. The effects of further automation of business paperwork and decision making are not far behind. It is not doom that we are facing, but it is the

150

possibility of vastly changed "rules of the game" of extracting a good life from our planet. For the first time mankind will have tools capable of processing sufficient data at high enough speed to make detailed economic decisions on the basis of detailed facts—provided he has adequate economic theories. There *are* a few other problems, too: data input technology lags data processing capability. The need to detect and discount corrupt or erroneous data becomes essential. The need to correct faulty theory and procedures before they do a vast amount of damage becomes crucial. The art of communication between man and the machine is still primitive.

Despite all of these (and other) difficulties, the economic payoff is sufficiently attractive that the ingenuity of man is undoubtedly equal to the task of devising the needed procedures and techniques.

The implications of the computer evolution in the social and political spheres are also profound. A highly probable result is an increasing concentration of economic power in the hands of organizations large enough and progressive enough to make effective use of decision machines. A major continuing problem then will be to maintain an adequate balance of power between these various forces—governmental and private—that operate with the machines at their elbow. Doctrinaire answers will not suffice.

How well will fallible, hypocritical, slightly dishonest man make out in partnership with machines that are models of probity? It would be naive to say that machines will prevent dishonesty, but properly used, they will require a high order of knowledge and intelligence from the rascal with turpitudinous intent! Well controlled machines will alibi cheerfully for their master.

These problems—ethical, social, economic, and political—will involve the generation now in our universities and schools, and may be quite basic to their way of life. Hence it seems desirable to make available a "cultural" course that explores for nonscientists the contexts in which decision machines can operate, their scope and properties, and their achievements and limitations to date. Such a course could also effectively illustrate the algorithmic and heuristic methods, certain principles basic to linguistics, and a portion of the rhyme and reason of modern science, technology, and mathematics. Such a course does not exist today, to our knowledge.

3.7 Standards and Accreditation

With such diverse need and goals apparent, can we expect any degree of standardization in university level computer education? Standardization is probably most desirable in the major sequences, where pre-professional computer education is the concern. Will a recognized and established discipline, complete with traditions, established standards, and a few sacred cows, arise? Not without pain and effort, and not in any thoroughgoing way; the dynamics of the situation are too dominant. The field is still developing and changing too rapidly to admit of much immediate standardization.

However, much good can come out of the efforts of the various bodies now seeking to determine a consensus that will permit the eventual establishment of standards, and possibly accreditation of undergraduate computer curricula. At the moment their goals may realistically be only to exchange mutual advice and moral support, but that is most valuable, too, and leads to definitive action when the time is ripe. One such group is the Southern Regional Education Board composed of computer people from Delaware to Texas. ACM and AFIPS Committees are also concerned.

One business society, the Data Processing Management Association, has proceeded to establish its own form of accreditation for individuals rather than curricula, as will be discussed in the next section.

3.8 EDP, or ADP, or BDP

In the world of business education, computers are not called computers; instead they are EDP or ADP or BDP machines. The acronyms stand for Electronic, Automatic, or Business Data Processing, respectively. The distinction between EDP machines and computers is, in a sense, real in that a computing machine optimized for business use will be rich in high-speed versatile input-output, and relatively poor in rapid or sophisticated mathematical manipulations. Basically, however, the machines are still computers—i.e., blood siblings of the mathematical machines.

The educational needs of the business student are somewhat different than the needs of the engineer or scientist, although management science and operations research are bringing these needs closer together.

A recent survey of computing in schools of business indicates that the use of machines is firmly intrenched, but that EDP techniques, as such, still make up only a small part of the student's education [61]. This is quite proper and understandable.

There also appears to be a significant need for vocational programs of two years' duration centered on EDP technology. The State of California, for example, with NDEA support, offers a comprehensive program including five major courses, Introduction to BDP, Electric Accounting Machines, Stored Programming, Business Systems and Procedures, and Data Processing Mathematics. The program is offered at fifteen public junior colleges throughout the state, and in 1962–63 there were about 500 students majoring in it. A detailed description of their courses is available [62].

Suitable vocational courses have also been outlined by other authorities [63, 64]. A program of this nature is also being developed in Springfield, Ohio, with NDEA support, under Mr. R. O. Brinkman (1115 North Limestone Street).

Unsuitable course programs also exist [65].

The DPMA (Data Processing Management Association) has taken an active role in setting standards and encouraging development of adequate educational programs in EDP at all levels. A "Certificate in Data Processing" is awarded by DPMA to those applicants who have three years of experience in the data processing field, and pass a comprehensive examination administered by the association. Formal academic (college level) requirements will go into effect in 1965 [66]. Comment on the program has been quite favorable.

DPMA also sponsors a popular "Future Data Processors" program, which provides instructional manuals and student handouts at modest cost to enable interested local groups or individuals to present organized data processing courses to high-school students. These courses are planned to be extracurricular and noncredit [67].

Selected texts suitable for college-level work are listed in the Bibliography [14, 30, 68–71]. Many others, on systems analysis, punch card methods, etc., are beyond the scope of this survey.

3.9 Short Courses

Special university short courses designed primarily for engineers and scientists in industry and government are a feature of the computer educational scene. The largest and longest-lived examples are the Engineering Summer Conferences at the University of Michigan every June, and the irregularly scheduled specialized short courses offered by U.C.L.A. and M.I.T. Other significant programs of this sort have been mounted by the University of Pennsylvania, the University of North Carolina at Chapel Hill, and Wayne State University, to name but a sample.

Various research institutes and industry associations also sponsor seminars for management and executive personnel.

4. Computer Education in the High Schools and Community

4.1 School Curricula

It is a most interesting happenstance—probably fortuitous—that the past decade, the decade of emergence of the computer, has also been a period of intense activity in school mathematics. New curricula and new courses have been born in substantial numbers [72] and many have prospered, amid alarum, enthusiasm, and controversy. Computer mathematics as such has been a small part of a few of these programs, and not a major overt factor. The revolution in school mathematics has rather centered on the fundamental approaches to the subject, with relatively "pure" mathematics as a guiding light, and abstraction rather than representation of the physical world as an often dominant influence.

The modern trends in school mathematics have tended to make the interested students' transition into computer mathematics easier. For example, most of the new programs introduce number representation in other bases than ten (but why must they choose base seven?) and modular arithmetic. Enough set theory crops up to make Boolean algebra and computer logic seem very straightforward, in the hands of a good teacher.

Computer programming, as such, has not made its way into these new mathematics curricula, except in rare instances. The reasons for this are many. Few high schools have access to a computer. Few high school mathematics teachers know how to program. There is no generally accepted notation and language for describing programs and programming that is usable at high school level other than flow charting, and *that* art is as yet undisciplined. Programming is not required or expected of high-school graduates by colleges and universities, so the able student often (properly) is advised to spend his time on more classical topics such as the beginnings of calculus, or analytic geometry, which will give him an edge in beginning college mathematics.

Arguments and considerations such as these have ruled in many cases, but there are notable exceptions [73, 74]. The William Howard Taft High School in New York City offers a regular senior course in computer mathematics, under Mr. George Grossman. An extracurricular honors program for outstanding students from other New York City high schools is also managed by Mr. Grossman, and uses the facilities of the Watson Computing Laboratories at Columbia University. The Bronx High School of Science also offers an outstanding curricular program in computer usage.

The National Council of Teachers of Mathematics, with financial assistance from the IBM Corporation, has prepared a 200-page book on Computer Oriented Mathematics, to assist high school teachers in preparing courses in this field. The project has been directed by W. Eugene Ferguson of Newton High School, Newtonville, Massachusetts. The book should be available late in 1963, from N.C.T.M. [75].

4.2 Volunteer Programs

Many of the programs in computer education at high school level have been carried out by amateur educators who are computer professionals [76]. For example, Joe H. Ward, Jr., Chief of the Computer Analysis and Programming Section at Lackland Air Force Base, Texas, has for five years been giving noncredit computer courses for high school teachers and students. A typical course in 1962 included eighty students, and ran for twenty-four instruction hours over an eight-week period. FORTRAN is used as the major vehicle in Mr. Ward's courses.

A major program in high-school computer education was sponsored by the Washington, D.C., Chapter of ACM in the schools of nearby Maryland

154

and Virginia. Organized by George G. Heller, a programming specialist from IBM Federal Systems Division in Bethesda, Maryland, course sequences were offered during 1960–61 and 1961–62 in over a dozen high schools on a noncredit extracurricular basis [77, 78]. About thirty volunteer lecturers participated in the program, which reached about 500 students during the two academic years. The volunteer program is continuing on a reduced schedule. Many of the high schools in the area are now offering some of the material of the program in regular courses taught by regular teachers who attended the volunteer lectures.

The author had the privilege and pleasure of teaching part of one course in George Heller's program, and it was most rewarding. Only the best students are willing to expend the extra effort to attend Saturday classes that require homework, and can qualify for a program such as this. As a result the level of class interest and achievement is very high, and provides a stimulating and demanding experience for the teacher.

Other high-school programs have been organized and taught by university faculty who have had an appropriate "concern." For example, Professor Richard V. Andree, Head of the Mathematics Department at the University of Oklahoma, has carried out an extensive program of summer institutes and Saturday school-year courses for high school teachers and students in the central Oklahoma area. College faculty members have also participated in summer programs specifically designed for them.

Another effort worthy of mention is the "Special Summer Session for Secondary School Students in Computer Mathematics and Programming" organized and presented during the summer of 1962 by Andries van Dam, an Instructor in the Moore School of Electrical Engineering of the University of Pennsylvania in Philadelphia. The Moore School provided a classroom and free time on their educational computer, an RPC-4000, but did not officially sponsor the program. A group of 39 students, obtained by contacting high school mathematics chairmen, began the program, which ran for seven full Saturdays. Of the starters, 29 finished the course, and 20 "passed" the final exam, which was nominally at college achievement level. Five of the students submitted projects to the 1962 Fall Joint Computer Conference educational session, all were accepted, and two won prizes.

During the summer of 1963, the Engineering Schools at Pennsylvania presented a more extensive program, with two courses aimed at high-school students.

What does it take to put on a successful educational program of that sort? At least three things: talent, access to a computer, and a desire to work with youth. All three need not be concentrated in one person, but it usually takes one dedicated person to spark the program. Indeed, a better course can be achieved if two qualified teachers are available, one for the lectures and one to help with problems at the machine—assuming that the course is centered about a small computer and that part of the enjoyment is actually working the computer.

A major need for programs of this sort is for more adequate text and lesson material, to make the best possible use of the available teaching talent. It is desirable that such material be keyed to the type of computer used by the students. Several general books and pamphlets are available that cover parts of the field at an appropriate level, and more can be expected to appear during the coming months [69, 79–92].

4.3 Computer Hardware Education

The major emphasis in computer education at the high-school level (both in school and in volunteer programs) has been on programming, for several reasons, among which are relevance, cost, preparation of the student, and availability of teachers and instructional materials. By relevance is meant the fact that programming, well taught, is fundamentally the subject matter of "problem solving," in a very basic and general sense. Hence programming is relevant to both high-school mathematics and physics, and will help both, if taught in a general way.

Most high-school students are unprepared to learn much about circuit engineering, for they lack adequate background in electrical theory. However, the concepts of logic are accessible to them, if carefully presented, and a good high school class can make great strides in logic design. A good teacher, with experience in avoiding the pitfalls of both over-formalism and under-formalism, is a major ingredient to success of this kind.

The cost of electronic components is high, and only a limited number of high-school instructional projects can hope to have parts donated by manufacturers. Several local groups have managed to do just that, however, and have built small computers at quite small investments. A high-school group in Lower Merion, Pennsylvania, under the guidance of Professor Morris Rubinoff of the Moore School of Electrical Engineering, University of Pennsylvania, is currently hard at work designing and building a small machine.

A similar group at Hinsdale, Illinois, under the direction of David M. Boyd, Chief Instrumentation Engineer of Universal Oil Products, Des Plaines, Illinois, built a computer from gift parts in 1960–61. So it can be done.

The rarity with which logic design and circuit engineering enter into high school programs is in part a scholastic-cultural manifestation. Mathematics, physics, and chemistry appear in the high-school curriculum, and good teachers exist in the high schools in these subjects. Engineering does not appear at high-school level, although some students and high-school faculty undoubtedly—if mistakenly—interpret technical-vocational courses as being representative of engineering.

In the university, electrical engineering courses do not begin until the middle of the sophomore year, in a typical curriculum. Prior to these courses, the student gets courses in physics, chemistry, and mathematics that lay the foundation for engineering, but do not, in many cases, provide much application of these tools to engineering situations.

As a result, the study of electronic circuits gets pushed back to later years, in spite of the fact that much of the basic material in this field is well within the grasp of younger students. We therefore see a strange dichotomy—electronics taught early as a nonmathematical technician subject, often to less able students, whereas superior students wait until their junior year in college to be introduced to the subject!

Electrical circuits and electronic circuits provide many elementary applications suitable as examples for principles of physics, and for exercise of mathematical techniques. Computer switching circuits are among the simpler electronic circuits to analyze, involving, for the most part, simply algebra and a basic understanding of Ohm's Law and Kirchhoff's Laws. The dynamic aspects of circuit analysis are, of course, more difficult, but static analysis is certainly not beyond the able senior high school student. A problem in this regard is the absence of suitable text material.

4.4 Age of Students, and Teaching Techniques

How young can students be, and yet be taught computing successfully? Much can be done at junior high-school level, with talented students, as has been firmly demonstrated by the experience of Fred Gruenberger of the Rand Corporation in teaching 1620 programming to selected seventh and eighth graders in the Santa Monica, California, schools [93].

Some work has even been done with elementary school children by a research team from System Development Corp. [94, 95]. Success was partial.

In many ways, junior high school is an excellent time to teach programming to talented students. The normal demands of the typical junior high school program are not adequate to challenge the better student. Properly taught, programming not only stimulates the student to use his mentality at a time he would normally be lazy, but also provides a basis of practice and understanding of the algorithmic method that makes superior work in senior high school science and mathematics more likely.

In teaching students of any age, but particularly younger students, teaching techniques are important. Dr. Douglas Engelbart has evolved a technique of game playing that is invariably well received by audiences young and old [96]. (We used a simplified form at an adult party—it was a howling success.) Reprints of his paper are available from him. His game is based on the logic of a machine, and teaches how machines do arithmetic, but there is no reason why it should not be adapted to the teaching of programming fundamentals, also.

An alternative approach has been described by G. W. Horton [97].

4.5 Home Study

Correspondence courses in computer programming are quite practical, since a computer could be located at school headquarters. In some such courses, however, this is not done, and the results are understandably less than perfect. Available home study courses have been listed in the March issue of the *Journal of Business Education*. The National Home Study Council, 200 K Street, N.W., Washington 6, D.C., which accredits home study courses, may also be contacted for detailed information.

At least one extensive home study course in programming is sponsored by a university, specifically, by Pennsylvania State University, University Park, Pennsylvania. This course features proctored final examinations in the student's home city.

Computer electronics is included in many of the advanced correspondence courses from schools of radio engineering. No college level engineering courses are available on a correspondence basis.

In the area of public education, television has not been neglected. In addition to the election eve highjinks with computers, which are, in their fashion, educational, there has been at least one planned educational series on computers, "The Computer and the Mind of Man," produced by KQED, San Francisco, for NET, National Educational Television, and shown over its tape network as a series of six half-hour programs. Richard Hamming of Bell Telephone Laboratories was host, and many visiting experts participated in the lectures and demonstrations.

5. Programmed Instruction

The art of programmed instruction (teaching machines) has attracted many practitioners and even more protagonists during the last five years. About fifty companies now market teaching materials for use in machines of various sorts, or programmed books that do not require a machine, according to a 1962 survey for the U.S. Office of Education and NEA (National Education Association) [98].

Not all authorities agree that programmed instruction is a "good thing." See, for example, the review of W. Christian's paper [99] by H. N. Laden [100]. Part of the current difficulty of evaluating programmed texts is that many poor programs have been written, in the rush of a new, exciting, and potentially profitable field. Many of the program writers have been

158

themselves inadequately prepared in the subject matter they were programming, and that can be disastrous, for the programmed method is a demanding mistress. The situation should improve as the field matures. Selected references for background and achievement in the field are listed in the reference list [101–112].

An ASEE (American Society for Engineering Education) committee, reporting on the status of programming efforts in progress in engineering schools as of June, 1962, indicated that 72 faculty members at 38 U.S. universities were writing, testing, or using programmed text material for segments of their engineering specialty [113]. By contrast, the number of research efforts in programmed instruction that involve a digital computer directly is small, only eight replies indicating that "hardware" development and testing were in progress.

Two projects in which a large scale digital computer has been harnessed to one or more students will be discussed here. The first is not at a university at all, but is at the IBM Research Center in Yorktown Heights, New York. The Behavioral Sciences Group there, under Dr. William Uttal, has prepared programs for an adapted 650 computer to teach stenotypy, German, and psychological statistics [114]. Transfer of the programs to a much faster 1410 computer was planned, and should by now be accomplished. It is estimated that up to 20 students could have been handled simultaneously on the 650, had that number of input-output stations been available, but that the corresponding saturation point for the 1410 lies between 100 and 200 students.

Unfortunately, fairly expensive terminals (input-output stations) are required, and, at this point in the development of the method, are not the same for all of the different courses being taught. For the German and stenotypy courses a modified computer discfile is used at the central machine to store audio sound traces, and so permit the computer to pronounce German words, or English dictation words, for the student. (Who says that a computer can't talk? And in two languages, too!) For the statistics course, and many others, a computer controlled typewriter can be used as the terminal.

The computer programs are designed to vary the pace of the learning process so that the rapid learner moves ahead rapidly in large steps, whereas the slow learner gets the supplementary exercises, and repeated explanation, that he needs. The computer is used in conjunction with text material, the student, at approximate points in his progress, being told to "read your text."

An important by-product of using the computer is that a complete record of each student's progress through the course material is available. These data are the best possible guides to improvement of the teaching programs. Unforeseen difficulties and obscurities can be pinpointed, and areas of needed

159

modification identified. The computer, of course, can also give tests, and automatically mark the papers, a true boon for teachers.

Dr. Uttal reports excellent results with the programs, particularly the one in statistics, where direct comparison with a conventionally taught course covering the same material was possible (albeit not under fully satisfactory experimental controls). It is also suggested that the economics of modern computer usage in teaching will compare favorably with conventional methods, because of much more efficient use of professorial talent. The preliminary evidence is favorable.

The PLATO (Programmed Logic for Automatic Teaching Operations) project in the Coordinated Science Laboratory of the University of Illinois is also of interest [115]. In this project involving the ILLIAC computer a closed circuit television system is used to enable the computer to present displays to the student. This is less expensive than it sounds, for closed circuit industrial television is a competitive production business that delivers a lot of electronic sophistication for relatively little money. Input to the closed circuit video system is either from slides or from characters generated by the computer on a buffer cathode-ray storage tube. Only one slide selector is required for a set of students, but a separate cathode-ray storage tube is needed for each student, which is costly. The experimental PLATO system was limited to serving only two students because of the small 1024-word storage capacity of ILLIAC. PLATO's designers estimate that perhaps 1000 students could concurrently use a large modern computer. That figure appears high to us. In such a situation, clearly, the major cost of a large teaching installation is going to be the terminals—the input-output stations with all their buffering.

As in the IBM project, the teaching program adjusts the presentation of new material to the progress of the student. The logic of PLATO is slightly different. The student must request HELP sequences as they are needed, by appropriate keying from the keyboard. He may jump back to the main sequence when he thinks that he has had enough help. The program will not let him go on until he has mastered his current difficulty, by HELP or crook.

Also, detailed student records are produced and used for teaching program improvement.

At this point, the case for digital computer assistance in programmed instruction has not been proven, but the initial indications are that the technique has definite value for some subjects under some conditions. Even if it does not prove practicable to use computers routinely for established courses, it may prove eminently feasible to use a computer during the development of a new programmed text, to record the paths that students take, and the difficulties they encounter, thus permitting dynamic teaching program improvement. The final product might be a programmed book, usable without the computer. Clearly the structure of such a book will be more complex than the one-line programs of the Skinner school of thought. The Crowder Tutor-Texts are examples of branching programmed books.

The Educational Science Division of U.S. Industries, the publisher of Tutor-Texts, also produces a small machine that affords some flexibility in inserting auxiliary practice or correctional material. Unfortunately, the step from book to special electromechanical machine reduces the flexibility of programming, even though control of student "cheating" is far better than with programmed books. In neither case is there a detailed record of the student's course of progress, to help with teaching program improvement. The cost of the machine is far less than the cost of a digital computer, however.

Mention should also be made of the extensive work at System Development Corporation on automated classrooms [116].

6. Conclusions

Much has been done. There is yet a lot to do.

ACKNOWLEDGMENT

The author wishes to thank the Department of Health, Education, and Welfare for permission to prepare this article. The views expressed herein are not to be considered in any way as expressions of the point of view of the Department.

ANNOTATED BIBLIOGRAPHY

Section 1

1. *The Bible of the World* (R. O. Ballou, ed.), pp. 277–279. Viking Press, New York, 1939.

Section 2

2. Bryan, G. L., *et al.*, The Role of Humans in Complex Computer Systems, Technical Report No. 24, Psychology Dept., Univ. of Southern Cal., Los Angeles, California, Jan. 1959. (Also contains valid comments on programmers.)
3. The People Problem, and The Computer Personnel Research Group, *Datamation*, **9**, No. 1, pp. 37–39 (Jan. 1963). (Discusses steps toward useful measures of programmer characteristics.)

Section 3.1

4. Computing in the University, *Datamation*, **8**, No. 5, pp. 27–30 (May 1962). (Combines data from surveys by Dr. C. B. Lindquist of the U.S. Office of Education and Dr. Roy F. Reaves of Ohio State Univ.)
5. Lindquist, C. B., Guide to Undergraduate Programs in Mathematics, U.S. Office of Education Report OE-56008, 1962. (Brief survey of college mathematics curricula, and bibliography on careers in mathematics.)

6. Keenan, T. A. (ed.), Fifth Annual Survey of University Computing Activities, University of Rochester Computer Center, 1961. (Publication omitted in 1962; a valuable survey.)

7. Foecke, H. A., and Tolliver, W. E., Engineering Enrollments and Degrees in Institutions with ECPD-Accredited Curriculums: 1962, *Jour. Engg. Educ.*, **53**, 354–377 (1962–63).

Section 3.2.1

8. Alt, F. L., *Electronic Digital Computers, Their Use in Science and Engineering.* Academic Press, New York, 1958. (Old, but authoritative, clear, and concise. Last 2 out of 5 parts require substantial mathematical background; first three are quite accessible.)

9. Bartee, T. C., *Digital Computer Fundamentals.* McGraw-Hill, New York, 1962. (Compact presentation of broad area.)

10. Chu, Y., *Digital Computer Design Fundamentals.* McGraw-Hill, New York, 1962. (Comprehensive detailed presentation of arithmetic, logic, basic circuit configurations, and design techniques.)

11. Gotlieb, C. C., and Hume, J. N. P., *High-Speed Data Processing.* McGraw-Hill, New York, 1958. (Widely used; now somewhat out of date.)

12. Hohn, F. E., *Applied Boolean Algebra—An Elementary Introduction.* Macmillan, New York, 1960. (Brief, clear, mathematically oriented paperback.)

13. Hurley, R. B., *Transistor Logic Circuits.* Wiley, New York, 1961. (Widely read; many good sections.)

14. Ledley, R. S., *Digital Computer and Control Engineering.* McGraw-Hill, New York, 1960. (Comprehensive; heavy style; much unique material.)

15. Maley, G. A., and Earle, J., *The Logic Design of Transistor Digital Computers.* Prentice-Hall, Englewood Cliffs, New Jersey, 1963. (Selective coverage. Specialties include a no-nonsense transform treatment of NOR logic and chapters on asynchronous circuits.)

16. Marcus, M. P., *Switching Circuits for Engineers.* Prentice-Hall, Englewood Cliffs, New Jersey, 1962.

17. Phister, M., Jr., *Logical Design of Digital Computers.* Wiley, New York, 1958. (A classic; widely used.)

18. Pressman, A., *Design of Transistorized Circuits for Digital Computers.* Rider, New York, 1959. (Much material of sound engineering value, presented in detail.)

19. Richards, R. K., *Arithmetic Operations in Digital Computers.* Van Nostrand, Princeton, New Jersey, 1955. (Old, but still of value.)

20. Scott, N. R., *Analog and Digital Computer Technology.* McGraw-Hill, New York, 1960. (Good coverage of engineering aspects.)

21. von Handel, P. (ed.), *Electronic Computers: Fundamentals, Systems and Applications.* Prentice-Hall, Englewood Cliffs, New Jersey, 1961. (Includes Tantzen, R. G., Digital Computers; Jaenke, M. G., Analog Computers and Computing Control Systems; and Gschwind, H. W., Digital Differential Analyzers.)

Section 3.3

22. Wiesner, J. B., Communication Sciences in a University Environment, *IBM Jour. Res. & Dev.*, **2**, 268–275 (1958). (States the philosophy of the MIT graduate program in areas related to the computer sciences.)

23. Miller, C. L., and Seifert, W. W., The Faculty and the Computer—Some Problems and Goals, *Jour. Engg. Educ.*, **50**, 839–845 (1959–60). (Asserts that the entire faculty should get into the act.)

24. Arden, B. W., *An Introduction to Digital Computing*. Addison-Wesley, Reading, Massachusetts, 1962. (Sophomore text at Michigan; the language is MAD and the emphasis is on numerical methods.)
25. Organick, E. I., *A Computer Primer for the MAD Language*. Addison-Wesley, Reading, Massachusetts, 1963. (Short-lecture-course text at Michigan.)
26. Galler, B. A., *The Language of Computers*. McGraw-Hill, New York, 1962. (Also MAD, a clear exposition of the language in terms of several interesting classes of problem.)
27. Galler, B. A., Arden, B. W., and Graham, R., *The Michigan Algorithm Decoder*. Univ. of Michigan Bookstore, Ann Arbor, Michigan, 1963. (Defines the MAD Language.)
28. Pehlke, R. D., and Sinnott, M. J., Computers in the Undergraduate Teaching of Metallurgical Engineering, *Jour. Engg. Educ.*, **52**, 573–577 (1961–62). (Analog and digital, as used at Michigan.)
29. Streeter, V. L., Use of Digital Computers in Teaching Hydraulic Design, *Jour. Engg. Educ.*, **53**, 284–288 (1962–63). (Five problems worked out in detail.)
30. Scott, N. R., Computer Design Courses in the Engineering Curriculum, *Jour. Engg. Educ.*, **50**, 852–855 (1959–60). (Proposed content of computer engineering courses for different engineering majors.)
31. Brainerd, J. G., Setting up a Computer Faculty in a School of Engineering, *Jour. Engg. Educ.*, **50**, 846–851 (1959–60). (Recognizes and lists many aspects of the problem.)
32. Machol, R. E., The Computer Revolution in Engineering Education, *Proc. Natl. Electronics Conf.*, **16**, 305–307 (1960), or *IRE Trans.*, **E-4**, 67–70 (1961). (Purdue's philosophy.)
33. Atchison, W. F., Numerical Analysis and Computers in Engineering Education, *Jour. Engg. Educ.*, **50**, 856–859 (1959–60). (The need to tie mathematics to reality in undergraduate study is stressed.)
34. Karplus, W. J., and Kovach, L. D., The Use of Computers in Analysis, in *Proc. 1962 Spring Joint Computer Conf. (AFIPS Proc.*, **21**), pp. 225–234. National Press, Palo Alto, California. (The other side speaks up; utilization of analog computers preferred.)
35. Tukey, J. W., The Teaching of Concrete Mathematics, *Amer. Math. Monthly*, **65**, 1–9 (1958).
36. Hollingsworth, J., An Educational Program in Computing, *Commun. ACM*, **2**, No. 8, 6–7 (1959). (Describes the program at Rensselaer Poly.)
37. Forsythe, G. E., The Role of Numerical Analysis in an Undergraduate Program, *Amer. Math. Monthly*, **66**, 651–662 (1959). (Stanford.)
38. Forsythe, G. E., Engineering Students Must Learn Both Computing and Mathematics, *Jour. Engg. Educ.*, **52**, 177–188 (1961–62). (Stanford.)
39. Gilchrist, B., University Computer Courses, *Jour. Engg. Educ.*, **49**, 342–346 (1958–59). (Argues for mathematics department supremacy.)
40. Thompson, G. L., Computers and the Mathematics Training of Engineers, in *Undergraduate Physics and Mathematics in Electrical Engineering, Proc. Sagamore Conf., Sept. 1960*, pp. 55–69. Dept. of Electrical Engg., Syracuse Univ., 1960.
41. Luck, L. D., The Use of a Modern Computer as a Teaching Aid in Structural Analysis and Design, *Jour. Engg. Educ.*, **50**, 860–862 (1959–60). (He's strongly in favor of it.)
42. Block, H. D., and Ruoff, A. L., *Differential Equations in Engineering Analysis*. Merrill, Columbus, Ohio, 1960. (Text that presents a balance of analytical, analog, and digital techniques.)

163

43. Dijkstra, E. W., *A Primer of ALGOL 60 Programming*. Academic Press, New York, 1962.
44. Evans, G. W., II, and Perry, C. L., *Programming and Coding for Automatic Digital Computers*. McGraw-Hill, New York, 1961.
45. Gotlieb, C. G., General-Purpose Programming for Business Applications, in *Advances in Computers, Vol. 1* (F. L. Alt, ed.), pp. 1–42. Academic Press, New York, 1960.
46. Halstead, M. H., *Machine-Independent Computer Programming*. Spartan Books, Washington, D.C. (1962). (Describes NELIAC, a used and usable dialect of ALGOL; some gaps in the explanations.)
47. Iverson, K. E., *A Programming Language*. Wiley, New York (1962). (Thorough presentation of a universal notation for describing algorithms that include manipulative as well as mathematical steps. Graduate level.)
48. Leeds, H. D., and Weinberg, G. M., *Computer Programming Fundamentals*. McGraw-Hill, New York (1961). (Widely used.)
49. McCracken, D. D., *A Guide to FORTRAN Programming*. Wiley, New York (1961). (An 88-page paperback, condensed but clear.)
50. McCracken, D. D., *A Guide to IBM 1401 Programming*. Wiley, New York (1962).
51. Ralston, A., and Wilf, H. S. (eds.), *Mathematical Methods for Digital Computers*. Wiley, New York (1960). (A unique compilation of algorithms and techniques on varying levels; some errors noted.)
52. Sherman, P. M., *Programming and Coding Digital Computers*. Wiley, New York, 1963.

Section 3.5

53. Katz, D. L., Organick, E. I., Navarro, S. O., and Carnahan, B., The Use of Computers in Engineering Education, Final Report of the Ford Foundation Project at the University of Michigan, Ann Arbor, 1963. (Issued in parts for each engineering discipline containing many suggested student problems; main text contains many recommendations, and much data on University of Michigan Computer Center operation.)
54. Katz, D. L., et al., Integration of Electronic Computers into the Undergraduate Educational Program. First Annual Report of the Ford Foundation Project on Computers in Engineering Education, University of Michigan, Ann Arbor, 1960. (Many student problems described.)
55. Katz, D. L., et al., Use of Computers in Engineering Education, Second Annual Report of the Ford Foundation Project, University of Michigan, Ann Arbor, Michigan, 1961. (Many additional student problems.)
56. Katz, D. L., and Organick, E. I., Use of Computers in Engineering Undergraduate Teaching, *Jour. Engg. Educ.*, **51**, 183–205 (1960–61). (Brief statement of the philosophy of the Ford Foundation project staff at Michigan.)
57. Carnahan, B., Luther, H. A., and Wilkes, J. O., Numerical Methods for Digital Computers, Ford Foundation Project Report, University of Michigan, Ann Arbor, 1963.
58. Carnahan, B., Copi, I. M., et al., The Use of Logic in Solving Engineering Problems, Ford Foundation Project Report, University of Michigan, Ann Arbor, Michigan, 1962.
59. Wilson, R. C., Use of Computers in Industrial Engineering Education, Ford Foundation Project Report, University of Michigan, Ann Arbor, Michigan, 1962. (Good discussion and many worked-out problems.)

Section 3.6

60. Committee on the Undergraduate Program in Mathematics, Mathematics Assn. of America, Recommendations on the Undergraduate Program for Engineers and Physicists, *Jour. Engg. Educ.*, **52**, 716–731 (1961–62).

Section 3.8

61. *Data Processing*, **4**, August 1962.
62. *Business Data Processing Technical Courses*. Calif. State Dept. of Educ., Business Educ. Publication No. 105, Sacramento, California, May 1962. (Detailed syllabi of several courses for two-year vocational program.)
63. *General Information Manual—Data Processing Courses in Vocational and Secondary Schools*. Document No. F20-8087, IBM Corp., New York, 1962. (Thorough two-year course outlined; includes much work with punch card systems, elementary accounting, etc.)
64. *Electronic Data Processing: A Suggested 2-year Post High School Curriculum for Computer Programmers and Business Application Analysts*. Technical Education Branch, U.S. Office of Education, Washington, D.C., 1962. (Detailed.)
65. Young, D., Beware the Phony EDP Schools, *Business Automation*, 14–19 (Feb. 1962). (Evidence that the diploma mills have started.)
66. Study Guide: Certificate in Data Processing, Data Processing Management Assn., 524 Busse Highway, Park Ridge, Illinois. (Undated.)
67. "Future Data Processors" Instruction Manual and Student Handout Kits, Data Processing Management Assn., Park Ridge, Illinois. (Undated.)
68. Gregory, R. H., and Van Horn, R. L., *Automatic Data Processing Systems*. Wadsworth, San Francisco, California, 1960. (Comprehensive.)
69. *Introduction to IBM Data Processing Systems*, IBM Corp., 1960. (Covers equipment types and programming concepts, within a somewhat generalized framework.)
70. Martin, E. W., Jr., Electronic Data Processing. Irwin, Homewood, Illinois (1961).
71. McCracken, D. D., Weiss, H., and Lee, T-H, *Programming Business Computers*. Wiley, New York, 1959. (Has some excellent chapters, and Chapter 3 is a must.)

Section 4.1

72. *The Revolution in School Mathematics*. Natl. Council of Teachers of Mathematics, Washington 6, D.C., 1961. Good summary of various new high-school mathematics programs, with discussion of problems of implementation.)
73. Littlefield, D. G., Computer Programming for High Schools and Junior Colleges, *The Math. Tchr.*, **51**, 220–223 (1961). (Gives a detailed course outline.)
74. Van Tassel, T., Digital Computer Programming in High-School Classes, *The Math. Tchr.*, **54**, 217–219 (1961). (Describes a "blackboard digital computer.")
75. Ferguson, W. E., *et al.*, *Computer Oriented Mathematics*. Natl. Council of Tchrs. of Mathematics, Washington 6, D.C., 1963.

Section 4.2

76. Armerding, G. W., Gruenberger, F., Marks, S. L., and Parkin, T. R., A One-Day Look at Computing, *Commun. ACM*, **5**, 486–487 (1962). (Report of an eight-hour session for high school students.)
77. Heller, George G., A Computer Curriculum for the High School, *Datamation*, **8**, No. 5, 23–26 (May 1962). (Describes the Washington, D.C., volunteer program.)
78. Heller, G. G., Organizing a Local Program in Computing Education, *Datamation*, **9**, No. 1, 57–59 (Jan. 1963). (Basic manual on how to do it.)

79. Crowder, N. A., and staff, *The Arithmetic of Computers; An Introduction to Binary and Octal Mathematics.* U.S. Industries, Educational Science Division, New York (1960). (Well done, in Crowder's traditional scrambled-book multiple-choice question format; said to be of "average 10th grade" level.)

80. Reference Manual—Glossary for Information Processing, IBM Technical Publication C20-8089, no date.

81. Gorn, S., and Manheimer, W., *The Electronic Brain and What it Can Do.* Science Research Associates, Chicago, Illinois, 1956. (Well done booklet, fundamental enough to be relatively ageless.)

82. *Yes, No—One, Zero—The Language of Computers.* Humble Oil & Refining Co., Eastern Esso Region, 60 West 49th Street, New York, no date. (Booklet, readable and free.)

83. Johnson, D. A. and Glenn, W. H., *All about Computing Devices.* Webster Publishing, St. Louis, Missouri, 1961. (Booklet by school skilled teachers.)

84. Johnson, D. A. and Glenn, W. H., *Understanding Numeration Systems.* Webster Publishing, St. Louis, Missouri, 1960. (Designed for high school enrichment, discusses base 7, base 5, and base 2. All in fun.)

85. Kenton, R. G., *I Can Learn about Calculators and Computers.* Harper, New York, 1961. (Designed for grades 6 to 9.)

86. McCormick, E. M., *Digital Computer Primer.* McGraw-Hill, New York, 1959. (A real book, for adult and intelligent youth, with good introductory treatment of a broad range of topics. Recommended.)

87. Murphy, E. A., Jr., *Do You Talk Computerese?* Minneapolis-Honeywell Regulator Co., Philadelphia, Pennsylvania, 1960. (Booklet, well done.)

88. Murphy, J. S., *Basics of Digital Computers,* Vols. 1, 2, 3. Rider, New York, 1958. (Designed for technicians, profusely illustrated with teaching diagrams, much use of analogy. Suitable for technically oriented high school students. An outstanding example of its type.)

89. Samuel, A. L., Computing Bit by Bit, *Proc. IRE,* **41,** 1223–1230 (1953). (An excellent introductory article, surprisingly modern for its date of publication. See also other articles in this October, 1953, Special Computer Issue of *Proc. IRE.*)

90. Siegel, P., *Understanding Digital Computers.* Wiley, New York, 1961. (Variable, but generally excellent for the talented high school student. Starts from scratch but moves to reasonable use of Boolean algebra and mathematics. Not for kidders.)

91. Stibitz, G. R. and Larrivee, J. A., *Mathematics and Computers.* McGraw-Hill, New York, 1957. (Adult book quite accessible to high school students; selective coverage of topics.)

92. Young, F. H., *Digital Computers and Related Mathematics.* Ginn, Boston, Massachusetts, 1961. (Booklet of 40 pages, written with clarity and taste; outstanding of its type.)

Section 4.4

93. Gruenberger, F., A Diary for Tomorrow's Programmers, *Datamation,* **9,** No. 1, 48–54 (Jan. 1963). (No one should try to teach programming to junior or senior high-school students without having read this blow-by-blow report of the trials, tribulations, and techniques of the 1962 seventh-grade summer class in Santa Monica.

94. Dobbs, G. H., Myer, E. P., and Perstein, M., A Course in Computer Programming and Advanced Mathematical Concepts for Elementary School Students, System Development Corp. TM-494, May 27, 1960. (Details of the 1959 summer program for selected fourth to sixth graders.)

95. Pelton, W. and Vaughn, L., Programming—An Approach to Problem Solving, System Development Corp. SP-167, April 7, 1960. (Philosophy of program of Reference 94.)

96. Engelbart, D. C., Games that Teach the Fundamentals of Computer Operation, *IRE Trans.*, **EC-10**, 31–41 (1961). (How to make a human computer system using students as flip-flops and gates; reprints free from author. It's fun and it teaches all sorts of things.)

97. Horton, G. W., HOBLADIC, *The Math. Tchr.*, **54**, 212–216 (1961). (A blackboard digital computer for class participation.)

Section 5

98. Finn, J. D. and Campion, L. E., *Teaching Machines and Programmed Learning, A Survey of the Industry, 1962*. U.S. Office of Education, 1962. (Available from Supt. of Documents, 55¢.) (Good basic discussion, photos of equipment, lists of available programs, basic bibliography.)

99. Christian, W., Private Tutor for Business, *Business Automation*, **7**, No. 2, 26–31 (Feb. 1962). (Simplified presentation of basic principles of teaching machines. See next item.)

100. Laden, H. N., Review of "Private Tutor for Business," by W. Christian, *Computing Rev.*, **10**, 287 (1962). (Expressive and forceful statement of the hazards of relying too much on programmed learning. Not a moderate point of view.)

101. Coulsen, J. E. (ed.), *Programmed Learning and Computer-Based Instruction*. Wiley, New York, 1962.

102. Eurich, A C., Engineering the Teaching of Engineering, *Jour. Engg. Educ.*, **53**, 273–278 (1962–63). (Good restatement of the basic arguments for using programmed instructional materials.)

103. Galanter, E. (ed.), *Automatic Teaching: The State of the Art*. Wiley, New York, 1959. (A wide spectrum of early papers.)

104. Green, E. J., *The Learning Process and Programmed Instruction*. Holt, Rinehart & Winston, New York, 1962. Reviewed by J. L. Rogers, *Computing Rev.*, **3**, 287–288 (1962). (Very favorably reviewed.)

105. Hughes, J. L., Effect of Changes in Programmed Text Format and Reduction in Classroom Time on the Achievement and Attitude of Industrial Trainees, *Jour. Programmed Instr.*, **1**, 43–54 (1962). (Describes training of IBM 7070 maintenance technicians.)

106. Lysaught, J. P., *Handbook of Programmed Instruction*. Wiley, New York, 1962. (Techniques of writing, evaluating, and using programmed texts.)

107. Margulies, S., and Eigen, L. D. (eds.), *Applied Programmed Instruction*. Wiley, New York, 1962. Reviewed by J. L. Rogers, *Computing Rev.*, **3**, 288 (1963). (Compilation of 25 papers; uneven.)

108. Pask, G., Electronic Keyboard Teaching Machines, *Educ. & Commerce*, **24**, 16–26 (1958).

109. Roe, A., Research on Teaching Machines and Programmed Learning, *Jour. Engg. Educ.*, **52**, 439–446 (1961–62). (Describes work in progress at UCLA. "Explodes" many theories, but concludes that programmed learning works well, when properly used.)

110. Rogers, J. L., Programmed Instruction in Computing, *Datamation*, **8**, No. 8, 33–36 (Aug. 1962). (Good discussion of trends and results in programmed instruction; application to training programmers.)

111. Skinner, B. F., Teaching Machines, *Science*, **128**, No. 3330 (Oct. 24, 1958); also *IRE Trans.*, **E-2**, 14–22 (1959). (The word.)

167

112. Stolurow, S. M., *Teaching by Machine*. U.S. Office of Education, Cooperative Research Monograph OE-34010, 1961. (Available from Supt. of Documents, 65¢.) (Extensive discussion of many aspects, including citation of many research results; highly recommended for the serious student.)
113. ASEE Combined Committee on Programmed Instruction, A Report on Programmed Instruction, *Jour. Engg. Educ.*, **53**, 117–123 (1962–63). (Full report of data from 125 engineering schools.)
114. Uttal, W., *My Teacher Has Three Arms*, IBM Research Center, 1963.
115. Bitzer, D., Braunfeld, P., and Lichtenberger, W., PLATO: An Automatic Teaching Device, *IRE Trans.*, **E-4**, 157–161 (1961); also PLATO-II: A Multiple-Student Computer-Controlled Automatic Teaching Device, *Proc. Conf. on Applic. of Digital Comp. to Automated Instruction*, Oct. 10–12, 1961.
116. Bushnell, D. D., Computers in the Classroom, *Data Processing*, **4**, No. 3, 9–14 (April 1962). (Description of System Development Corp. Project CLASS, Computer-Based Laboratory for Automated School Systems.)

Digital Fluid Logic Elements

H. H. GLAETTLI

IBM Research Laboratory Zurich
Rüschlikon ZH, Switzerland

1. Introductory Part

1.1 Introduction

Within a relatively short period, i.e., almost since the beginning of their existence, electronics and semiconductor technique have penetrated the field of control devices and computing elements thoroughly. One is, therefore, likely to believe that computing is only possible due to the existence of these more or less recent developments. This widespread belief, however, neglects the fact that purely mechanical devices were the forerunners of present day computers, and we can easily find the historical sequence confirmed by pointing to our preference in using the expression "to mechanize" instead of "to electronize."

"Forerunner" is not synonymous with obsolete; the contrary is true: mechanical elements have been in constant use up to now, and are an object of continuous research and development efforts. This is mainly due to some of their unique properties to be discussed in the following section.

It is interesting to see that until recently not too many thoughts were spent on hydraulic or pneumatic circuits. This is in sharp contrast to the fact that, for example, valves are very suitable for setting up logic circuits to be used in not too flexible machines of the lower speed range. During the past few years a new section was added to the catalog of mechanical elements: amplifiers using liquids or gases and containing neither moving nor deformable parts (except the fluid itself) were invented. A variety of amplifiers, storage devices and switching elements now exists, of which not too much is known. A great deal of the difficulties in understanding is due to the complexity of the hydrodynamic equations describing the phenomena in question, and due to the fact that all three dimensions play an important role. Furthermore, complicated geometries are used which cannot be easily described by analytic expressions. A lot of the present insight is rather qualitative than quantitative.

The survey given herein should, therefore, be understood as a state of the art report, and the next few years may be expected to result in considerable additions, at least as far as applications are considered.

1.2 Some Special Properties of Mechanical Elements

Lifetime always seems to be a major point of interest. It is therefore justified to discuss this aspect, as well as some others related to it, separately. (A more general discussion of special properties of mechanical element is given toward the end of this contribution: see Closing Remarks, Section 3.) Lifetime or life expectancy alone, however, is not necessarily a good criterion for evaluating components; it is also not directly related to reliability. The important thing is to know whether the lifetime of a certain component is to be understood as an average value, where large deviations are possible, or whether it represents a minimum value, which cannot be exceeded considerably. In the first case one speaks of "life expectancy" and in the second of a "well-defined lifetime."

High reliability does not necessarily require a high life expectancy: a well-defined lifetime may result in high reliability as well. There is, however, a remarkable difference as to the possibility of preventive maintenance: preventive maintenance may have little, or even an adverse effect in the first case, depending on how the failure rate varies with time. In the second case, preventive maintenance represents the means for prolonging the period of trouble-free service.

Mechanical elements (in contrast to electron tubes, for example) belong to the class of elements characterized by a well-defined lifetime. Death is caused by wear, erosion, corrosion or fatigue. This implies another interesting fact about mechanical elements: as far as wear, erosion or corrosion are concerned, inspection becomes possible and one can evaluate the further trouble-free period to be expected, without knowing what happened before. No such tests or procedures are known for nonmechanical components.

Summarizing it can be said that mechanical elements allow high reliability over a limited period of time, which can be prolonged indefinitely (at least in principle).

1.3 Note on Classifying Fluid-Mechanic Elements

To classify fluid-mechanic elements according to whether they contain moving or deformable parts beyond the fluid itself, is certainly an obvious thing to do. It may be helpful as far as cataloging is considered; its physical meaning, however, is very limited: it may be justified to think of a certain correlation between moving and deformable parts on the one hand, and design difficulties, when elements are to be miniaturized, on the other. There is no proof available at this time to support the opinion according to which devices with moving or deformable parts are inherently slower. One is likely to think of inertia; but as soon as thin diaphragms are considered, it can easily be realized that they represent no more inertia than a few millimeters of air. This is about the same order of magnitude as the minimum effective length of pure fluid amplifiers as will be shown later.

A much more meaningful classification is introduced by distinguishing between static and dynamic elements. This distinction is analog to the one made between hydrostatic and hydrodynamic transmissions: in the first case, forces are transferred and exerted by the (preferably relatively high) static pressure of the fluid. No power expenditure is involved except during the time when the fluid is in motion, if leakage losses are neglected. In the second case, forces are exerted by momentum changes in the fluid which is always in motion. Viscous friction and turbulent losses are the counterparts of leakage losses in static systems. The maximum operating pressure is usually limited to a few atmospheres. To keep down losses during standby periods is more difficult in dynamic than in static systems, because in devices running temporarily at high Reynolds numbers tight valves can be used, but no inviscous fluids nor turbulence-free ducts exist.

Dynamic elements may contain moving and/or deformable parts or they may not. Examples are given later. No static device working without moving or deformable parts is known at present, although this is not excluded by principle. One could imagine non-Newtonian fluids which could be used to control fluid flow in a really static manner. Valves are the only known static switching means at present..

There are, however, much more important differences between static and dynamic elements than the one concerning standby power expenditure, which is, in most cases, rather quantitative because many static elements are not free from appreciable leakage.

One such major difference is represented by the requirement of a minimum Reynolds number in dynamic systems. There is no analog in static circuits: no minimum pressure, for example, is required for proper performance (static friction, as well as spring forces to be overcome, are neglected). A minimum operating power is the immediate and expected consequence of the necessity of such a minimum Reynolds number. A less expected consequence is represented by the way the minimum operating power depends on the size: smaller elements require a higher minimum power.

Another important difference concerns the maximum allowable static pressure. Dynamic systems, as will be explained later, often show an upper pressure limit that is of the order of a few atmospheres (1 atm = 14.5 psi) and depend heavily on the pressure in the return line (e.g., atmospheric pressure if an exhaust line is in direct connection with the atmosphere). Static systems may be run at pressures mainly determined by material strength and leakage considerations.

Further differences are found in the design technique. Whereas static systems make use of rather conventional devices that are easily recognized, dynamic systems are often composed of elements that, in some cases, seem to have nothing in common with their static counterparts, and are even no longer easily recognized as passive or active elements.

1.4 Remarks Concerning the Survey Part

The whole field of fluid logic is just being explored and survey would be better replaced by status report. Even in these days of preparation of the report, new fluid amplifiers have been published. Therefore a certain risk of being incomplete is almost unavoidable, and the fact that not enough time has elapsed to become familiar in the same manner with the latest development as with earlier investigations, explains why some elements are treated more in detail than others. The length at which an element is discussed has no significance in respect of its technical or economical value; it merely reflects the author's experience and the general trend of publications. Last but not least, there is something like "easily recognizable application potential" which calls for an uneven distribution of research efforts.

Most of the general properties are discussed in the subsections dealing with specific arrangements. On the one hand, the importance of many effects depends on the elements, on the other hand, they become clearer in some cases than in others. There is, however, also a didactic reason behind this procedure: the field of fluid dynamics is mathematically more complicated than electronics (most elements are three-dimensional by their nature). Therefore exact analytical representations are beyond the reach of most methods commonly applied to electronic problems. Elementary estimates and similarity considerations which appear to be an especially powerful tool, play an important role and this is best demonstrated by application examples. Thus information contained in many sections adds up to a better understanding of a single element under consideration. It must also be emphasized that due to the different characteristics of the various elements, an optimum solution will probably make use of more than one kind of basic unit.

Compatibility requirements will be discussed several times. This is due to peculiar circumstances in fluid logic circuits: in order to build large circuits with fluid elements it is not sufficient to have elements that amplify pressure, flow rate and hence power. There is no practical equivalent for coupling condensers: the relatively large volume required is one reason against such an element; the fact that such a coupling condenser would be at least as complicated as the active elements themselves is another argument; dc-transformers are possible in fluid circuits. They would consist of a Venturi-tube or of a diffusor followed by a nozzle. Unfortunately the efficiency of diffusors is limited to a relatively low value, if no special measures are taken. Such measures, e.g., suction or vanes, however, make these elements again more complicated than the active elements, and serious difficulties arise when such measures have to be applied to miniaturized components. Therefore, and because of the limited pressure changes that can be achieved by such arrangements, the difference between input and output pressure levels needs special attention. If only one single species of elements is used to set up a whole circuit, the range of input pressure must lie within the range of output pressures obtained directly or with pressure dividers. In the latter case the step down factor must not reduce pressure amplification below one, nor must the efficiency of such an arrangement seriously interfere with flow rate amplification.

An element having a pressure amplification greater than one, a flow rate amplification greater than two (this makes branching easy) and a control pressure level that can be covered completely by the range of output pressures has, without doubt, a higher application potential than other elements which do not fulfill all these requirements. An alternative choice is to combine various kinds of elements in order to achieve the above-mentioned properties within small building blocks and this possibility is another great stimulus toward further exploration of fluid amplifiers and logic elements.

2. Survey Part

2.1 Approaches Using Moving or Deformable Parts

Moving and deformable parts were recognized a long time ago as being an efficient means for controlling fluid flow. In fact, the technique based on such elements was satisfactory and until very recently there was no sufficient stimulus to create interest in other possibilities of flow control.

Another historical fact, however, is much less easily understood, namely, the complete lack of interest in hydraulics or pneumatics for applications in the field of digital computing, especially in connection with mechanical input and output signals. Desk top calculators or early calculators for punched card machines work not only on a purely mechanical basis, but are restricted to the choice of conventional elements such as bars, shafts, linkages, interposers, etc.

The main task to be performed in mechanical arrangements is that of transporting mechanical energy from a location A to a location B. The forces to be encountered in A and B may differ not only in respect of their magnitude, but also their direction. Such tasks can very easily be performed with the aid of fluids: no complicated parts are required, and lubrication is inherent if proper fluids are chosen. Another advantage of using fluids is that this technique helps in distributing stresses more uniformly, and last but not least, there is great ease in effecting power amplification and doing logic.

Computing elements using fluids in connection with moving or deformable parts are not based on recently discovered new effects. The purpose of investigations in this field was mainly to explore the possibilities, to verify or improve the status of understanding and to get experience.

2.1.1 Spool Valves

The notion "spool valve" implies statical balance, i.e., no static forces are exerted on the valves by the controlled fluid. Dynamic forces, however, may be present.

Switching action and driving principle are clearly separated. Spool valves, therefore, may be classified under static or dynamic elements depending on whether the fluid at the control inputs (driving surfaces) exerts mainly static or dynamic forces.

The fact as to whether a system works statically or dynamically can easily be recognized by observing the type of switches: a single "make" or "break" contact is used in dynamic systems, whereas static systems require a transfer contact if speed and efficiency are of importance. This is due to a finite amount of leakage that must always be taken into account. Every signal line in a static system must always be connected by a relatively low impedance to a high or low pressure-carrying line, otherwise leakage could slowly change the pressure level.

As this section deals only with static systems (power consumption is one of the main reasons) the basic element is introduced by Fig. 1. Information is represented by the static pressure: h = high pressure stands for the binary "1," r = low pressure (return line) for the binary "0."

In addition to these two pressure levels a third pressure m defined by

$$m = \frac{h + r}{2} \tag{1}$$

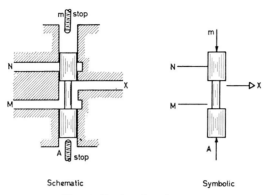

Schematic   Symbolic

FIG. 1. Basic valve element.

is used. It has no logical meaning. It serves to define unequivocally the position of the valve without necessitating springs.

A, N, M, and X represent input and output terminals. The same symbols, however, are also used to describe the signals and enter as variables the expressions in Boolean algebra for the logic behavior throughout this report.

For $A = 0$ (low pressure at A) the spool is in the down position, for $A = 1$ (high pressure at A) it goes into the upper position. The output terminal X correspondingly is connected to M or N, respectively. As M and N may also be connected to the high or low pressure line, the signal at X is described by

$$X = A'M + AN. \tag{2}$$

This function comprises the AND-gate ($M = 0$) and the OR-gate ($N = 1$). Only the signal A is amplified (a minor pressure difference at A may result in a larger difference at X for $M = 0$ and $N = 1$). Inversion and amplification may occur simultaneously for $M = 1$ and $N = 0$.

Expression (2) compares favorably with what can be achieved by a single transistor; a relay with one transfer contact, however, is logically somewhat superior to a valve, especially in view of the fact that it allows generation of the EXCLUSIVE OR-function.

N, M, and X on the one hand, and A on the other, can be kept well separated if leakage is neglected. This possibility is as important as the fact that signal degeneration from M or N to X is almost negligible.

As far as power amplification is considered, its dependence on the response time is easily verified: the energy required to displace the valve increases with decreasing response time, whereas the energy that can be delivered to a load is proportional to the available time, if inertia can be neglected.

175

A bistable device derived from the basic element discussed above is shown in Fig. 2. The two end positions are stable equilibrium positions; the center position represents unstable equilibrium. There is almost no application for an element in this form. Figure 3, therefore, gives an example of a complete memory cell.

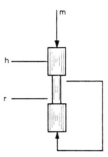

FIG. 2. Bistable valve element.

Write-in and read-out are independent of each other and may occur simultaneously. Read-out is nondestructive. To prevent loss of information pressure must be maintained all the time. Figure 4 shows a first example of a simple circuit. It generates the EXCLUSIVE OR-function.

The general impression created by valve circuits is that of simplicity. Only the active elements are shown explicitly. Inertia (self-inductance) is contained in the lines, whereas capacitors (pressure vessels) are seldom used. Elastic tubing and the compressibility of gases represent almost the only practical solutions for capacitors. Coupling condensers cannot be

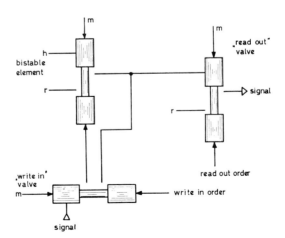

FIG. 3. Memory cell including valves for write-in and read-out.

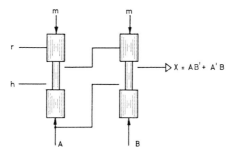

FIG. 4. Spool valve circuit to generate the EXCLUSIVE OR.

miniaturized without difficulties. Leakage also speaks against coupling condensers, and it is fortunate enough that quite different pressure levels may occur at the terminals A on one side and M, N, and X on the other. Thus coupling condensers are not a necessity. Figure 5 shows a circuit to generate the carry signal in a binary full adder.

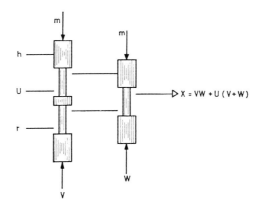

FIG. 5. Generation of the carry signal in a binary full adder.

To produce the carry signal is only one of the possible functions of this simple building block. The same physical arrangement can be used to produce other functions such as the negated carry (see Fig. 6), the sum (see also Fig. 6), or the negated sum.

It can also be used as a convertible gate (OR-gate into AND-gate) or as an amplifier which can be transformed into an inverter by applying a pressure signal to the driving surface of the left-hand valve.

A very powerful arrangement is shown in Fig. 7.

Matrices contain a relatively low number of leakage paths. They are especially suited for decoding or table look-up. Addressing is easily done with valve trees, an example of which is given in Fig. 8.

177

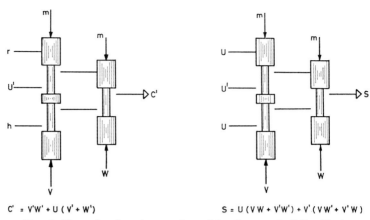

$$C' = V'W' + U(V' + W')$$ $$S = U(VW + V'W') + V'(VW' + V'W)$$

FIG. 6. Two other functions performed by the same building block.

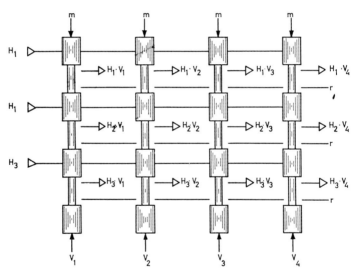

FIG. 7. Three by four matrix.

Considerably more "transfer contacts" are required than in a relay tree. A very effective solution of the topological problem becomes obvious as soon as all three valves are arranged in parallel bores.

Figure 9 shows a binary counter stage.

It comprises switching and memory elements. Valves I and II correspond more or less to the triodes in an electronic scale-of-two circuit. Valve III acts as an intermediate amplifier.

A full operational cycle is shown in the table of Fig. 10.

178

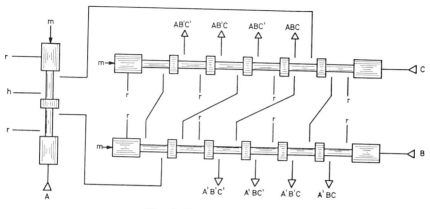

Fig. 8. Pyramid of valves.

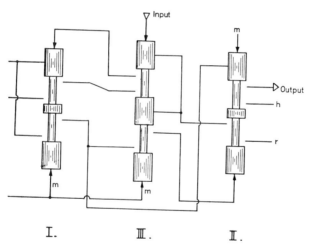

Fig. 9. Binary counter stage.

Input	III	I	II	Output
h	0	0	0	h
r	1	1	0	h
h	0	1	1	h
r	1	0	1	r

Fig. 10. Full cycle of the binary counter.

179

The positions of the valves are described by numbers: "0" means down, "1" up. The output signal is as short as the input pulse.

Figure 11 shows a shift register cell. The main and the intermediate storage parts are identical. Shift pulses are applied to the terminal S. If shifting in only one direction is required, the lowest valve may be omitted.

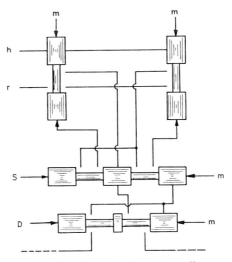

FIG. 11. Binary shift register cell.

Figure 12 shows a simple multivibrator with an interesting symmetry: the connections h and r to the power supply may be interchanged without affecting the performance.

The frequency is proportional to the square root of the pressure. There is, however, an upper limit where cavitation effects first cause random variations of the frequency and finally prevent any further increase. As

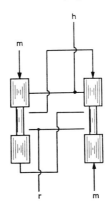

FIG. 12. Multivibrator.

will be explained later, this limit depends strongly on the size of the elements. Additional switching sections allow an output signal to be obtained, the amplitude of which is not determined by the supply pressure of the multivibrator. It is also possible to double the frequency by an arrangement similar to an EXCLUSIVE-OR circuit.

No purely passive element has been mentioned so far. There seems to be a relatively low interest because valves are logically quite powerful and do not require additional elements, and last but not least, no passive elements with moving parts appreciably simpler than a valve have been shown. This latter remark also applies to the element shown in Fig. 13.

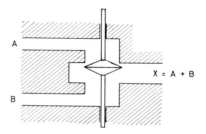

FIG. 13. Passive element serving as an OR-gate.

An OR-gate especially suited for static systems (because it prevents "short-circuits"), where every signal line is always connected to a pressure source, is represented. A great variety of designs is possible (see also Fig. 22 of the following section).

As far as manufacturing technique is concerned, investigations have shown that a technique similar to that of printed circuits can be applied: basic configurations containing channels and bores in only one plane can be molded in plastic materials. Several of these single layers can then be stacked up to form a small building block.

Due to the important role of inertia "molded circuits" present more difficult problems than printed circuits: the longest channel determines the minimum response time. Therefore, power lines projecting perpendicularly through the single layers have to be distributed over the whole area in order to allow short connecting channels. Thus, the layers of a building block must fit together not only along one edge but over the whole area. This represents an additional complication beyond the requirement of short connections within the single layers.

Figure 14 shows single elements as examples of the "molded circuit" technique. The sizes are 30 × 34 × 6 mm and 19 × 22 × 4 mm, respectively. The bores are 2 and 1.3 mm. By designing odd and even layers it becomes possible to build multistage units without intermediate layers. Figure 15 shows such a unit.

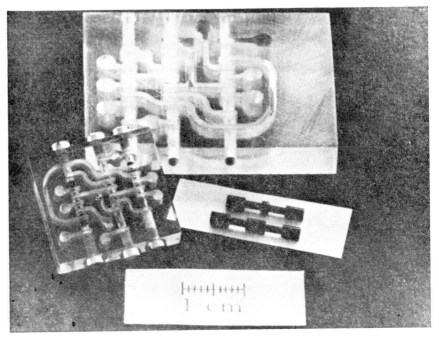

FIG. 14. Binary counter stage adapted to "molded circuit" technique.

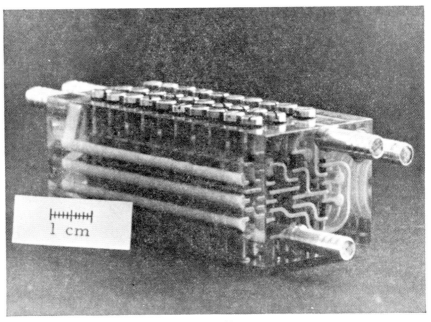

FIG. 15. Ten-stage binary counter.

Ten stages of the larger size shown in Fig. 14 are put together. The model was tested successfully with low viscosity liquid up to 300 cycles per second. (The first two stages are slightly modified compared with the circuit of Fig. 9 in order to improve speed.)

Topological problems become more difficult if more than one type of circuit has to be incorporated in a block. Figure 16 shows a solution of the topological problems in a binary parallel adder:

One stage consists of three layers generating the sum, the carry or the negated carry signal, respectively. Corresponding layers of odd and even stages are mirror images.

Figure 17 shows an experimental four-stage binary adder.

It uses the circuits shown in Fig. 5 and Fig. 6, arranged as shown in Fig. 16. The repetitive pattern with a period of six layers is easily recognized.

The response time of valve circuits consists of two parts: the signal propagation time and the time required to displace the valve over a significant portion of its total stroke after a pressure signal has appeared at its driving surface. As far as compact circuits in connection with liquids are considered, the signal propagation time can be neglected. The acceleration $\ddot{x}$ obtained when a pressure difference $p = 10$ atmospheres is applied to a column of fluid (density $= \rho = 1$ gm/cm^3; length $= l = 20$ cm) is

$$\ddot{x} = \frac{p}{\rho \cdot l} \approx 5 \cdot 10^3 \text{ meters/sec}^2. \tag{3}$$

Such an acceleration needs to be maintained only during the time t until a displacement $s = 2.5$ mm has occurred:

$$t = \sqrt{\frac{2s}{\ddot{x}}} \approx 10^{-3} \text{ sec.} \tag{4}$$

The velocity $\dot{x}$ reached after the same displacement is

$$\dot{x} = \sqrt{\frac{2ps}{\rho l}} \approx 5 \text{ meters/sec.} \tag{5}$$

The limiting velocity v_∞ (all potential energy converted into kinetic energy, no viscous losses, no static pressure recovery) is

$$v_\infty = \sqrt{\frac{2p}{\rho}} \approx 45 \text{ meters/sec.} \tag{6}$$

This justifies the use of the elementary expressions given above. In fact they represent first order approximations of the solutions of the differential equations describing the interdependence of x, $\dot{x}$, and $\ddot{x}$.

Even if fluids of a relatively high viscosity are used, the above figures are not affected appreciably: the pressure drop Δp occurring in a tube

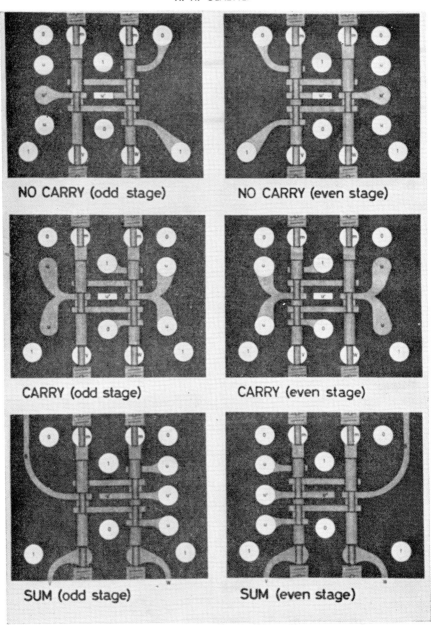

FIG. 16. Topological design of a binary parallel adder.

FIG. 17. Four-stage binary adder.

having a diameter $2r = 4$ mm at the highest velocity $v = 5$ meters remains negligible if a fluid of a viscosity $\eta = 10$ cp is chosen:

$$\Delta p = \frac{8\eta v l}{r^2} \approx 0.2 \text{ atm.} \tag{7}$$

The pressure drop due to viscous friction between the pistons and the cylinder wall may be somewhat higher, but of the same order of magnitude.

Any displacement of a valve or piston represents an expenditure of energy. This energy E can easily be evaluated if an incompressible fluid is used; it becomes for a bore diameter $2r = 4$ mm

$$E = \pi \cdot s \cdot r^2 \cdot p \approx 30 \cdot 10^{-3} J. \tag{8}$$

This relatively high value is characteristic for the high ratio power per unit volume in hydraulics.

Leakage losses are proportional to the third power of the gap between the piston and the cylinder wall. On the one hand this makes it difficult to give generally valid figures, on the other hand a most effective means to reduce leakage losses is indicated: close tolerances. Depending on the manufacturing technique it may become important to reduce leakage losses by proper system planning.

If gases are used, the density ρ in Eq. (3) has to be adjusted in order to

185

incorporate also the mass of the valves or pistons to be moved. A similar remark applies when liquids are used, the densities of which differ considerably from those of the pistons.

If branching is considered, the pressure drop through the controlling valve due to the increased flow rate may become appreciable. It may easily become a limiting factor. Equations (3), (4), and (5) then no longer hold. A saturation flow rate $\dot{Q}_{sat}$ determined by the control valve can then be introduced for high enough branching numbers n. This results in a response time

$$\tau_{n \to \infty} = \frac{n \cdot \pi r^2 \cdot s}{\dot{Q}_{sat}}. \tag{9}$$

For smaller values of n the response time τ approaches a square-root dependence on n:

$$\tau_{n=small} = \sqrt{\frac{2nsl}{p}}. \tag{10}$$

In many cases branching is not easily recognized. It is, for instance, present in adders and shift registers. The fact that the add time depends on the result to be indicated, or that the maximum shift frequency depends on the information contained in the shift register, is due to branching effects.

The relatively high expenditure of energy when a valve is to be displaced can be reduced considerably by decreasing the size. As far as viscous losses can be neglected and if all linear dimensions are reduced by the same factor, the response time is reduced by the same factor. There is, however, somewhere a limit, where viscosity can no longer be neglected, and a simple similarity consideration, taking into account viscosity effects, leads to the results illustrated in Fig. 18.

The relative size α with reference to that of a (tested) model is shown on the abscissa. The ordinate represents the reduction factor γ for various conditions β_0 found in the original model (of larger size). β_0 is the ratio of the (maximum) velocity reached at the end of the stroke s to the maximum possible velocity due to viscous friction. Low viscosity helps to keep down β_0, but increases power losses due to leakage. The pressure has been assumed to be constant.

Figure 18 shows that possible reduction of the response time by miniaturizing hydraulic devices is limited even in the ideal case where the gap between piston and cylinder wall represents a constant fraction of the bore diameter. Branching increases β_0. The speed of a miniaturized system, therefore, is determined by the speed of the circuit with the highest branching number.

If technical difficulties require larger gaps between pistons and cylinder wall in miniaturized elements, the response time may show a minimum.

186

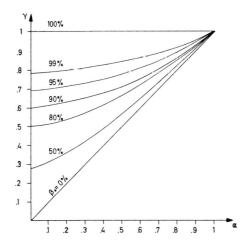

FIG. 18. Reduction of the response time as a function of relative size.

Experience has shown that manufacturing difficulties start at bore diameters of about 1 mm. Down to this size the curves of Fig. 18 give a good description of the influence of miniaturization.

No publication reporting commercial use of valves for doing logic is known. There is a general feeling that one single technique will not be applied before a much larger field comprising other moving and nonmoving part approaches is explored.

2.1.2 Ball Elements

A very interesting approach to logic devices using moving parts works with balls. Its obvious simplicity probably cannot be exceeded. Figure 19 shows the basic arrangement:

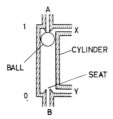

FIG. 19. Basic ball element. [From ref. 18.]

A ball moves freely, but not loosely, in a cylindrical housing having four tubular connections A, B, X, and Y. The best way to explain its operation is to consider the element incorporated in a complete circuit as shown, for instance, in Fig. 20. The terminals A and B are supplied through separate

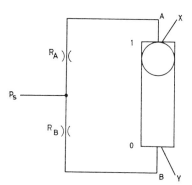

FIG. 20. Bistable circuit with ball element. [From ref. 18.]

flow restricting orifices R_A and R_B by a common pneumatic supply at a pressure p_s. The radial connections X and Y are open to the atmosphere.

The ball is assumed to be initially in the "1" position (up). Inlet A is then closed by the ball. As there is no flow through R_A the pressure at A equals the supply pressure p_s. Flow is present, however, through R_B, inlet B, and out through Y. There is also a finite flow from B around the ball and out through X. The pressure at B is appreciably lower than p_s due to the pressure drop through R_B. The fluid exerts on the ball, on the one hand, a force f_- in the downward direction

$$f_- = p_s \cdot F_{\text{seat}} \tag{11}$$

and on the other hand, a force f_+ in the upward direction

$$f_+ = \frac{R_y(\dot{Q})}{R_B(\dot{Q}) + R_y(\dot{Q})} \cdot p_s \cdot F_{\text{ball}}. \tag{12}$$

R_y is the ratio of pressure drop to flow rate of the connection Y, R_B is the same ratio valid for the flow restricting orifice. R_y and R_B may depend on the flow rate. F_{seat} is the area of the seat and F_{ball} is the cross-sectional area of the ball. Leakage around the ball has been neglected. A force in the upward direction can easily be achieved by choosing F_{seat} relative to F_{ball} in such a way that it fulfills the condition:

$$\frac{F_{\text{seat}}}{F_{\text{ball}}} < \frac{R_y(\dot{Q})}{R_B(\dot{Q}) + R_y(\dot{Q})}. \tag{13}$$

Symmetry within relatively wide tolerances, therefore, leads to bi-stability as the same relation is also true when R_x is substituted for R_y, and R_B for R_A.

Leakage around the ball, however, can no longer be neglected if the connection X (the ball being in the upper position) is closed. The pressure then rises on the upper side of the ball. A net force downwards results (even before the same pressure is reached as below the ball), which causes the ball to move downwards. By leaving the end position the ball, however, opens the corresponding axial connection. Therefore, a further fast increase of the pressure above the ball occurs. The ball is driven into the other end position where it remains stable also after X has been reopened.

Leakage around the ball plays an important role in determining the response. A small response time calls not only for the highest possible ratio $F_{\text{seat}}/F_{\text{ball}}$ but also for a high leakage rate around the ball. Condition (13) has then to be replaced by

$$\frac{F_{\text{seat}}}{F_{\text{ball}}} < \frac{R_y \cdot R_{\text{ball}}}{2R_y R_B + R_{\text{ball}}(R_B + R_y)}, \tag{14}$$

where R_{ball} represents the resistance (pressure drop per unit flow rate) around the ball, which may also depend on the flow rate. Small values of R_{ball} also tend to decrease $F_{\text{seat}}/F_{\text{ball}}$. Therefore, a compromise between response time and stability becomes necessary for a given pressure, a fact that is true for all bistable elements.

An alternative possibility of control exists by applying trigger pulses to X or Y, respectively, rather than closing one of these connections. This avoids the leakage path around the ball as a way to introduce the energy required to start switching. The fact that a control signal of a finite power is necessary can be disregarded. Pressure gains of up to 100 are reported to be feasible [18].

An interesting variant of the element in Fig. 19 is shown in a symbolic representation in Fig. 21.

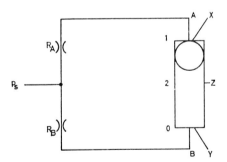

Fig. 21. Tristable ball element circuit. [From ref. 18.]

A third connection Z allows a third stable position, a very rare fact in the world of memory elements (no commercial use of tristable elements is known at this time).

The same method of obtaining bi- or tristability with the aid of resistances can also be applied to valves. They, however, can then no longer be considered as purely static switching means under these circumstances, and tristability requires a more complicated geometry for valves than for ball elements. The simplicity of ball elements is also demonstrated by Fig. 22.

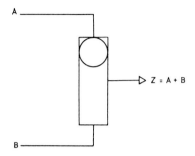

FIG. 22. Passive ball element OR-gate.

This OR-gate is identical, as far as its performance is considered, to the device shown in Fig. 13. Therefore, it can also be used as a passive element in static circuits.

A multiple AND-gate is shown in Fig. 23.

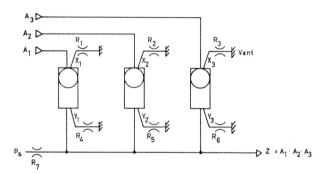

FIG. 23. Active multiple AND-gate. [From ref. 18.]

The resistances R_1, R_2, and R_3 can be omitted and X and A terminals connected together if fluid can escape through the input lines A_1, A_2, or A_3 when no signal is applied. A minimum load must be provided at Z in order to return the ball fast enough and safely (in spite of disturbances such as accelerations or gravity). Figure 24 shows a multiple OR-gate.

Circuits using ball elements, in contrast to those set up with valves, are quite similar to electric circuits: appropriate measures must be taken to satisfy impedance matching and loading requirements. "Blocking condensers" can easily be represented by cavities if compressibility is high

190

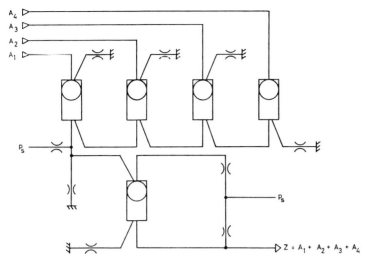

FIG. 24. Active multiple OR-gate. [From ref. 18.]

enough. "Selfinductance" can be simulated by the inertia of the fluid (especially when liquids are used) or by moving parts, such as the balls, for instance. Many nonlinear effects provide diode action. Hence, there are many possibilities for multivibrator, oscillator, shift register, counter circuits, etc. For the sake of completeness a simple example of a multi-vibrator circuit is given in Fig. 25.

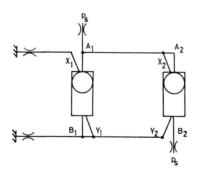

FIG. 25. Multivibrator circuit.

There is only a limited similarity between this circuit and the spool valve multivibrator shown in Fig. 12: for dc operation the output signal obtained at A_1 is in phase with the input signal fed to B_1 and Y_1, and the output signal of the second element obtained at Y_2 is inverted with reference to the input signal present at A_2 and X_2. The two elements, however, are not as symmetrical as the two spool valves: the pressure at A_1 varies between p_s

191

and a certain minimum value, whereas the pressure at Y_2 varies between 0 and a maximum pressure lower than p_s.

To a certain extent, the ball elements shown in Fig. 25 represent a variation of the basic element shown in Fig. 19 and Fig. 20. Leakage around the ball is no longer required, and only one seat must be provided since the element is used as a three terminal device. Input and output paths are well separated as far as fluid flow is considered; proper relations, however, must exist between the pressure levels. As there is fluid flow only in one position, and as no steady control flow is required, the element may be called semi-static.

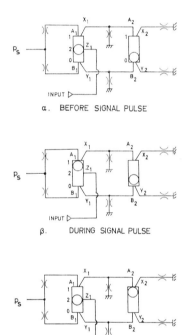

Fig. 26. Binary counter stage and its operation. [From ref. 18.]

Figure 26 shows a binary counter stage in three operating conditions. A four and a five terminal element are used, the latter allowing three different positions to be taken by the ball, according to the set of signals applied to the element. (This is not identical with tristability, which requires three stable positions for one and the same set of input conditions.)

With no pulse applied to Z_1 the five-terminal element is monostable, the ball being forced to its center position. As the ball of the bistable element at the right is in the lower position, the pressure at B_2, Y_1, and B_1 is some-

192

what higher than that at A_2, X_1, and A_1, respectively. This does not affect appreciably the first ball in its number two position, as long as connection Z_1 is open. Closing Z_1, or applying a pulse to it, however, makes the center position in the left-hand element unstable, and the ball is driven to the upper end, where the pressure is lower. This cuts off the pressure from X_1 and A_2. Thus the second element becomes monostable with the ball in the upper position. After the signal pulse, the bistability of the element at the right is restored; the ball remains in its upper position, now causing a somewhat higher pressure at A_2, X_1, and A_1 than that at B_2, Y_1, and B_1, by closing A_2.

Construction and packaging uses layers stacked up to form small blocks. In contrast to the technique applied to the construction of spool valve units, the axis of a single element is perpendicular to the single planes, one element protruding through several layers.

Figure 27 shows a photograph of such a block consisting of eight layers.

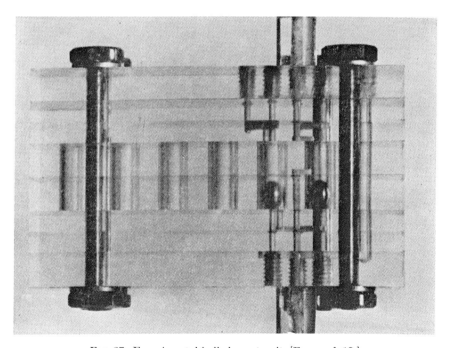

FIG. 27. Experimental ball element unit. [From ref. 18.]

The block contains two ball elements (one with four, the other with five connections). Cylinders are provided for four additional elements.

A much smaller unit than the one in Fig. 27 is shown in ref. 18, where the following characteristic dimensions are proposed:

Cylinder diameter	0.5 mm
Ball diameter	$d = 0.48$ mm
Port and orifice diameters	0.1 to 0.25 mm

Assuming a stroke $s = 0.5$ mm, an effective pressure $p = 1$ atm, a density $\rho = 8$ gm/cm³ a response time

$$\tau = \sqrt{\frac{2s\rho d}{p}} \approx 2 \cdot 10^{-4} \text{ sec} \tag{15}$$

can roughly be evaluated. It is, therefore, easily possible to get below one millisecond. Plastic balls instead of steel balls allow a further reduction. It must, however, be borne in mind that sound velocity also becomes a limiting factor. A pressure signal in air travels only 3 cm in 10^{-4} sec, which limits synchronous action at high speeds to a small volume.

To estimate a characteristic volume per element includes the difficulty of providing enough space for connecting lines. Last but not least, there is a problem similar to that in sensitive electronic and solid state circuitry: the problem of effective ground connections. In the opinion of the author, a volume of 50 mm³ per ball element seems to represent a lower limit, especially if capacitors are also to be included.

As far as resistances are to be considered, there may be a conflict between small size and the tolerances afforded by the available manufacturing technique: the flow rate through a tube is proportional to the fourth power of its diameter. For reproducibility reasons, a relatively large diameter calling for a much greater length may be required. Similar remarks apply to nonlinear elements, where additional volume may also be required.

No publications dealing with the limitations of ball elements, with the design or miniaturization problems are available, although more light and especially more fundamental investigations in the field of "conventional" mechanical elements (i.e., with moving parts) would be greatly appreciated, at least from a scientific point of view.

2.1.3 Diaphram Valves

Diaphragm valves represent another approach to reduce the influence of friction between moving elements with the aid of deformable parts, by providing sufficiently high forces to overcome friction even at very low pressures, or by avoiding it completely. Investigations along the first line [see ref. 21] comprise elements based on the arrangement shown in Fig. 28.

The device uses three pressures h, m, and r, related by Eq. (1) and of which only h and r are logically meaningful. The device is semistatic: even for a load of infinitely high impedance there is air flowing out through the nozzle if the pressure applied to the terminal A is lower than m. The

194

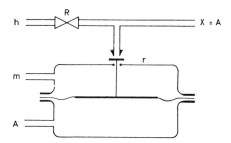

FIG. 28. Basic diaphragm valve element, type 1. [From ref. 21.]

impedance of the load to be connected to x must be properly chosen with regard to the resistance R.

By applying the signal to the upper chamber and the auxiliary pressure m to the lower one, a negated output signal is obtained.

Depending on the effective areas, a high pressure gain is possible in spite of the absence of static balance. This gain, however, goes at the expense of response time, as a larger area requires more flow to effect the necessary displacement. Figure 29 shows an approach along the second line, according to ref. 22.

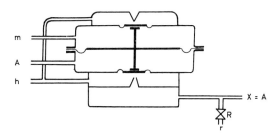

FIG. 29. Diaphragm valve, type 2. [From ref. 22.]

Friction and leakage is avoided by the consequent use of deformable elements (diaphragms). The displacement of the rigid centerpiece is limited: upwards by a stop, downwards by the nozzle of the flapper valve arrangement. This reduces the danger of mechanical overload and keeps the response time down. A certain amount of balance is provided by applying high pressure symmetrically with respect to the actuating chambers.

Another flapper valve can be substituted for the stop, thus providing a second output signal which is the negation of the first one. If the load provides a path for dc, the bypass via the resistance R can be omitted.

Several actuating chambers may be combined into one block in order to generate various logic functions. Figure 30 gives an example. An AND-

195

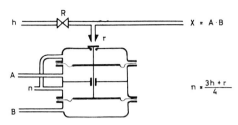

FIG. 30. Diaphragm valve AND-gate. [From ref. 21.]

gate is shown. A second intermediate pressure n, halfway between m and h is required. Figure 31 shows a memory element. A binary "0" is written in by a high pressure pulse arriving at the upper input terminal, a "1" has to proceed through the lower input line.

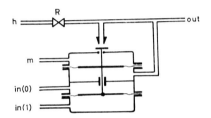

FIG. 31. Memory unit. [From ref. 21.]

Figure 32 gives an example of hardware according to ref. 22. The element shown corresponds to that of Fig. 29. A modular construction can easily be recognized. It allows the building of double contact units merely by substituting another (identical) valve section for the "stop" section (thinner section in the rear with only one connection).

Diaphragm valves represent relatively complicated structures. Their speed is limited to about 100 cps. They have, however, some unique properties: they are very sensitive and they work reliably at very low pressures because there is no static friction. They allow complete separation of input and output circuits, thus being really analog to relays in this respect. Diaphragm valves, however, differ logically from relays: special measures have to be taken (and it is uncertain whether this can be done successfully in practice) to generate the EXCLUSIVE-OR function with one single unit, whereas any relay having one transfer contact may be used to do this.

As far as applications are considered, the diaphragm valve has special merits as a "transducer" from very low to medium pressures. Last but not least, it can be used as a proportional device which, however, is beyond the scope of this article.

FIG. 32. Single contact air relay. [From ref. 22.]

2.2 Pure Fluid Elements

Pure fluid elements are the results of the most recent developments. It is interesting to see how long it took from the time when the basic observations and investigations on boundary layer phenomena were made until inventions like that of the turbulence or wall interaction type amplifier occurred.

It is even more astonishing to see that pictures of arrangements very similar to or identical with present amplifier configurations have constantly been published in textbooks during the last 40 to almost 60 years (compare, for example, the photographs on page 32 of ref. 31 with diffusor-like wall interaction amplifiers, or with the efficiency controlled diffusor). One should also remember the famous Kármán's vortex street, which demonstrates how dc is transformed into ac with the aid of an oscillator, which in turn must comprise an active element. Last but not least, the fact that boundary layer suction allows reduction of the overall resistance of an airplane (i.e., the power required for suction is transformed into resistance and included) can also be interpreted in terms of power amplification.

In order not to duplicate again the above-mentioned textbook figures an observation made by the author is given below.

During observations made on a wall interaction type amplifier at low

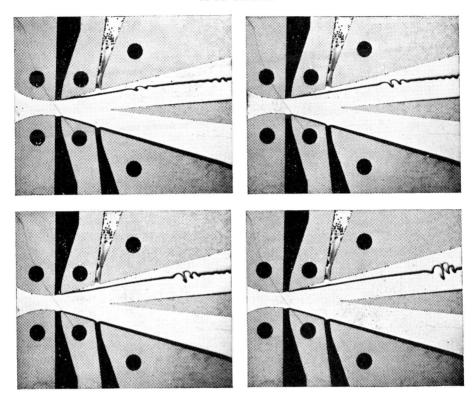

Fig. 33. Disturbance growing when carried downstream.

Reynolds numbers it happened that vibrations of the floor introduced small disturbances into the boundary layer marked with ink. Moving downstream, these disturbances which were too small to be recognized at the moment when they were caused by pressure changes in the control channel, grew appreciably beyond what could be expected considering the opening angle of the two-dimensional diffusors. This example is certainly not conclusive as to power amplification because of the low Reynolds number involved: no power could be taken off; no detectable pressure signal is left over at the output terminal. The initially growing disturbances, however, are the beginning of the amplifying action which sets in at higher Reynolds numbers.

Two basic principles to effect amplification without moving or deformable parts (except the fluid itself) are known at present: (1) momentum control and (2) boundary layer control. In the first case, control flow adds momentum which significantly changes the direction of the main flow. In the second case, only the boundary layer is affected by introducing or extracting fluid. Thus flow separation is easily controlled, which eventually allows directing of the fluid to certain ducts, or allows changing of the pressure drop at will.

To a certain extent some amplifiers discussed in the following sections are treated as ideal and pure cases. Practical embodiments actually behave not only in a different way when the operating conditions are changed, but even represent mixtures of various amplifier types. Momentum action, for example, occurs in "wall interaction" amplifiers at high operating pressures. Loads are of special interest because of their wide variety. There are not only linear and nonlinear loads (among the latter there are also typical diodes) but also loads, the pressure drop of which depends strongly on the direction of the velocity vector at the inlet. In many cases the load also becomes geometrically such an important part that the underlying amplification principle is no longer obvious.

2.2.1 Free Jet Interaction Amplifier Based on Momentum Control

Free jet interaction amplifiers based on momentum changes appeal to the very elementary physical concepts. There is such an ease in explaining how amplification is achieved that this type of amplifier s used as a model in cases where the underlying assumptions are far from being true and where additional effects are far more important. The main reason for all this is that hydrodynamics is almost not involved.

The basic arrangement is shown in Fig. 34. Amplification occurs by

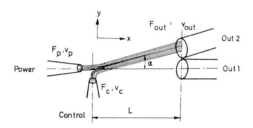

FIG. 34. Principle of jet interaction amplifier.

adding momentum in the y-direction to the power jet (index p) with the aid of a control jet (index c). Thus the jet no longer leaves the amplifier through output terminal 1, but is displaced to impinge on receiver "out 2." The changes in both flow rate and pressure available at the output terminals may exceed the corresponding changes at the control input at the same time. Thus power amplification is easily achieved, and there are no difficulties in getting output pressure levels matched with input pressure levels. Branching (i.e., one unit drives several others) also becomes easily possible.

Quantitatively, the position looks as follows: F denotes the cross-sectional areas of the jets near the power nozzle (p), at the control nozzle (c) and in front of the receiver or output terminals (out). If v denotes the jet velocities at the locations determined by the indices and α the deflection angle, momentum conservation requires:

$$F_p \cdot v_p{}^2 = F_{out} \cdot v_{out}^2 \cdot \cos \alpha \qquad (16a)$$

and

$$F_c \cdot v_c{}^2 = F \cdot {}_{out} v_{out}^2 \cdot \sin \alpha. \qquad (16b)$$

The density of the fluid has been assumed to be constant. Continuity requires

$$F_p \cdot v_p + F_c \cdot v_c = F_{out} \cdot v_{out}. \qquad (17)$$

By introducing the ratios

$$\kappa = \frac{F_c}{F_p} \qquad (18a)$$

$$\chi = \frac{v_c}{v_p} \qquad (18b)$$

the following expressions are obtained with regard to the two output terminals indicated by * and **:

Flow rate amplification: $\mu_Q{}^* = \dfrac{1}{\kappa\chi} \qquad \mu_Q{}^{**} = 1 + \dfrac{1}{\kappa\chi}$ (19)

Pressure amplification: $\mu_p{}^* = \dfrac{1}{\chi^2} \qquad \mu_p{}^{**} = \dfrac{1 + \chi^2\chi^4}{(1 + \kappa\chi)^2 \cdot \chi^2}$ (20)

Power amplification: $\mu_p{}^* = \dfrac{1}{\kappa\chi^3} \qquad \mu_p{}^{**} = \dfrac{1 + \kappa^2\chi^4}{(1 + \kappa\chi)\kappa\chi^3}$ (21)

Although this type of amplifier shows a relatively good linearity compared with others, integral amplification factors have been used. The reason is that many fluid amplifiers show a pronounced nonlinearity which requires special measures (e.g., negative feedback) to make them suitable for proportional amplification, and finally at least this presentation deals with principles and orders of magnitude which are barely changed by considering these elements as analog instead of digital devices.

It is clear that χ must be smaller than one in order to fulfill the compatibility requirements without the use of an additional element with other properties. It is also evident that the expressions marked with one asterisk can be considered representative as soon as $\kappa\chi$ and $\kappa\chi^2$ are small compared with one. Therefore these simpler expressions will be used further.

The necessary angle α_0 by which the jet has to be deflected for full discrimination (no flow-through out 1, full flow-through out 2) is determined by

$$L \cdot tg\ \alpha = l. \qquad (22)$$

L is roughly the length and l the width of the power jet. The response time τ of the whole amplifier consists of three parts:

$$\tau = \tau_1 + \tau_2 + \tau_3. \tag{23}$$

τ_1 is the time required to accelerate the fluid in the control nozzle (including connecting channels) to the velocity required to displace the jet properly. τ_2 is the so-called transport time and τ_3 is the time required to accelerate the fluid in the receiver and output duct in order to make not only a pressure but also a flow signal available. Otherwise no power is delivered.

τ_2 is given by

$$\tau_2 = \frac{L}{v_p}. \tag{24}$$

Bearing in mind that

$$tg\ \alpha = \kappa\chi^2 \tag{25}$$

and combining (19), (20), (22), and (24), leads to

$$\tau_2 = \frac{l}{v_p} \cdot \mu_{\dot{Q}} \cdot \sqrt{\mu_p}. \tag{26}$$

As l is varied (especially in the case of miniaturization) various laws governing similarity are to be remembered. Two dimensionless numbers, which are to be kept constant, are more important than others.

The first one is the Reynolds number which is a measure for the ratio inertia forces/viscous forces. It is defined by

$$R = \frac{\rho \cdot v \cdot l}{\eta} \tag{27}$$

(ρ = density of the fluid, v = flow velocity, l = representative length, η = dynamic viscosity). The inverse of the Reynolds number indicates to a certain extent the amount of damping. As useful mechanical energy must be available at the output terminal of any mechanical device the Reynolds number of fluid dynamic elements must exceed a certain minimum value R_{min}. In the case of the free jet amplifier the Reynolds numbers for the nozzle and for the receivers are important. Obviously both vary in the same way with the size and as critical Reynolds numbers usually differ for various geometries, only one Reynolds number for the whole device is given.

Elimination of v_p by introducing the Reynolds number into (26) leads to an expression that will be encountered again in several variations:

$$\tau_2 = \frac{\rho \cdot l^2}{R \cdot \eta} \cdot \mu_{\dot{Q}} \cdot \sqrt{\mu_p}. \tag{28}$$

The Weber number W is another important dimensionless figure. It is defined by

$$W = \frac{\rho v^2 l}{\sigma}, \tag{29}$$

where σ represents the surface tension constant (e.g., for water/air $\sigma = 72.5$ dyn/cm). W corresponds to the ratio of inertia forces to surface tension forces.

The role of W is the following: if a free jet impinges on another free jet there is a great danger that the jet disintegrates. It may happen that no reasonable power can be developed through receiver 2 or that amplification remains considerably below the estimated value because a great deal of the control fluid momentum is lost. There are two means to avoid this: on the one hand the Weber number can be chosen small enough. Surface tension forces then allow the jets to combine into one jet and keep it together until full momentum exchange has taken place. On the other hand walls may be used to conduct the fluid to the receiver and to introduce saturation effects. A small Weber number may seriously restrict the choice of fluids and operating conditions. It may even result in a conflict between the requirement

$$\frac{\sigma}{v} W_{\max} - \eta R_{\min} > 0, \tag{30}$$

fluid properties and gravity, which has not yet been taken into consideration. As far as low flow velocities are considered, walls are likely to introduce new effects (e.g., Coanda effect), which may become more important than momentum control.

Therefore it may be concluded that the free jet interaction amplifier in its purest form has little chance to be applied. More optimistic predictions can be made for the modified version using walls and allowing high flow velocities: wall interaction type amplifiers run at sufficiently high Mach numbers, or showing heavy cavitation-effects actually perform in the way of momentum control amplifiers. As far as "saturation"-effects due to the walls are neglected, their behavior is the same as that of an ideal free jet amplifier.

2.2.2 Turbulence Amplifiers

The turbulence amplifier published by R. Auger [27] is one of the latest additions to the family of pure fluid elements. The arrangement is given in principle by Fig. 35. It resembles very much Figure 34, related to the free jet interaction amplifier.

The underlying principle of amplification, however, differs remarkably. A laminar main jet is developed through the relatively long inlet tube. (This necessitates a Reynolds number well below 2000.) In the absence of any disturbance (no control flow) the jet remains laminar until it reaches the receiving tube, where an appreciable static pressure recovery becomes

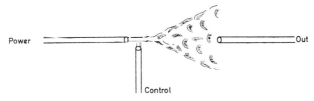

Power　　　　　　　　　　　　　　　　　　　　　　　Out

Control

FIG. 35. Principle of the turbulence amplifier. [From ref. 27.]

possible. If the Reynolds number related to the main jet is maintained at a proper value (approximately 300–1200) laminar flow can be converted into turbulent flow by a relatively weak flow signal through the control tube or even by acoustic disturbances. Strong mixing then takes place, the energy initially contained within the narrow jet is distributed over a much larger cross-sectional area and the pressure detectable in the receiving tube is greatly reduced.

This action is shown in the two photographs of Fig. 36. Smoke is blown through the power tube. In both cases, with and without control signal, no load is connected to the output terminal.

The control signal required to cause transition from laminar to turbulent flow is not strong enough to cause an appreciable deflection of the jet. Boundary layer control therefore allows higher gains than momentum control. In fact, almost any amplification factor may be obtained by approaching the upper critical Reynolds number, where white noise appears at the output.

In contrast to the free jet amplifier where it is advantageous to have the jet different from the surrounding fluid, as to fluid properties such as density and viscosity (e.g., water or oil jet in air), the turbulence amplifier is well suited for conditions corresponding to a submerged jet. The turbulence amplifier draws a constant current from the power sources as the jet interaction type amplifier, based on momentum control, does. In fact, no dynamic amplifier is known at present, which deviates appreciably from such a behavior, as will be seen later.

Not too many data concerning the turbulence amplifier are known. 10 mw is reported to be a representative value for the power consumption. The amplifier may be made sensitive to acoustic disturbances by increasing the length of the free jet. The pressure gain then rises from approximately 50 up to about 1000. An optimum tube diameter of 0.75 mm is reported; no reasons are given for this.

As far as compressibility effects can be neglected, linear acceleration does not affect the operation of the amplifier. (Such a statement cannot be made for the momentum control amplifier if a submerged jet of the same density as the surrounding fluid is not used.) It must, however, be borne in mind that, in principle, any fluid dynamic amplifier may be affected by Coriolis-

203

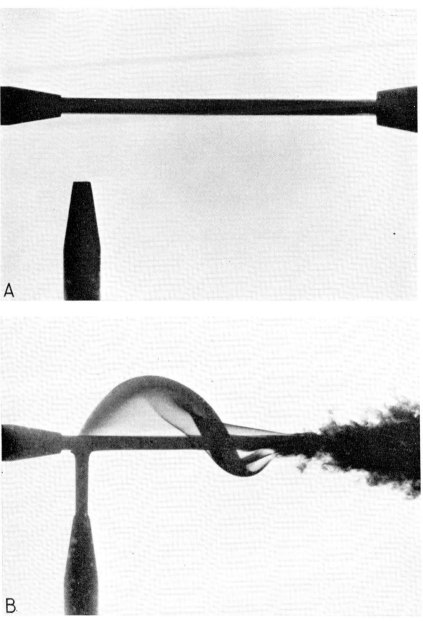

FIG. 36. Operation of a turbulence amplifier. (a) Without control signal. (b) With control signal

forces. Therefore presence of rotational motion requires special attention.

Figure 37 helps to describe the logic functions that can be performed by the turbulence amplifier.

$$A \qquad\qquad X = AB'C'$$

FIG. 37. Turbulence amplifier as a logic element. [From ref. 27.]

More than one control input can easily be used. The logic power, however, seems somewhat limited: an AND-gate requires at least two consecutive stages, which in turn also (at least) double the response time. The situation is much like that of the momentum controlled jet interaction type amplifier, where the chance to get a useful signal at the second output terminal is rather hypothetic.

2.2.3 Efficiency Controlled Diffusor

It is shown in many textbooks that pressure recovery in diffusors can be increased considerably by applying suction. Very instructive photographs (such as for instance on page 32 of ref. 31) have been taken at least forty years ago. It never occurred, however, that such a device was interpreted as an amplifier, and so far no experimental investigation is known to the author.

Basically two arrangements are possible: suction may be used to increase the efficiency by preventing flow separation in an overcritical diffusor, or injection may be applied to disturb the boundary layer in an undercritical diffusor. The generally accepted limit between over- and undercritical is given by an opening angle between 8° and 12°. More detailed investigations taking into consideration other important geometrical data such as the nozzle width and the wall length are given in ref. 32.

The following consideration is intended to throw some light onto two important aspects in connection with compatibility, namely pressure amplification factor μ_p and the pressure levels at the input and output terminals. Figure 38 clarifies the assumptions by showing the static pressure along a line through the amplifier and load resistance. The scale on the abscissa is arbitrary, and not even linear along this above-mentioned line.

Both cases, suction and injection, are treated at the same time. Therefore the indexes + and − have two different meanings: + means "injection" if an undercritical diffusor is concerned and "no suction" in the case of an overcritical one. − means "no injection" or "suction," respectively. A

205

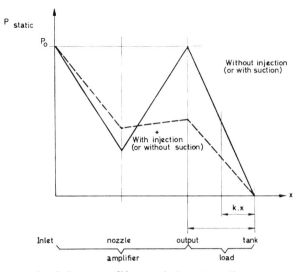

FIG. 38. Pressure levels in an amplifier consisting of an efficiency controlled diffusor and a load resistance.

nonlinear load resistance is assumed, the pressure drop p_L being defined by

$$p_L = c_L \cdot \frac{\rho}{2} \cdot v^2. \tag{31}$$

(v is the mean flow velocity taken at an appropriate location, ρ the density of the fluid and c_L a dimensionless constant.)

The static pressure at the nozzle, p_N, is assumed to be representative for the pressure to be applied in order to effect suction or injection. p_N can be described by

$$p_N = p_0 - c_N \cdot \frac{\rho}{2} \cdot v^2, \tag{32}$$

where c_N is another dimensionless constant (in close relationship with the contraction ratio of the nozzle.

The controlled variable, i.e., the static pressure recovery $\Delta p_r = p_L - p_N$ is given by

$$\Delta p_r = c_r \cdot \frac{\rho}{2} v^2. \tag{33}$$

Again, c_r is dimensionless: it assumes, however, two different values depending on whether the $+$ or $-$ condition holds. If v is taken at the nozzle, c_r may vary between the two values c_{r-} for an ideal diffusor and c_{r+} for Porda tube action. These two values can be described by the cross-sectional areas F_N at the diffusor entrance (nozzle) and F_{out} at the output:

206

$$c_{r^-} = 1 - \left(\frac{F_N}{F_{\text{out}}}\right)^2 \tag{34a}$$

$$c_{r^+} = 2 \frac{F_N}{F_{\text{out}}}\left[1 - \frac{F_N}{F_{\text{out}}}\right]. \tag{34b}$$

The ratio κ of maximum to minimum pressure recovery is, therefore,

$$\kappa = \frac{1}{2}\left(1 + \frac{F_{\text{out}}}{F_{\text{in}}}\right) \tag{35}$$

The mean velocity v in the amplifier taken as a base for Eq. (33), however, is not constant. Assuming a constant supply pressure p_0, v is determined by

$$p_0 = (c_N - c_{r^-} + c_L) \cdot \frac{\rho}{2} v_-{}^2 \tag{36a}$$

or

$$p_0 = (c_N - c_{r^+} + c_L) \cdot \frac{\rho}{2} v_+{}^2. \tag{36b}$$

The pressure amplification μ_p is easily calculated to be

$$\mu_p = \frac{c_L}{c_N}. \tag{37}$$

As there are no principal difficulties in making c_L larger than c_N, pressure amplification seems to be possible.

This evidence can be combined with generally available experience [see refs. 28 to 30] which states that the necessary amount of suction or injection to change appreciably the efficiency of diffusors is about one order of magnitude below the flow rate through the diffusor.

The consequence so far is that the efficiency controlled diffusor is an amplifier allowing not only power, but also pressure *and* flow rate amplification. It fulfills, therefore, some of the necessary requirements for compatibility.

Another aspect in connection with compatibility, namely the question concerning the control and output pressure levels is investigated in the following:

If an amplifier has to drive other amplifiers connected to the same power supply and being of identical construction, the following conditions must be met for direct coupling:

$$p_0 - c_N \cdot \frac{\rho}{2} v_+{}^2 < k \cdot c_L \cdot \frac{\rho}{2} v_-{}^2 \tag{38a}$$

$$p_0 - c_N \cdot \frac{\rho}{2} v_-{}^2 > k \cdot c_L \cdot \frac{\rho}{2} v_+{}^2. \tag{38b}$$

k is between 0 and 1. It represents a tap on the load resistance which becomes necessary in order to apply enough suction to the following amplifier

207

stage or to stop injection there completely. (Another solution to circumvent the ever-positive value of c_L would be a dc transformer consisting of an ideal Venturi-tube or a pressure divider arrangement with an additional bias pressure.)

By assuming a sufficiently high Reynolds number it is justified to set $c_N = 1$. From the above two inequalities it can then easily be derived that

$$k \cdot c_L = k \cdot \mu_p > 1. \tag{39}$$

This is (unfortunately) a necessary condition and simple enough to be found independently with the aid of Fig. 38.

A sufficient condition can be derived by further treating (38a) and (38b). This is facilitated by making the following restriction concerning the load: the pressure drop is assumed to be proportional to the square of the mean flow velocity. Therefore the load corresponds to a nozzle with an inlet cross-sectional area F_{out} (the same as the output opening of the diffusor) and a cross section F_{ex} at the smallest diameter.

In the following, the abbreviations x and y, defined by

$$x = \frac{F_N}{F_{out}} \qquad 0 < x < 1 \tag{40}$$

$$y = \frac{F_{out}}{F_{ex}} \qquad y > 1 \tag{41}$$

are used. As v is measured at the diffusor entrance, c_L then becomes

$$c_L = x^2(y^2 - 1). \tag{42}$$

The final result of this rather theoretical investigation is an explicit formula which, on the one hand, guarantees that a finite value y exists for every value x according to (40), and which, on the other hand, establishes a lower limit for y by

$$y_{min} = \frac{1}{2x} \cdot \sqrt{2[2 - (1 - x)^2 + \sqrt{4 + (1 - x)^2}]}. \tag{43}$$

This does not state anything about the general characteristics of such an amplifier. A numerical example throws some light onto this: $x = \frac{1}{2}$ requires y to exceed 2.76. If y is chosen to be equal to 4, a pressure amplification μ_p

$$\mu_p = c_L = 3.75 \tag{44}$$

results and k must lie between 0.816 and 0.850. The ratio χ of maximum to minimum pressure is given by the ratio of v^2/v_+^2 and becomes

$$\chi = 1 + \frac{(1 - x)^2}{x^2 y^2} = \frac{17}{16}. \tag{45}$$

This is certainly not impressive and one may consider it to be a surprise

208

in so far as the efficiency controlled diffusor has been conceived as a variable resistance device.

Unfortunately χ is not changed substantially when other (allowed) values are chosen for x and y. Even in the case where the pressure amplification is reduced to one (in such a situation the compatibility requirements are no longer fulfilled because the input and output pressure levels do not match), χ, which for $\mu_p = 1$ is given by

$$\chi = 1 + \frac{(1 - x)^2}{1 + x^2} \qquad (46)$$

varies only between one and two.

A provisional evaluation of what can be expected, therefore, looks as follows.

The efficiency controlled diffusor allows a reasonable pressure gain. The fact that as many of these devices as desired may be coupled together directly, when loads with a pressure drop proportional to the square of the mean flow velocity are used, is rather interesting. Compatibility, however, which tends to keep the ratio of maximum to minimum flow rate down to a level corresponding almost to that of a constant flow rate device, leads to high load resistances. The picture does not change appreciably if compatibility is no longer a must: the simpler requirement of a pressure amplification higher than one provides only a minor improvement. The efficiency controlled diffusor is a poor switch.

No publication dealing with diffusors as amplifiers can be cited. No work has been reported to the author. The efficiency controlled diffusor, therefore, seems to be mainly of scientific interest at the present time. It is uncertain whether the positive difference output pressure level minus input pressure level can be used in connection with other types of amplifiers.

The logic function to be performed by an efficiency controlled diffusor depends to a certain extent on whether an undercritical diffusor with injection or an overcritical one with suction control is considered. More than one control input can be used.

The behavior is described in Fig. 39. The picture does not differ too much from that given in the preceding section on the turbulence amplifier. The

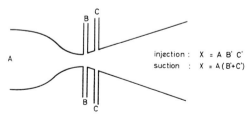

Fig. 39. Efficiency controlled diffusor as a logic element.

possibility, however, of having two different logic functions performed by elements based on the same principal arrangement is new.

Things become more complicated in a device where suction and injection are applied at the same time at the control input terminals. One control input may majorize the other, depending on the relative signal levels.

A variant to the arrangement shown in Fig. 39 exists in so far as it is also possible to precede a nozzle by a diffusor. This, however, is only advisable if a sufficiently high flow rate occurs at the entrance. Otherwise the ratio of cross-sectional area at the diffusor outlet to the one at the inlet has not a sufficient effect to get a useful pressure signal. Although such an arrangement helps to reduce the danger of reduced pressure recovery, due to cavitation, it also has disadvantages: a fully developed Poiseuille or turbulent velocity profile at the entrance limits the possible static pressure recovery in a diffusor to an appreciably lower value than that attainable by a rectangular profile.

As a sum: a limited logic power must be attributed to the efficiency controlled diffusor. More than one element is required to represent the basic logic functions, even if amplification is not a must. This is another reason why passive elements for doing logic are of great interest.

2.2.4 Wall Interaction Type Amplifiers

Wall interaction type amplifiers represent probably the elements on which more efforts have been spent so far, than on any other fluid element. A great variety of devices is possible. In most cases the geometry is not more complicated than that of other fluid dynamic amplifiers discussed previously. New fluid dynamic effects, however, introducing new aspects (especially as to the use of these devices for computing) are present. The result is that the same element may perform as an amplifier, memory and logic element simultaneously under the same operating conditions. It is even possible that a simple amplifier (monostable device) may be converted into a bi- or tristable device by simply changing the operating pressure.

It is, therefore, convenient to discuss at least amplifier and memory actions separately. Figure 40 serves to explain how amplification is effected.

In a first approach, the device can be interpreted as a two-dimensional diffusor, the divided downstream section being neglected. In contrast to the efficiency controlled diffusor, suction or injection is no longer applied symmetrically. Suppose that an undercritical diffusor is considered, i.e., a diffusor in which no flow separation occurs. Injection of slow particles through "Control I" increases the thickness of the boundary layer to the point where separation occurs. A large stall sets up, causing a correspondingly asymmetric flow pattern. A flow divider is now used to separate fast and slow particles before mixing becomes significant. Thus, two output

210

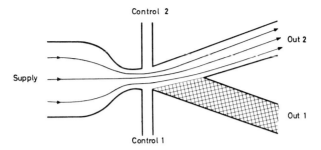

FIG. 40. Asymmetric boundary layer control.

ducts are obtained, one of which is "blocked" by a stall, whereas full flow proceeds through the other.

A similar picture is found if an overcritical diffusor is used: suction applied through "Control II" prevents formation of a stall along the upper wall by removing slow boundary layer particles.

Fortunately, the power required to inject or suck away slow particles is considerably smaller than the resulting difference of the power available at "Out I" or "Out II." Therefore, the element acts as an amplifier.

In principle, there exists a third method of controlling stall formation, namely, by accelerating the boundary layer with fast particles injected through a plurality of nozzles almost parallel to the wall. An overcritical diffusor would be required. This method, however, is not very promising: experience has shown that suction is much more effective and more easily obtained than uniform injection.

Injection of fast particles against the stream into the boundary layer does not introduce a qualitatively new concept. A photo showing the formation of a large stall and the corresponding displacement of the stream is shown in Fig. 41.

The boundary layer is marked by dye-injection through the first pair of control nozzles. A similar picture regarding stall formation is produced by applying suction on the opposite side. When more than one pair of control channels are available it makes almost no difference, whether the first or second pair or both are used for injection or suction.

The geometry can be varied over a wide range: starting with an undercritical diffusor the opening angle can be varied from a few degrees to almost 180° without affecting qualitatively the amplifier properties; the transition from the nozzle to the diffusor section may be smooth, steady, or show a sudden increase of the width, the diffusor walls may be straight or curved in both senses, etc. A preference can be justified by considering the quantitative data of the amplifier (not too much is available at present in a comprehensive form) or by taking into account other qualitative effects such as memory.

211

FIG. 41. Boundary layer control by injection.

Certain geometries show special effects in so far as there exists at least one set of input variables (flow rates and pressures at the supply end and control channels, the pressures being referred to the pressure at the output terminals) allowing two or three different flow patterns that are definitely stable against finite disturbances. Such a behavior is due to the phenomenon of attachment or reattachment of a jet. Figure 42 helps to describe this phenomenon.

In the two-dimensional arrangement shown above, a jet parallel to the lower wall induces a shear flow in the surrounding liquid by viscous friction

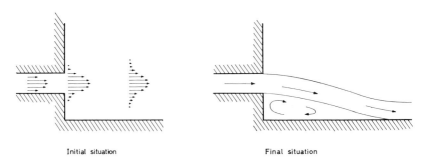

Initial situation   Final situation

FIG. 42. Attachment of a submerged jet to a wall.

or turbulent mixing. Beside the weakening of the jet and flattening of the velocity profile, its main effect is found in the space between the jet and the lower wall. The induced shear flow results in a transport of fluid out of this space. The pressure there decreases; a pressure difference across the jet occurs. The jet is bent toward the wall thus increasing the velocity gradient and the transport effects. The pressure in the volume between the jet and the lower wall decreases further, and as a consequence the rising pressure difference across the jet increases the curvature of the latter. The final situation is shown in the drawing at the right of Fig. 42. The jet attaches to the lower wall, and an equilibrium position is established, where no further pressure change in the now "enclosed" volume below the jet occurs. The whole phenomenon is also known for many other geometrical arrangements (e.g., aircraft wings) and generally referred to as "reattachment" (after separation at the exit in the vertical wall at left). The enclosed volume is called "separation bubble." Its presence depends on various circumstances.

It is interesting to see that the bubble pressure, and hence the position of the jet, can be controlled by introducing into it or taking out of it fluid through a control channel, as shown in Fig. 43.

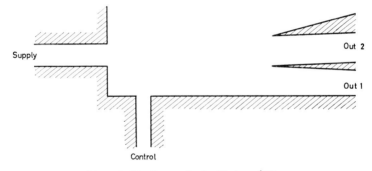

FIG. 43. Nonlinear single-sided amplifier.

Powergain is possible and it becomes almost a matter of personal taste, whether one should speak of boundary-layer control or whether a new notion such as "separation bubble control" should be introduced. The author is inclined to speak of boundary layer control and to refer to the attachment or reattachment phenomenon when stability or nonlinearity is considered.

Single-sided devices as shown for instance in Fig. 43 may be said to constitute the basic arrangement of a boundary layer amplifier; they are, however, of limited practical interest. Double-sided elements are preferred because of the symmetry they offer. Another consequence is found in the logic behavior, shown in Fig. 44.

213

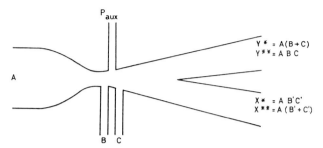

FIG. 44. Logic behavior of a double-sided element.

The device is made monostable by applying an auxiliary pressure on the wall opposite to the control ports. If no control signal is applied, i.e., if there is suction applied through B or C, or if there is no injection, neither through B nor C, the jet adheres to the lower wall. The logic functions are different for pure injection control (*) and pure suction control (**) in the same way as for the efficiency controlled diffusor. At the same time, however, two complementary output signals are obtained: one is the negation of the other, as far as input A equals 1. More complicated structures are easily possible. They require special attention as soon as there are control ports on both sides of the "diffusor," or if bi- or tristability is involved.

Figure 45 reviews the flow patterns possible in symmetric devices (geometry, input signals).

An arrangement having two output ducts is shown. It is easily possible to provide three output terminals, in order to make full use of the three stable states.

It is certainly true that it is more difficult to get the jet into the center position than along one of the walls of such a tristable element. Elements with three output ducts, however, also find great interest without offering tristability. This is illustrated by the example in Fig. 46.

A "diffusor" with a relatively large opening angle is chosen. Thus, as far as more or less equal signals are applied, free jet flow occurs [see ref. 32], i.e., the jet separates from both walls and proceeds through the center. Injection from one side facilitates separation and allows the jet to attach or reattach (after transition of the separated laminar shear layer into a turbulent one) to the other wall. The jet, however, falls back into the center position as soon as injection is stopped, or if injection occurs from both sides. Exact geometry and Reynolds number determine how far boundary layer or momentum control are involved. The important aspect, however, is the logic behavior: x and z fed to an OR-gate result in the EXCLUSIVE OR-function, whereas y represents the complement, the EQUIVALENCE. The versatility of this element is clearly demonstrated in

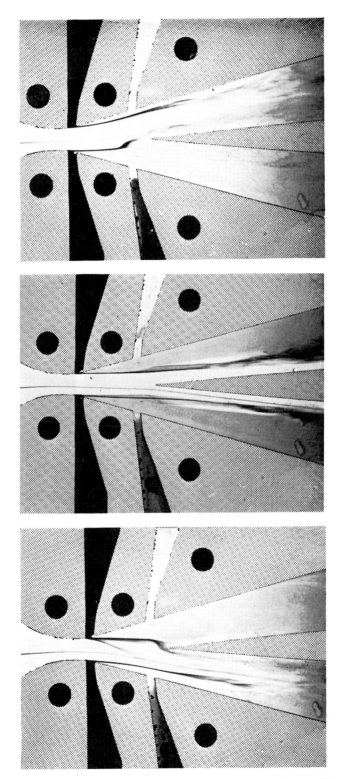

FIG. 45. Stable flow patterns in a symmetric wall interaction amplifier.

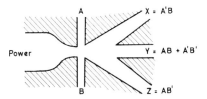

FIG. 46. Logic behavior of a monostable element with three output ducts.

connection with passive elements in the circuit of Fig. 67 in Section 2.2.6.

Amplification and, therefore, also multistability depend on the Reynolds number. Such a statement is generally true for every fluid-*dynamic* amplifier. The following considerations, therefore, are of a very general nature, although they are discussed mainly in connection with the wall interaction type amplifiers.

A first remark applies to the Reynolds number. It is defined by

$$R = \frac{\rho \cdot v \cdot l}{\eta} \tag{47}$$

where l is a representative linear dimension (usually in a significant direction perpendicular to the direction of the fluid in the undisturbed condition), v is the velocity of the fluid and ρ and η are its density and dynamic viscosity, respectively. The Reynolds number gives an idea of the ratio of kinematic forces to viscous forces. A low Reynolds number, therefore, generally means high damping and high losses. The influence of the Reynolds number is especially pronounced in the range where both kinematic and viscous forces are important. The dependence on the Reynolds number, therefore, can be neglected for very low and very high values. It is, however, possible, that other dimensionless figures such as Mach or cavitation number, etc. become important. A very typical example is given in Fig. 47.

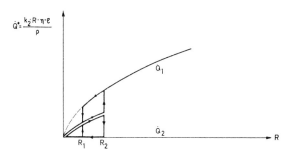

FIG. 47. Dependence of the performance of a wall interaction type amplifier on the Reynolds number.

The curves show the flow rates through the two output ducts when the amplifier discharges into the atmosphere. Amplification starts somewhere below R_1. Up to R_1 the element is monostable, between R_1 and R_2 it offers tristability and becomes bistable above R_2. The point where power amplification becomes greater than one cannot easily be detected and depends on the definition of the load conditions. Pressure and flow rate gain usually exceed the value 1 for different arguments R. R_2 is about equal to $2R_1$, whereas R_1 is of the order of magnitude 10^3.

Although no analytical representation of what is going on in a boundary layer amplifier is available (at least at this time), it is possible to describe important operating and design parameters and to estimate their limits with the aid of similarity considerations and a few experiments.

The operating pressure p for a dynamic amplifier is given by

$$p = k_1 \cdot \frac{\rho}{2} v^2. \tag{48}$$

k_1 is a constant taking into account a certain pressure recovery; it lies between 0 and 1, in most cases very near to 1. ρ and v have been defined earlier. The following expression is obtained if v is eliminated by introducing the Reynolds number as defined by (47):

$$p = k_1 \frac{R^2 \cdot \eta^2}{2\rho l^2}. \tag{49}$$

The fact that p is inversely proportional to l^2 reminds one of the difficulties in effecting measurements with smaller models at the same Reynolds number: models are subjected to the same forces as their larger counterparts. This fact becomes even more pronounced when the operating power P is represented in the same way:

$$P = k_1 \cdot k_2 \frac{R^3 \cdot \eta^3}{2\rho^2 l} \tag{50}$$

(k_2 is the aspect ratio, i.e., the ratio of channel depth to channel width). Equation (50) states that smaller elements running at the same Reynolds number require more power. Such a fact does not belong to the general experience in the field of electronics.

In order to give an expression for the response time, it is appropriate to assume a transport effect over a distance $k_3 \cdot l$ (the effective length of the element) at a speed

$$v_t = \frac{v}{k_4}. \tag{51}$$

The terms k_3 and k_4 are dimensionless constants. Their product represents the Strouhal number with reference to the nozzle width l. The response time τ is then given by

217

$$\tau = \frac{k_3 \cdot k_4 \cdot \rho \cdot l^2}{R \cdot \eta}, \tag{52}$$

or if (49) and (52) are combined, by

$$\tau = \frac{k_1 \cdot k_3 \cdot k_4 \cdot R \cdot \eta}{2p}. \tag{53}$$

Equation (52) mentions a fact of great convenience for model tests: large elements are a good substitute for a high speed camera. Equation (53) is especially useful in estimating the lower limit of the response time when the minimum Reynolds number is known and if there exists a maximum operating pressure that does not depend on the size. This is, in fact, true at least for the wall interaction type amplifier. It can be explained very easily be considering the pressure difference Δp across a reattached jet such as shown in Fig. 48 when an incompressible fluid is used.

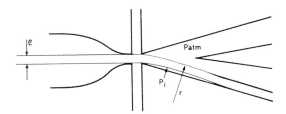

FIG. 48. Bending of a liquid jet.

This pressure is determined by

$$\Delta p = \frac{l}{r} \cdot \rho \cdot v^2. \tag{54}$$

If atmospheric pressure is present on the outer side of the jet, Δp is limited by

$$\Delta p = p_{\text{atm}} - p_i < p_{\text{atm}} - p_v \tag{55}$$

(p_v is the vapor-pressure of the liquid in question). Introducing (54) into (55) and combination with (48) results in

$$p < k_1 \cdot \frac{r}{2l} (p_{\text{atm}} - p_v). \tag{56}$$

The existence of such an upper pressure limit can easily be verified. Figure 49 shows a graph similar to Fig. 47. The pressure, however, instead of the Reynolds number is plotted on the abscissa.

The breakdown observed at p_{max} does not mean that amplification finds an end in principle: it is true that suction control is no longer possible. Momentum control, however, still works and another case is revealed,

218

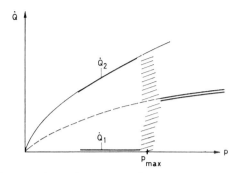

FIG. 49. Breakdown of bistability in a wall interaction type amplifier when the maximum operating pressure is exceeded.

where the same geometrical arrangement may be used to effect amplification based on two different principles, depending on operating conditions. In fact as far as injection control is considered, a steady transition from boundary layer control to momentum control is possible.

A similar effect can be realized when gases are used instead of liquids: although it is possible to work at Mach numbers higher than one, there exists an upper limit for the operating pressure where attachment is no longer possible if no special measures are taken such as a positive bias pressure on the return line. It is, therefore, justified to introduce a maximum pressure p_{max} (which can easily be verified to be of the order of magnitude of a few atmospheres) and a minimum Reynolds number of about 10^3 into (53) and (49). With the addition of a conservative value of 10^2 for the Strouhal number $k_3 \cdot k_4$ the first equation delivers the minimum response time obtainable with various fluids, whereas the second equation delivers the minimum size on which (53) is based implicitly.

A more general graph giving the minimum response time (at the maximum operating pressure) as a function of the linear size (in this case the nozzle width) follows in Fig. 50.

Sound velocity has been introduced as the maximum velocity in order to get figures for the minimum response time when gases are used. It would certainly be possible to run amplifiers at supersonic speeds. This, however, would necessitate a special nozzle design, and it is not clear whether this may result in a lower response time or whether the greater velocity is at least partly counterbalanced by the greater length of the element, which finally also reduces the packaging density and thus adds to the inertia and signal propagation time. Increased power consumption is another consequence to be taken into consideration.

The star at the lower end of the straight lines marks simultaneously the minimum possible size and the corresponding response time.

As far as the amplification factors (power, pressure, flow-rate) are kept

219

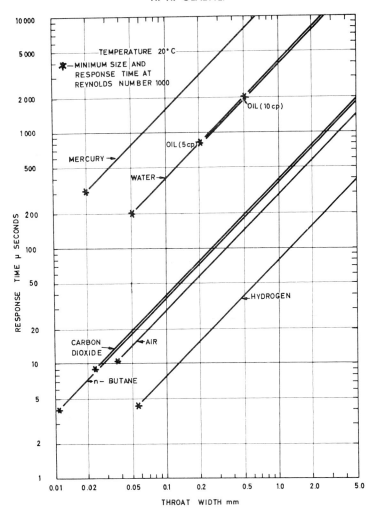

Fig. 50. Response time of a wall-interaction type amplifier as a function of the linear size.

constant, there also exists a maximum response time because of Eq. (52). The corresponding curves [straight lines with twice the slope of the ones shown, and also going through the points (l_{min}, τ_{min}) marked by asterisks] are not shown.

In order to give numerical values for the operating power, the interrelation between R and k_2 must be known: the definition (47) of the Reynolds number does not take into account the third dimension. Low aspect ratios k_2 introduce more damping and require, therefore, a higher Reynolds number (defined in the conventional way). Calculations and experiments have shown that a minimum occurs for the product $k_2 \cdot R^3$ near $k_2 = 2$, and that this minimum is only slightly lower than the value for $k_2 = 1$. It is, therefore, justified to introduce $R = 10^3$ and $k_2 = 1$ into (50).

Elimination of R by combining (49) and (50) allows specification of a maximum operating power at the same aspect ratio, if the maximum operating pressure is introduced.

Both curves (for minimum and maximum power) are represented by straight lines in Fig. 51. They intersect at $l = l_{min}$. The power range increases considerably with size.

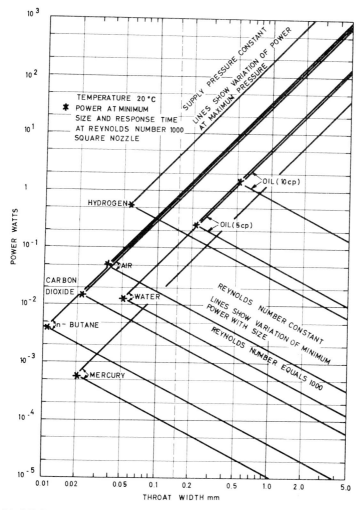

FIG. 51. Minimum and maximum operating power as a function of the linear size.

Figures 50 and 51 lead to the following conclusions: gases allow elements faster by about two orders of magnitude than liquids do; the minimum size for elements run with gases and liquids is the same; the minimum response time is not the only criterion to select the fluid. Power consumption or the question whether elements can be produced at the corresponding size and at the required quality are two other important aspects.

The wall interaction type amplifier probably has found the biggest publicity. Many publications deal with the wall attachment of jets. No details regarding response time and amplification are published at this time. Design parameters have been discussed very recently in [ref. 60].

Not too many circuits have been shown so far. In principle there exist two boundary cases of connecting wall interaction elements together: the first one may be considered to be the conventional way, using connecting channels in which an initially asymmetric velocity profile is made symmetric or where static pressure recovery may occur in order to reduce losses. The second possibility brings elements in such a close proximity that one complicated structure rather than several elements is likely to be spoken of.

A very attractive example of the first kind is shown in Fig. 52.

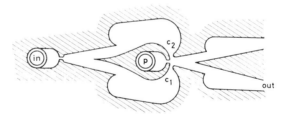

Fig. 52. Binary counter stage according to R. W. Warren (U.S. Patent No. 3,016,698). (From ref. 50.)

It shows a binary counter stage consisting of two wall interaction type elements designed and connected together in an ingenious way that makes full use of the versatility of these devices. The operation is as follows: assume that the submerged jet in the element at the right, which is connected to the supply all the time, adheres to the upper wall. The pressure at the upper control port c_2 is then lower than that at c_1. Thus a flow through the control channels, which form a loop through the amplifier at the left, in the direction from c_1 to c_2 is set up. The resulting flow rate is not sufficient to release the jet from the upper wall, and is not a necessary evil but performs an important task by conditioning the "amplifier" at the left. "Amplifier" in this case is set between quotation marks because the underlying wall interaction element is used as a nonlinear element

222

rather than an amplifier. An input pulse arriving at "in" results in a jet that, according to the preset flow pattern, tends to attach itself to the upper wall, thus increasing injection at c_2 and suction at c_1 to the point where the amplifier at the right is caused to switch over. An output signal is now available at "out." This condition is not affected if the input pulse at "in" terminates. A reverse flow in the control channel loop from c_2 to c_1 sets up, but again has no effect beyond that of conditioning the input element in order to direct the following input pulse to c_2. The same state as at the beginning is then restored after two input pulses.

A relatively simple, but instructive example of a complex structure according to ref. 62 is given in Fig. 53.

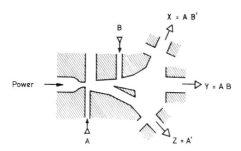

Fig. 53. Two-input/three-output logic structure.

The whole device consists of two wall interaction type amplifiers, each one with one control input. The upper output leg of the first one feeds directly into the supply end of the second one. The various corners along the outer wall demonstrate effectively the possibility of multiple separation and reattachment (Coanda effect!).

A more complicated example comprising six active elements is given by the photograph of Fig. 54.

A complete shift register unit consisting of a main and an intermediate storage cell is shown. Each cell is followed by a pair of pulsed gates which are monostable, the stable flow positions being along their outer walls. To shift the information step by step, pulses are applied to the outer control ports of the gates. These pulses may vary in length, different pulse lengths may be applied to both pairs. The only requirement other than that of a minimum pulse length is that the pulses should overlap or have only a very short interval between them.

The examples of the binary counter stage and of the two compound units are not only illustrative as to the combination of amplification and memory in one and the same element, or as to the formation of compact circuits, they also demonstrate the possibility of using the same physical arrangement in connection with a pulsed supply as an interesting variant.

223

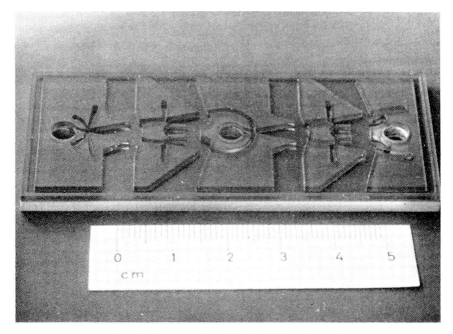

Fig. 54. Large scale model of a shift register cell.

The general tendency to attribute a great application potential to devices based on the geometry of double-sided wall interaction elements, therefore, is easily understood, and a general trend to concentrate on this type of fluid amplifier seems to be its natural consequence rather than its cause.

2.2.5 The Vortex Chamber Amplifier

The vortex chamber amplifier is not only a good example of how easily momentum and boundary layer control may be combined (it may become difficult to attribute the proper importance to each of the two principles!), it also illustrates how large a field hydrodynamics opens to the inventive mind looking around for active and passive, linear and preferably non-linear elements.

Figure 55 shows the basic arrangement in an early form. With no control signal applied, the main stream entering the cylindrical chamber radially flows through without an extraordinary pressure drop, developing a flow pattern that is symmetric with reference to a plane determined by the axis of the cylindrical chamber and by that of the power inlet tube. This behavior, however, changes if fluid is injected or sucked out through the control channel, depending on what type of control is favored by the geometrical layout: then the particles pass through along logarithmic

224

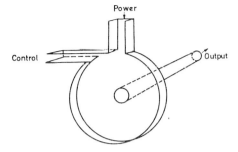

FIG. 55. Basic arrangement of a vortex chamber amplifier.

spirals, conserving their angular momentum. Thus they gain considerable kinetic energy at the expense of static pressure, and by preventing static pressure recovery in the axial exhaust tube as much as possible, a considerable net pressure drop results.

So far the device has been considered as a whole. Figure 56 introduces a new aspect in interpreting the vortex chamber amplifier by dividing it up into a switching device and a nonlinear passive element.

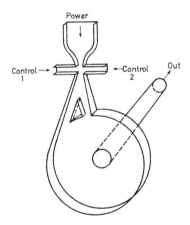

FIG. 56. Another interpretation of the vortex chamber amplifier.

A wall interaction type amplifier suited for boundary layer control is shown in connection with a cylindrical chamber. This cylindrical chamber represents a very interesting nonlinear device: the pressure drop is not only a nonlinear function of the flow-rate; it depends also on the direction of the flow at the inlet (omission of the wedge is possible and would make it easier to speak of *one* inlet), and it is this second phenomenon which is made use of in the vortex chamber amplifier. Therefore, the necessary

225

action to effect amplification is to provide a change of the direction of flow, and it makes no difference how this is done.

It is then also clear that a great many combinations of amplifiers and nonlinear elements such as the above mentioned cylindrical unit are possible. They easily allow bistability or tristability (the latter leading to the use of both senses of rotation) to be introduced.

As far as an arrangement based on momentum control as shown in Fig. 57 is considered, an elementary description is possible. Following ref. 66, one starts with the tangential velocity v_t at the entrance just after mixing of power and control stream:

$$v_t = \frac{\dot{Q}_c}{\dot{Q}_c + \dot{Q}_p} \cdot v_c \tag{57}$$

v_c is the velocity of the tangentially injected control fluid, $\dot{Q}_c$ the control and $\dot{Q}_p$ the power flow-rate.

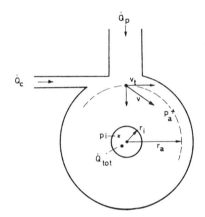

FIG. 57. Description of a vortex chamber amplifier.

As there are no gravity effects the Bernoulli's equation reduces to

$$p_a + \frac{\rho}{2} v^2 = p_i + \frac{\rho}{2} v_i^2. \tag{58}$$

Neglecting the radial velocity components and observing that

$$v \cdot r = \text{constant} \tag{59}$$

(conservation of angular momentum) the following expression for the controllable part of the pressure drop inside the cylinder is obtained:

$$\Delta p = p_a - p_i = \frac{\rho}{2} \left[\left(\frac{r_a}{r_i} \right)^2 - 1 \right] \cdot \left(\frac{\dot{Q}_c}{\dot{Q}_c + \dot{Q}_p} \right)^2 \cdot v_c^2. \tag{60}$$

Introduction of the control power

$$P_c = \frac{\rho}{2} \cdot \dot{Q}_c \cdot v_c^2 \tag{61}$$

allows to define a power amplification factor

$$\mu_P = \frac{\dot{Q}_c}{\dot{Q}_c + \dot{Q}_p}\left[\left(\frac{r_a}{r_i}\right)^2 - 1\right] \tag{62}$$

and a pressure gain

$$\mu_p = \left(\frac{\dot{Q}_c}{\dot{Q}_c + \dot{Q}_p}\right)^2 \cdot \left[\left(\frac{r_a}{r_i}\right)^2 - 1\right] \tag{63}$$

for an infinitely high load. It is interesting to see that the first and second power of the inverse flow gain

$$\frac{1}{\mu_Q} = \frac{\dot{Q}_c}{\dot{Q}_c + \dot{Q}_p} \tag{64}$$

enter the expressions for μ_P and μ_p. The total pressure drop p_{tot} through the amplifier is composed of two terms: one is represented by (60), the other takes into account that there is also a pressure drop with no control flow. As viscous effects can be neglected, a term quadratic in $\dot{Q}_p$ is justified. p_{tot}, therefore, is given by

$$p_{tot} = \frac{\rho}{2}\left\{\frac{1}{\Delta F^2}(\dot{Q}_c + \dot{Q}_p)^2 + \frac{1}{F_c^2}\left[\left(\frac{r_a}{r_i}\right)^2 - 1\right]\left(\frac{\dot{Q}_c^2}{\dot{Q}_c + \dot{Q}_p}\right)^2\right\}. \tag{65}$$

F_c is the cross-sectional area of the control jet; ΔF is a fictive cross-sectional area of the fluid flow at the output end of the amplifier in order to account for the pressure drop due to contraction and turbulent losses.

Careful use must be made of Eq. (65): it cannot be applied for $\dot{Q}_p = \dot{Q}_c$. In such a case, which is easily possible if the control pressure is varied independently of the supply pressure, the fluid in the chamber may rotate similarly to a rigid body and the pressure drop may then be described by

$$p_{tot(Q_p = -Q_c)} \approx \frac{1}{3F_c^2} \cdot \rho \cdot \dot{Q}_c^2. \tag{66}$$

Equation (65) also throws some light on the nonlinear behavior of the vortex chamber amplifier. The fact that there is no proportionality between changes of the pressure drop through the amplifier and changes of the control pressure needs no further discussion in a survey dealing with elements for digital control. Expression (65), however, contains also the possibility of negative resistance. Analogously to procedures followed by electronic engineers the pressure drop as a function of flow-rate would then be described by curves as shown in Fig. 58.

227

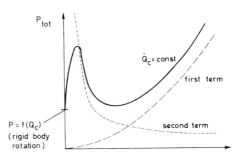

FIG. 58. Possibility of negative characteristic of the vortex chamber amplifier

No conclusions as to the future use of this effect are possible at the moment. The effect has been verified experimentally in ref. 66. It is, however, expected that other possibilities in connection with the interpretation suggested by Fig. 56 may be used more successfully to effect memory.

The great merit of the vortex chamber amplifier over other nonmoving part elements is the fact that it allows a more effective control of the flow rate. Contrarily to the efficiency controlled diffusor no change of the static pressure occurs if the vortex chamber amplifier is in the low resistance condition. This avoids the troubles usually encountered in recovering the static pressure.

As to the use of the vortex chamber amplifier for doing logic it must be remembered that only one output signal is obtained out of one element. There is, however, more freedom than for instance in the case of the turbulence amplifier or efficiency controlled diffusor: referring to Fig. 56 it can easily be seen that due to the symmetry in the active part, a positive or negated output signal may be obtained.

Although the vortex chamber amplifier projects into the third dimension, it can be considered as being essentially a two-dimensional device, which fits it to production techniques mentioned earlier.

As far as means for improving or preventing pressure recovery are considered (for instance vanes) there is an interesting possibility making use of the two different senses of rotation. No publication concerning minimum Reynolds number, maximum pressure, response time, etc., is known to the writer.

Due to the fact that a finite pressure recovery in the axial outlet cannot be avoided, a behavior similar to that of the efficiency controlled diffusor may be expected: as the static pressure cannot be reduced to zero, cavitation should occur if an incompressible fluid is used and this should affect the performance. In fact, a cavitating core can be easily observed if vortex motion is present. Its influence, however, is not destructive concerning the performance because no pressure recovery is intended. Cavitation becomes important only when it occurs under "normal flow" conditions. It then limits the maximum operating pressure relative to the pressure at the output terminal, and this latter pressure (fortunately) may reach relatively high values, especially if nonlinear loads are used. It is, therefore, not easy to estimate an upper limit for the operating pressure.

The response time of the vortex chamber amplifier is determined partly by the time it takes to change the flow pattern. The transition time $\tau_{n \to v}$ from normal to vortex flow can be evaluated by the time required to replace the fluid in the cylindrical chamber by fresh fluid. This time is given by

$$\tau_{n \to v} \approx \frac{2V}{\dot{Q}_{\max} + \dot{Q}_{\min}}. \tag{67}$$

V is the volume of the cylindrical chamber, and $\dot{Q}_{\max}$ and $\dot{Q}_{\min}$ are the maximum and minimum total flow rates through the amplifier. The transition time from vortex to normal flow may become longer because of the possibility of positive feedback by shear forces. No publication is known dealing with the question whether positive feedback, based on shear forces sufficient to cause bi- or tristability, may occur or may be prevented.

2.2.6 Passive Elements

As indicated earlier there is considerable interest in passive elements: on the one hand the logic power of many active elements is relatively low, whereas amplification and memory are easily effected; on the other hand hydrodynamics offers many phenomena involving nonlinear interrelations.

The simplest passive elements are represented by resistance, capacitance and selfinductance. All are linear and their realization by viscous friction, compliance and inertia is obvious. Perhaps it may be pointed out that capacitance may be represented by elastic tubing or by the compressibility of the fluid itself.

Nonlinear elements are logically far more powerful. A diode counterpart may be derived from every amplifier type discussed in Sections 2.2.1 to 2.2.5. Figure 59 shows the principle of the so-called jet diode according to ref. 68.

Fig. 59. Principle of the jet diode. (From ref. 68.)

Only flow from A to B is possible. Other elements such as C etc. may be added. The ratio forward flow/backward flow approaches infinity. The flow rates at A and B may differ in one or both directions, a fact that makes a considerable difference compared with electronic or solid state diodes. It must also be borne in mind that the arrangement shown in Fig. 59 cannot be simulated either by one or by two electronic diodes. The device must be operated above a certain minimum Reynolds number. Especially in the case of a submerged jet a certain maximum Reynolds number must not be exceeded; otherwise the element works at a low efficiency in the forward direction and at an increased back current.

A turbulence diode is shown in Fig. 60 in its two operating conditions.

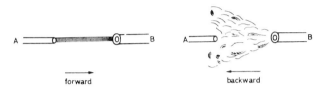

FIG. 60. Turbulence diode in its two operating conditions.

The tube at the left is smooth, whereas the one at the right contains an obstacle similar to a trip wire. A jet remains laminar if it originates at A; it becomes, however, turbulent if it originates at B. In the latter case only a minor product of pressure and flow rate is received at A.

Different resistances on the sides of A and B, possibly in connection with different tube diameters, allow basing of the operation completely on Reynolds number effects. On the one hand this avoids mechanical obstacles, on the other hand it sets even narrower limits for the range of useful Reynolds numbers than is the case in the arrangement of Fig. 59. The obtainable ratio of forward to backward flow is easily affected by the Reynolds number; its optimum value is lower than that of the jet diode.

A combination of an overcritical and an undercritical diffusor can also be used to perform diode action. Figure 61 shows the corresponding arrangement.

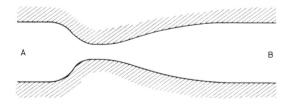

FIG. 61. Diode consisting of an asymmetric Venturi tube.

If the flow proceeds in the direction from A to B the static pressure first decreases, but is recovered again to a great extent. In the reverse direction the same decrease in static pressure is found. The velocity profile, however,

230

is less rectangular. Together with the overcritical opening angle of the left hand diffusor a considerably lower pressure recovery occurs. As to its behavior this type of diode resembles electronic or solid-state diodes. The major difference is due to the Reynolds number dependence and due to the relatively low backward resistance. High flow rates, in addition, may result in cavitation which tends to equalize forward and backward resistance.

The pressure drop through the Venturi-diode may be evaluated in the following way: efficiency factors commonly used to describe diffusor losses may be introduced to calculate the forward resistance. The backward resistance may be evaluated roughly by subtracting the pressure recovery due to Borda tube action from the pressure drop in the nozzle. The backward pressure drop p_{back} becomes then

$$p_{\text{back}} = \frac{1}{2} \rho v^2 \left[1 - \left(\frac{F_N}{F_0} \right)^2 \right] - 2 \frac{F_N}{F_0} \left[1 - \frac{F_N}{F_0} \right]. \tag{68}$$

F_N is the cross-sectional area in the nozzle, F_0 the one at the inlet or outlet. Compared with the forward pressure drop

$$p_{\text{forward}} = \frac{1}{2} \rho v^2 (1 - K_1) \cdot \left[1 - \left(\frac{F_N}{F_0} \right)^2 \right], \tag{69}$$

where K_1 is the dimensionless efficiency factor for pressure recovery, the following discrimination ratio is obtained:

$$\frac{p_{\text{back}}}{p_{\text{forward}}} = \frac{1}{1 - K_1} \cdot \frac{1 - F_N/F_0}{1 + F_N/F_0}. \tag{70}$$

As soon as the ratio F_N/F_0 is small, the ratio of backward to forward pressure drop depends solely on K_1. K_1 values of 90%, however, can barely be exceeded, which accounts for the relatively low discrimination figures to be expected. It must also be borne in mind that low ratios F_N/F_0 favor cavitation.

Wall attachment can also be used to produce diode effects. An example is given in Fig. 62. Flow from A to B is easily effected. Flow in the reverse direction tends to attach to the upper or lower wall. Thus it is prevented from reaching A. A double-sided element is shown, although a single sided device could be used as well. The increase in cross-sectional area at B is not

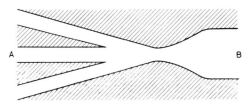

Fig. 62. Wall attachment diode.

necessary. It is shown because of didactic reasons: it reminds one of the wall interaction type amplifier shown in Fig. 46, to which the diode shown above represents the "two"-terminal counterpart.

The same remarks as to the analogy with electronic and solid-state diodes as made in connection with the jet diode apply. A minimum Reynolds number is a must, but the maximum flow velocity is also limited in much the same way as is the case in the wall interaction amplifier.

Figure 63 gives a last example of a diode. The device represents a lower

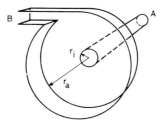

FIG. 63. Vortex chamber diode.

resistance for flow in the direction from A to B than vice versa. Although it is difficult to get numerical data by calculation it is nonetheless interesting to derive an expression for the diode action based on very simple assumptions.

It is assumed that the terminals A and B are connected to reservoirs through inlet arrangements introducing minor losses and outlet arrangements allowing no static pressure recovery.

The pressure drop in the forward direction may then be described by

$$\Delta p_{\text{forward}} = \frac{1}{2}\,\rho\,\cdot\,\frac{\dot{Q}^2}{K_2{}^2\cdot F_B{}^2}. \tag{71}$$

F_B is the cross-sectional area at B; K_2 is a dimensionless constant accounting for the increased pressure drop due to the increase of the cross section after A, as well as for losses due to secondary currents, by a virtually reduced F_B; $\dot{Q}$ is the volumetric flow rate. The pressure drop in the backward direction consists of two terms: the reduction in static pressure from the tank to the "nozzle" at B and the further reduction in the vortex chamber according to Eq. (60) when $\dot{Q}_p$ equals zero:

$$\Delta p_{\text{backward}} = \frac{1}{2}\,\rho\,\frac{\dot{Q}^2}{F_B{}^2}\left\{1 + \left[\left(\frac{r_a}{r_i}\right)^2 - 1\right]\right\}. \tag{72}$$

The radii r_a and r_i are defined in Fig. 63. The ratio of backward to forward pressure drop at constant flow rate becomes then

$$\frac{\Delta p_{\text{backward}}}{\Delta p_{\text{forward}}} = K_2{}^2\cdot\left(\frac{r_a}{r_i}\right)^2. \tag{73}$$

K_2, as indicated earlier, is expected to be smaller than one; it depends in such a way on the ratio r_a/r_i as to limit the obtainable forward to backward pressure ratio. Although this effect can be explained qualitatively, neither quantitative predictions nor results are available. It is uncertain whether the vortex chamber diode is superior to the Venturi diode under ideal conditions, and in order to obtain an idea of the actual performance the losses in the axial inlet tube have to be evaluated in connection with the requirement of preventing static pressure recovery when the direction of flow is reversed.

So far only the stationary behavior of diodes has been discussed. Remarkable differences may occur if the dynamic performance is considered: if for instance pulses are applied to the jet diode of Fig. 59 in the backward direction, the flow rate at A is constantly zero. This is, however, not true in the case of the Venturi or vortex chamber diode: it takes a noticeable time to set up the stationary flow pattern. Thus a much higher flow rate occurs at the beginning of a pulse than the steady state one. Due to the smaller deviation of the transient flow pattern from the stationary picture the same effect is less pronounced in the forward direction. The slight improvement in this direction is more than counterbalanced by the much more increased initial back "current."

Two or more diodes can easily be combined to form logic elements such as for instance or-gates. Fig. 64 gives an example. The element makes use

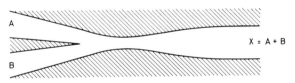

A

B

X = A + B

FIG. 64. or-gate.

of the reduction of static pressure by narrowing the duct. Thus it can be achieved that no appreciable signal occurs at B when input A is activated, which is due to some diode action occurring in this device if the load connected to X is limited. A signal applied to X, however, could be sensed at A, at B or at both locations, depending on further circumstances. If this possibility is to be avoided, a solution along the lines of Fig. 62 should be chosen.

Passive logic elements are not restricted to diode arrangements. Figure 65 shows a two-input/two-output device which is especially useful in adders. Basically the device contains two logic elements: the one at the left is a two-input/three-output arrangement, generating A'B, AB and AB'. Two of these output signals are then combined in the or-gate at the upper right to form AB' + A'B. The device is based mainly on momentum action.

233

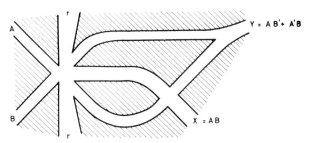

FIG. 65. Passive two-input/two-output device suited for a half adder. [Partially from ref. 52.]

Therefore, a minimum Reynolds number must be maintained, and in addition the signals A and B must be of the same level within relatively close tolerances. The available output power, however, is not the same at the two output terminals.

There are two more peculiarities in the above arrangement: on the one hand connections to the return line r (or to the open atmosphere) are provided in order to define the static pressure in the heart of the element and to prevent wall attachment or transport effects; on the other hand, two ducts cross one another in a single plan without interference. This is possible due to the fact that only one of these ducts may carry a signal at a time.

The performance of the two-input/three-output device contained in the arrangement of Fig. 65 is illustrated by the photographs in Fig. 66. The element discharges into the atmosphere. The jets leaving the output ducts can be clearly recognized; they demonstrate the good discrimination.

In designing circuits containing passive elements, special attention must be paid to the problem of signal degeneration: passive elements not only result in no amplification but usually reduce signal level and increase "noise."

Figure 67 shows a full adder circuit consisting of active and passive elements arranged in a way to preserve a sufficient signal level for the carry signal and to provide strong signals for the sum digits.

There is no general assent at this time as to the representation of fluid logic circuits. Therefore, the symbolism adopted by the author's group is used.

A and B are the two digits to be added. C_{in} is the incoming and C_{out} is the outgoing carry signal, whereas S is the output signal indicating the sum.

The element at the upper left corresponds to the device shown in Fig. 65. It is used as an AND-gate. $A \cdot B$ represents the strongest output signal that can be obtained from this device: its power level is high enough to allow it to be fed directly into another passive element, the OR-gate at the upper right.

234

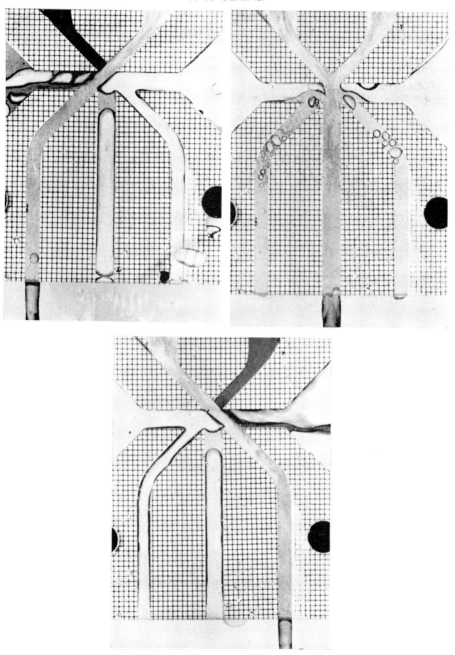

Fig. 66. Performance of a passive two-input/three-output device.

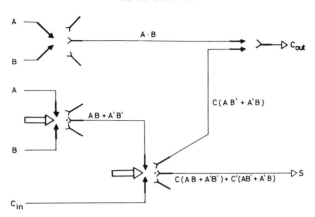

FIG. 67. Full adder circuit using active and passive elements.

Active elements are characterized by wide arrows representing the power jet. Dots in front of a receiver mark stable positions of the jet when equal signals at the control ports provide symmetric conditions. Both active elements in Fig. 67 are identical and correspond to the element shown in Fig. 46. As the incoming carry-signal is fed directly into a control port only very moderate power requirements are to be met by C. This is in good agreement with what can be expected to come out of the OR-gate at the upper right. Any number of stages as shown in Fig. 67 can be cascaded without additional intermediate amplifiers to form a binary parallel adder. The only exception may be found at the end of the carry line, where an amplifier may be used to generate an overflow signal of the same power as that of the S-signals.

The same symbolism, possibly with some minor additions, can be used for all types of fluid dynamic elements. It does not distinguish between the basic principles involved in getting amplification and memory, or used to do logic. "Ground" connections (i.e., exhaust lines) as well as connections to the power supply are not shown.

3. Closing Remarks

The present situation in the field of digital fluid logic elements can be summarized as follows.

A great deal of exploratory work has been done in a relatively short period of three to six years: elements with and without moving or deformable parts have been proposed and investigated. The information obtained is mainly of a qualitative rather than a quantitative nature. This is especially true for pure fluid elements where a great deal of knowledge and

236

experience is required in order to recognize the principles and effects involved. (Last but not least, the methods developed to evaluate the characteristics of these elements also represent qualitative information.)

As far as quantitative data are to be considered, it must be emphasized that they rely on assumptions or evidence which may become obsolete before long: there is, for instance, some evidence now that, due to a finite period during which tensile forces may persist in liquid, the maximum operating pressure for wall interaction elements may be considerably higher for very small elements. Depending on the results to be delivered from investigations on turbulent reattachment and laminar attachment presently going on, it may also happen that the value of the minimum Reynolds number for bistability in the same type of element decreases considerably from the generally accepted (at this time) 10^3.

A comparison of the various types of elements is barely possible at the moment: the amount of available experience differs among the various devices, and it would be unfair to compare theoretically derived limits of one element with what can be considered a practical figure for another.

The easiest way to make comparisons is, on the one hand, to stay within the group of elements with or without moving parts, respectively, or, on the other hand, to compare the general aspects of the two groups.

Spool valves and ball elements are the simplest devices having moving parts. Their response time (as a practical figure) lies around 1 msec or somewhat below. For logic applications, the greater logic power of spool valves may counterbalance the higher speed of balls. Spool valves are subject to static and gliding friction, balls to rolling friction. The dust problem seems to be more serious for ball elements. Valves offer more freedom in respect of impedance matching by varying the driving surface with regard to the cross section in the switching part; ball elements require a lower volume per element. To summarize: there is no obvious and generally valid reason to direct preference toward spool valves or ball elements without requiring many details to be taken into account.

Diaphragm valves are much more complicated devices. They are slower by about an order of magnitude (response time $\approx 10^{-2}$ sec) and require appreciably more volume. Therefore their use is restricted to a considerably lower number. Reliability at low operating pressures is their main merit.

As far as elements without moving or deformable parts are considered, it is better to speak of a certain geometry than of an amplifier type, because momentum control or boundary layer control may work in the same geometry, depending on Reynolds, Mach, and cavitation numbers.

The geometry introduced in connection with wall interaction elements probably has the greatest application potential: amplification can be obtained within a large range of characteristic numbers, and the logic power is considerable, especially in connection with passive elements.

Matching of input and output pressure levels requires special attention.

The geometry of the free jet amplifier is logically not too powerful: a multiple NOR-gate is easily possible. Additional stages, however, are required in order to produce other logic functions. Momentum control is bound to a low Weber number, whereas boundary layer control causes the amplification factor to be strongly dependent on the Reynolds number, thus allowing only a relatively narrow Reynolds number range to be used.

The efficiency controlled diffusor and the vortex chamber amplifier show a marked difference between input and output pressure levels: the first results in a step up, the latter in a step down. The vortex chamber amplifier, however, has a great advantage over other elements without moving parts, in as much as it represents the most effective means for controlling flow rate. This is especially true in the case where boundary layer control is present.

Special care is required to compare the two groups of elements, the one with and the one without moving parts. "No moving parts" can easily be used as a great lure. It is, however, not synonymous with "no inertia" or "much shorter response-time." Elements with no moving parts certainly have the potential of a short response time, but whether it can be realized depends largely on to what extent manufacturing problems can be solved. Last but not least, one should not forget about the power consumption, which is appreciable for these elements.

The author would not be surprised if future applications would comprise more than one group or type of element in the same housing, making full use of their partially quite different characteristics.

More problems to be solved have been left over to the field of elements without moving parts: there is no amplifier theory available at this time, there is even no agreement on how to characterize a pure fluid amplifier. Design optimization is only possible to a certain extent by "empirical iteration."

In addition to these more or less application-oriented questions, there are also more basic questions: what is the influence of a finite surface roughness? What are the possibilities offered by non-Newtonian fluids?

One additional word should be said concerning the relative position of electrical and fluid dynamic components: due to their highly different characteristics, it cannot be generally stated that electronic or solid-state devices have a new competitor. It is certainly true that a new aspect has arisen and from this point of view it can be deduced that there are, on the one hand, some misapplications of non-fluid mechanic elements and, on the other hand, some new possibilities where the new components will represent more economic or the only (technically) feasible solution.

Although single units of fluid mechanic amplifiers are now commercially available, it seems premature to speak of commercial application. As far as predictions can be made with regard to future applications, the intrinsic properties of these elements must be borne in mind:

α Simplicity (one fluid, one solid material; two-dimensional layout).

β Insensitivity to external influence (temperature, electromagnetic disturbances, nuclear radiation, linear accelerations).

γ Potential reliability (nondestructive tests possible).

δ Mechanical signals (no transducers necessary).

Applications in computers, therefore, may be expected in cases where mechanical input signals are available, where mechanical output signals are required, and where a limited amount of data processing at a limited flexibility and at a limited speed has to be achieved. This points in the direction of small size computers handling tape or cards, of automated machine tool and process control.

ACKNOWLEDGMENTS

The author wishes to express his appreciation to the many people who have contributed to this article in one form or another. Particular thanks are due to the members of the author's group, Messrs. H. R. Müller (who provided for the extensive bibliography kept up-to-date until February, 1963), A. E. Mitchell, J. E. R. Young, and R. Zingg. Their ideas and results entered into this contribution. The author also wishes to thank Mrs. D. Brüllmann for the careful preparation of the manuscript, and last but not least, he is grateful to all the other members of the IBM Research Laboratory who did their best in working on the many details contained in this survey.

BIBLIOGRAPHY

(An extensive bibliography is also contained in ref. 57.)

Short Surveys

1. R. N. Auger, "Pneumatic Computer Research in the USSR," *Automatic Control*, **13**, No. 6, p. 43–48 (December, 1960).
2. A. E. Mitchell, H. H. Glaettli, H. R. Müller, "Fluid Logic Elements and Circuits," *Transactions of the Society of Instrument Technology* (February, 1963).

Spool Valves

3. "Pneumatic Logic Circuit Surveys Control," *Control Engineering*, **2**, No. 9, p. 144–145 (September, 1955).
4. R. J. Cameron, "Pneumatics: Valve with a Memory Handles Logic Circuits," *Product Engineering*, p. 76–78 (May, 1958).
5. H. H. Glaettli, H. R. Müller, "Miniaturization of Hydraulic Devices, Part I," IBM Research Report RZ-34 (August, 1958).
6. H. R. Müller, "Miniaturization of Hydraulic Devices, Part II," IBM Research Report RZ-46 (August, 1959).
7. H. R. Rouom, Jr., "Hydraulic Switching Circuits," *Machine Design*, p. 140–145, 108–116 (February, March, 1959).

8. H. H. Glaettli, H. R. Müller, "Ueber die Moeglichkeit digitaler hydraulischer Rechenelemente" (On the Possibility of Hydraulic Digital Computing Elements), *Zeitschrift fur Angewandte Math. und Phys.* (ZAMP), **XI**, No. 1, p. 73–75, (1960).
9. H. H. Glaettli, H. R. Müller, "Vergleich hydraulischer digitaler Schaltelemente mit elektronischen und elektromechanischen Elementen," (Comparison of Hydraulic Digital Switching Elements with Electronic and Electromechanical Counterparts), *Zeitschrift fur Angewandte Math. und Phys.* (ZAMP), **XI**, No. 6, p. 535 (1960).
10. G. D. S. McLellan, A. E. Mitchell, D. E. Turnbull, "Flow Characteristics of Piston Type Control Valves," *Proceedings of the Symposium on Recent Mech. Engineering Developments in Automatic Control*, Inst. Mech. Eng. London (1960).
11. H. H. Glaettli, "Neuere Untersuchungen auf dem Gebiet digitaler mechanischer Steuerungs und Rechenelemente" (Recent Investigations in the Field of Digital Mechanical Control and Computing Elements), *Elektronische Rundschau*, **15**, No. 2, p. 51–53 (February, 1961).
12. H. H. Glaettli, "Hydraulic Logic: What's its Potential?," *Control Engineering*, **8**, No. 5, p. 83–86 (May, 1961).
13. R. N. Auger, "Spool Valve Hydraulic Computers," *Automatic Control*, **14**, No. 4 (1961).
14. E. L. Holbrook, "Pneumatic Logic," *Control Engineering*, **8**, p. 92–96, 104–108, 110–113, (August, July, November, 1961, resp.), **9**, p. 84–92, 85–88 (February, December, 1962, resp.).
15. H. H. Glaettli, "Hydraulische und pneumatische Rechenelemente" (Hydraulic and Pneumatic Computing Elements), *Automatik Katalog, 1962/63*, p. 6–12 (1962/1963).

Ball Elements

16. H. E. Riordan, "Pneumatic Digital Computer," *Electromechanical Design*, p. 36–40 (June, 1961).
17. H. E. Riordan, "Moving Ball Computers with Air," *Control Engineering*, **8**, No. 7, p. 22 (July, 1961).
18. H. E. Riordan, "A High Performance Pneumatic Digital Computer," Kearfott, Clifton, New Jersey, Technical Report.

Diaphragm Valves

19. V. Ferner, "Neue pneumatische bzw. hydraulische Elemente in der Mess- und Regelungstechnik" (New pneumatic or hydraulic elements in Measuring and Control Techniques), *Die Technik*, **9**, No. 6, p. 362 (June, 1954).
20. T. K. Berends, A. A. Tal, "Pneumatic Switching Circuits," *Automation and Remote Control*, **20**, No. 11, p. 1493 (Nov. 1959).
21. V. Ferner, "Anschauliche Regelungstechnik," VEB Verlag Technik, Berlin (1960).
22. T. K. Berends, A. A. Tal, "Pneumatic Relay Circuits," *Proceedings of the IFAC Congress, Moscow 1959*, **4**, p. 1641 (1960).
23. "Soviet Pneumatic Logic Elements," *Technical Survey*, **17**, No. 34, p. 599 (September, 1961).

Free Jet Elements

24. M. O. Meetze, Jr., C. L. Strong, "How Streams of Water Can be Used to Create Analogues of Electronic Tubes and Circuits," *Scientific American*, p. 128–138 (August, 1962).

Turbulence Amplifier

25. "New Fluid Amplifier Principle Demonstrated," *Control Engineering*, **9**, No. 11, p. 21 (November, 1962).
26. E. J. Kompass, "The State of the Art in Fluid Amplifiers," *Control Engineering*, **10**, No. 1, p. 91 (January, 1963).
27. R. N. Auger, "Turbulence Amplifier Design and Application," Fluid Logic Control Systems, 456 Riverside Drive, New York, Technical Report.

Diffusors

28. H. Sprenger, "Experimentelle Untersuchungen an geraden und gekrummten Diffusoren," Diss. E. T. H., Prom. Nr. 2803, Zürich (1959).
29. W. Pfenninger, "Untersuchungen über Reibungsverminderung an Tragflügeln mithilfe von Grenzschichtabsaugung," Mitteilung Nr. 13 des Inst. f. Aerodynamik ETH, Zürich (1946).
30. K. Kaufmann, "Grenzschichtbeeinflussung bei Diffusoren von Strömungsmaschinen," Diss. T. H., Karlsruhe (1957).

Wall Interaction Type Elements (Basic Facts)

31. Hermann Schlichting, "Boundary Layer Theory," McGraw-Hill, New York, (1960).
32. S. J. Kline, "On the Nature of Stall," *Transactions of the ASME, Series D*, **81**, No. 3 (September, 1959).
33. C. A. Moore, S. J. Kline, "Some Effects of Vanes and Turbulence in Two-Dimensional Wide-Angled Subsonic Diffusors," N.A.C.A., TN 4080 (1958).
34. A. Voedisch, "Analytical Investigation of the Coanda Effect," Air Material Command USAF, Wright Field Technical Report F.TR.2155 ND (1948).
35. A. Métral, F. Zerner, "L'Effet Coanda," Publications Scientifiques et Techniques du Ministère de l'Air, No. 218 (1948).
36. A. Métral, F. Zerner, "The Coanda Effect," Ministry of Supply, Technical Information Bureau, No. TIB/T 4027 (November, 1953).
37. P. R. Owen, L. Klanfer, "On the Laminar Boundary Layer Separation from the Leading Edge of a Thin Aerofoil," Aeron. Res. Council (GB), Current Paper No. 220 (1955).
38. M. B. Glauert, "The Wall Jet," *Journal of Fluid Mechanics*, **1**, p. 625 (1956).
39. M. Reiner, "The Teapot Effect," *Physics Today*, **9**, p. 16–20 (September, 1956).
40. J. B. Keller, "Teapot Effect," *Journal of Applied Physics*, **28**, No. 8, p. 859 (August, 1957).
41. C. Bourque, B. G. Newman, "Reattachment of a Two-Dimensional Incompressible Jet to an Adjacent Flat Plate," *Aeron. Quart.*, **XI**, p. 201 (August, 1960).
42. B. G. Newman, "The Deflexion of Plane Jets by Adjacent Boundaries—Coanda Effect," *Boundary Layer and Flow Control*, edited by G. V. Lachmann, Pergamon Press, New York, p. 232–264 (1961).
43. J. Greber, "Bubble Pressures under Reattaching Laminar Jets and Boundary Layers," *Proceedings of the ASME Symposium on Fluid Jet Control Devices*, New York (November, 1962).

Wall Interaction Type Elements (Devices)

44. R. E. Bowles, *et al.*, "Pure Pneumatic Computers," DOFL Report 1959 (1959).
45. "Fluid Amplifier Handbook," DOFL Office of Techn. Services, Dep. of Commerce, Washington 25, D.C.

241

46. "Fluid Systems Operate Without Moving Parts," *Automatic Control*, **12**, No. 4, p. 15–19 (April, 1960).
47. R. E. Bowles, B. M. Horton, R. W. Warren, "Fluid Computing Elements Open New Doors in Control," *Control Engineering*, **7**, No. 5, p. 26, 28, 30 (May, 1960).
48. J. R. Greenwood, "The Design and Development of a Fluid Logic Element," Thesis M.I.T., M.E. Dept. B.S. (May, 1960).
49. B. M. Horton, "Amplification by Fluid Stream Interaction," N.E.R.E.M., Boston (IRE) (November, 1960).
50. R. W. Warren, "Fluid Pulse Converter," U.S.A. Pat. No. 3 001 698 (September, 1961).
51. A. E. Mitchell, "Reattachment of Separated Boundary Layers and Their Effects in Fluid Switching Devices," IBM Research Report RZ-81 (February, 1962).
52. F. T. Brown, "Pneumatic Pulse Transmission with Bistable Jet Relay Reception and Amplification," M.I.T. Sc.D. Thesis, Dept. of Mech. Engineering (May, 1962).
53. Corning Glass Works, "Fluid Logics and Amplifiers to be Photoetched in Glass," *Control Engineering*, **9**, No. 6, p. 30 (June, 1962).
54. H. H. Glaettli, "Grundsätzliches und Grenzabschätzungen betreffend hydrodynamische Verstärker," (Principles and Limitations of Fluid Dynamic Amplifiers), *Zeitschrift für Angewandte Math. und Phys.*, **XIII**, No. 5 (1962).
55. R. A. Comparin, A. E. Mitchell, H. R. Müller, "Qualitative und quantitative Aspekte des Grenzschichtverstärkers" (Qualitative and Quantitative Aspects of Fluid Switching Elements), *Zeitschrift für Angewandte Math. und Phys.*, **XIII**, No. 5 (1962).
56. F. T. Brown, "A Combined Analytical and Experimental Approach to the Development of Fluid Jet Amplifiers," *Proceedings of the ASME Symposium on Fluid Jet Control Devices*, New York, p. 1–6 (November, 1962).
57. R. E. Bowles, "State of the Art of Pure Fluid Systems," *Proceedings of the ASME Symposium on Fluid Jet Control Devices*, New York, p. 7–22 (November, 1962).
58. R. E. Norwood, "A Performance Criterion for Fluid Jet Amplifiers," *Proceedings of the ASME Symposium on Fluid Jet Control Devices*, New York, p. 59–64 (November, 1962).
59. R. A. Comparin, H. H. Glaettli, A. E. Mitchell, H. R. Müller, "On the Limitations and Special Phenomena in Fluid Amplifiers," *Proceedings of the ASME Symposium on Fluid Jet Control Devices*, New York, p. 65–74 (November, 1962).
60. R. W. Warren, "Some Parameters Affecting the Design of Bistable Fluid Amplifiers," *Proceedings of the ASME Symposium on Fluid Jet Control Devices*, New York, p. 75–82 (November, 1962).
61. W. A. Boothe, "Performance Evaluation of a High Pressure Recovery Bistable Fluid Amplifier," *Proceedings of the ASME Symposium on Fluid Jet Control Devices*, New York, p. 83–90 (November, 1962).
62. R. A. Comparin, A. E. Mitchell, H. R. Müller, "Fluid AND-Gate," *IBM Technical Disclosure Bulletin*, **5**, No. 6, p. 30 (November, 1962).
63. W. A. Boothe, J. N. Shiun, "A Suggested System of Schematic Symbols for Fluid Amplifier Circuitry," G.E. Report (1962).
64. E. J. Kompass, "The State of the Art in Fluid Amplifiers," *Control Engineering*, **10**, No. 1, p. 88–93 (January, 1963).

Vortex Chamber Amplifiers

65. E. M. Dexter, "Vortex Valve Development," DOFL Fluid Amplifier Handbook, (1961).
66. E. M. Dexter, "Vortex Valve Development," G.E. Report.

Passive Elements

67. F. D. Ezekiel, R. J. Greenwood, "Hydraulics Half Add Binary Numbers," *Control Engineering*, **8**, No. 2, p. 145, (February, 1961).
68. M. O. Meetze, Jr., C. L. Strong, *Scientific American*, p. 128–138, (August, 1962).

Multiple Computer Systems

WILLIAM A. CURTIN

Radio Corporation of America
Defense Electronic Products
Moorestown, New Jersey

1. Introduction

The ever increasing complexity of data processing tasks and the decreasing time allowed for their execution is gradually exceeding what the current generation of automatic computers can accomplish.

245

There are currently several large information handling systems in the planning or design stages, an appreciable number of which are of a real-time nature, and which are expected to perform a wide variety of functions. Such information systems would include, for example, Information Traffic Handling, Information Storage and Retrieval, Simulation, General Mathematical Computations, Data Processing and Reduction as well as combinations of these and other functions.

Further, the information handling systems must be capable of responding easily and rapidly to changes in operational requirements. Indeed, their usefulness is largely dependent upon a facility for timely adaptation to sudden and unexpected changes in the nature of the information as well as to constantly evolving information processing technology and user policies.

In order to provide for these functions, it is mandatory that a large and complex computer system be provided. The computer system will generally include several large-scale digital processors and a complex set of peripheral hardware including display equipment, operator and maintenance consoles, communication and switching equipments and the like. The gross information handling characteristics of the computer system should generally provide for:

(a) The well integrated usage of many reliable hardware components for reasons of reliability and economy.

(b) The capability for constant evolution. The system must possess a high degree of growth potential such that system expansion will not require "retooling."

(c) Coping with an extremely large volume of data. The organization of data will be complex with a great variety of data elements. The data file is dynamic and subject to constant updating. Hence the input-output system must have unprecedented flexibility and capability without interrupting the normal data flow and computational procedures and must have provisions for numerous real-time channels responsive to random commands external to the system.

(d) Operation in real-time. Fast response balanced against cost requires full and efficient use of all hardware components.

(e) Predominantly automated communication among individuals and groups and among system machine components.

(f) Ultrareliability. Thus no single element can perform so unique a function that its failure could disable the entire system but rather should at most decrease the on-line capability.

(g) Response to real world requests and demands and ability to dynamically schedule itself in accordance with priority rules.

For the satisfaction of the above general provisions the present day concept of single or central processing unit is rapidly approaching obsolescence simply because the demands exceed what the state of the hardware art has been able to produce, particularly in response time, reliability and capacity. New system logical organizations and programming concepts, within the state of the component art, are required to cope with these information handling system requirements. Larger single processor machines having vastly extended computational capabilities resulting from unique logical design techniques may offer temporary refuge but will not solve the long term problem. Such systems are not seen to offer any advantage in the way of reliability, cost and growth potential.

The development of new computer systems always lags the conception of larger and more complex tasks requiring computer solution. To bridge this gap in the near future will require some fundamentally new ideas of computer system logical organization rather than revolutionary advances of the hardware art, although in the future such available hardware coupled with new system organizations will undoubtedly have a profound impact upon the computer art. To be sure, the more efficient use of logical elements, as now known, will be exploited to the fullest in deriving any advanced system organization.

System organizations characterized by a multitude of independent control units, the multiple computer, is envisioned as providing the ultimate satisfaction of the demands for vastly increased capacity and capability. The multiple computer approach is not new but has been given impetus only within the past few years and this has been almost exclusively in the area of implementation. The literature is almost void of any fundamental work on the theory of multiple computers [1] or evaluations of the pros and cons of the various ways in which multiple computers could be organized [2]. The exploitation of new logical design techniques for conventional machines has been rather slow and cautious which might account for the delay in the appearance of multiple computers in large numbers. Some of these techniques could be expanded to include larger system components but the awareness of this seems to follow their successful usage on a smaller scale. For example, Bauer [2] points out how parallel processing and modularity have gone through numerous evolutionary stages and today form the foundation for the development of multiple computers.

2. Outline of the Paper

A definition for a multiple computer system would appear to be in order to provide a framework for the discussion. Some thoughts in this regard will be forwarded, but a formal all-inclusive definition is not possible. Some of the motivations for building multiple computers will be considered, from which will emerge some general concepts for the design of a multiple

247

computer system. Incidental to this discussion are the pros and cons of various possible methods of mechanization, one of which will be explained in detail from a strictly functional point of view. However appealing or clever a hardware solution may appear, the total solution is incomplete unless the programming and scheduling tasks are equally powerful. Hence a brief discussion will follow on these topics. Finally, examples of different types of multiple computers which have been built and reported in the literature will be reviewed.

3. Definition of a Multiple Computer

Much controversy exists in this regard and rather than attempt to define a multiple computer, it is far simpler to state what most workers in the field would agree is not a multiple computer system.

The term multiple computer has been used to designate a broad spectrum of computer systems. These range from a low order group of conventional general purpose digital computers (not necessarily but usually identical) interconnected via their input-output channels to effect intercomputer communications, to a higher order group wherein several (identical or different) processing units are interconnected on an integrated basis. The low order group is conceptually the simplest and most logical way of organizing existing hardware to function as a group and today is the most prevalent method of simultaneously utilizing two or more computers. Such a system is called a multiple computer solely by virtue of including more than one computer but possesses no unique features for being so named. Since an unlimited variety of this type of system is possible, this type of installation will not be considered a multiple computer system in the present context. Consequently, by this consideration, duplexed systems [3] are also excluded from here being considered multiple computers even though the standby machine may, at times, be used simultaneously with the normally on-line machine.

Most modern day computers are capable of simultaneous operation, i.e., internal computations are interleaved in time with input-output operations so that in effect it appears as if multiple operations are being executed. In this paper, machines having this characteristic will not qualify as being multiple computers.

Some existing systems which have been called multiple computers will be reviewed in this paper, but the judgment of whether they are or are not multiple computers must remain an individual responsibility.

To illustrate the controversy of a multiple computer definition, Bauer [2] presents four criteria which a system should satisfy to be so classified and categorizes existing systems accordingly as they satisfy all the criteria.

Criterion 2, "There are two or more independently operating random access memories," would eliminate from consideration any system having one large random access memory capable of being sequentially addressed by several processors. This seems to be an unnecessary restriction since such a system would have several unique features closely analogous to a group of people communicating the results of their work to each other via a medium available to all, such as a blackboard. Such a system should qualify for multiple computer status equally as well as a system consisting of several smaller memories. For the public memory concept, control logic and programming could be easily devised to effect orderly memory access and so realize a desirable form of data communication between all of the processors.

Criterion 3, "Communication among major elements of the system is of the memory-to-memory type at memory access speeds," does not differentiate between serial or parallel information transfer at memory speeds, although the latter is certainly more desirable. Systems which provide only for transfer of control and/or status information between registers, for example, or which provide for access to a common memory (as noted above) should be respected as contenders for multiple computer status.

Minimum communication time via memory-to-memory transfer at memory speed, serial or parallel, is extremely desirable and indeed a sought after objective of a multiple computer system. While it is agreed that a worthwhile multiple computer should possess this virtue (see Section 5) it is questionable whether it is a factor which makes one system a multiple computer and another not. Although systems which satisfy these criteria would be deemed multiple computer systems, other systems not satisfying one or more of the criteria will also be considered multiple computer systems in this paper.

4. Motivation for Multiple Computers

Several reasons exist as justification for a multiple computer system. Reliability and expandability features in themselves are sufficiently valid reasons for wanting to progress beyond the single computer concept. However, the duplex computer concept was fostered from a reliability standpoint while the primitive input-output connected system is certainly expandable. Since these are not here considered to be multiple computer systems, additional motivations must exist for progressing beyond these concepts, although both reliability and expandability features should accrue from the more sophisticated multiple computer system.

Certainly the applications aspect mentioned in the introduction is a strong motivation, i.e., to what class of problems should we address a multiple computer? It is well known that, in theory at least, it is possible for any automatic computer to solve any computable problem given sufficient time to do so. Consequently, if a multiple computer is worth building at all, it should at least solve some class of problems within some specified time limit, which limit would be exceeded by any single computer working on the same task. Also, if a multiple computer is worth building at all, it should, at least some of the time, be used to execute a single task which requires all or most of the available equipment, otherwise several smaller computers, operating autonomously, would serve the purpose equally as well. Furthermore, the frequency of use of all or most of the machines on one problem must be sufficiently high to justify a multiple computer approach otherwise, from a time standpoint, the primitive input-output coordinated system would suffice.

Problems requiring a large amount of input-output data transfer (including communication between processors) relative to the number of internal operations would benefit most from a system which minimized interunit communication time. If the amount of data transfer is small in comparison, then the need for high-speed data communication is not so urgent. In the former case time is saved by providing for rapid transfer of large volumes of data—but this provision would be inefficient in the latter case, particularly if the expenditure of time in preparing the data for transfer is an appreciable percentage of the total transfer time. It is quite probable that the tasks to be executed will be of both types and, depending on the system organization, will inevitably be more time consuming in the execution of one type than the other. In general, all that can be said is that the system organization should be such that both time and hardware efficiency be significantly better than what could be achieved on a single processor or groups of processors operating autonomously.

Very often the impetus for a new computer or data processing system is derived from a particular set of problem requirements or class of problems and the machine is designed to be most useful in their execution. Additionally, certain features may be added to enhance the machine performance for collateral tasks at little additional expense. Hence we find computing machines designed for general business applications (data processor) with extensions, for example, to communication data processing, or for scientific applications (arithmetic type machine) with extensions, for example, to radar data processing, but usually not both. In other words it is difficult to conceive of one machine which can handle widely divergent tasks with equal facility. But in considering a multiple computer structure an initial minimum requirement would be that it be capable of handling a much broader spectrum of tasks than a single machine but yet not so broad that its over-all efficiency in the execution of any of its tasks be seriously impaired.

250

The question to what extent a multiple computer utilizes its hardware more efficiently is however secondary to the time factor since it is inevitable that it will be equipment-wise inefficient in the execution of some problems. Herein lies the most essential reason for the differences which exist in the various approaches proposed for multiple computer systems. If the class of problems is restricted and fairly well known in advance, then it is reasonable to integrate a small number of specialized units to minimize equipment inefficiency and to mechanize communication facilities between the units to optimize information transfer time. This is especially true of tasks having a high frequency of use and high urgency. If system versatility is sought, then general-purpose machines are called for and the attendant inefficiency in performing some tasks must be accepted. This type of organization would tend to increase the total execution time of some tasks; however versatility has its price.

With a given state of the hardware art the only way one can effectively decrease execution time is by truly concurrent processing of different phases of the same task. This implies a multi-unit processing system with a built-in communication system to minimize total execution and transfer time. This division of the work load to decrease the time expenditure along with reliability and expandability features emerges as the primary motive for a multiple computer system which promises more computing per unit time per dollar.

The idea of dividing the work load however bears some thought since such a division is both problem and machine dependent.

It is problem dependent because the problem must be divisible in such a way that concurrent operation on the different problem segments is possible. Classes of problems of this type would favor a multiple computer system composed of a group of general purpose machines—and if a majority of problems cannot be so classified, a multiple computer approach becomes questionable.

It is machine dependent by virtue of the fact that a majority of the problem segments which would result from problem division are most likely to be unique and so require quite different operational machine characteristics which would favor the use of special purpose processors. However this same consideration has also led to the specialized machine approach as a means of increasing efficiency. The fallacy here is that there will be problem segments which do not readily fit the abilities of any of the "specialist" machines, which confirms the previous conclusion that this type of organization should be reserved for a restricted, well defined class of problems. Clearly it would be uneconomical to build special purpose machines to handle any eventuality.

An alternative to providing machines designed to optimize the execution of special problem types is to divide the structure to optimize certain gross machine operations. For example, one machine would be used for input-output editing, data format conversion, file searching etc., while another machine would form comparisons to direct the data flow to the proper unit and yet another machine would be required to execute all arithmetical and logical operations and so on. Yet all of these functions are within the capabilities of a general purpose processor which, because of its versatility, could be expected to handle a wider variety of such functions with about the same or increased efficiency of time and equipment.

5. A System Design Approach for a Hypothetical Multiple Computer

In the previous section some of the pros and cons of specialized vs general purpose computers as the constituent parts of a multiple computer complex were presented. The preference for and advantage of a system composed of general purpose machines was stated. In this section some general considerations pertinent to the mechanization of a multiple computer organization based on the use of versatile, general purpose machines are proposed. The system organization described here is hypothetical but serves to illustrate how the integrated system design approach to this problem can achieve interesting results.

It is fundamental to a multiple computer system that in order for the system to be effective there must be complete cooperation between the computers under the control of an executor (usually a program) which schedules tasks and makes computer assignments. Individual computer responsibility for programs is avoided by providing the means for such a system to transfer rapidly segments of a program or an entire program from one computer to another. This suggests a modular memory scheme such that the system memory is an aggregate of several smaller memory units as opposed to one large memory common to all of the computers. This is one of Bauer's criteria for a multiple computer and it should be noted that exception was not taken on the desirability of this feature but rather on its necessity for constituting a multiple computer. Such a scheme can provide for the parallel transfer of large volumes of data which could be accomplished easily by merely transferring electronically an entire memory module or modules from one computer to another. This form of parallel data transfer is in contrast to the current practice of serially transferring memory data from one machine to another, either directly or via the input-output tape channel, or to some multiple computers which effect serial data transfer between computers via some intermediate high-speed storage device. Furthermore, it is desirable for any of the constituent computers to have memory units available to it at any time so that, in general, the number of modular memory units will be greater than the number of computers. The main advantage of such a multi-processor-memory organization is that programs and data can be shared by several computers on a *high-speed basis* and consequently the full computing power of the entire installation can be applied to high priority tasks.

Additionally, peripheral equipments should also be totally shared, on a demand basis, between all computer units but in such a way that any peripheral device is available to only one computer at a time and then only on a priority basis. The obvious advantage of shared peripheral equipment is instantaneous availability of large data files to all computers without replicating the files. In the event one computer requires access to a busy device then, by an executive routine, the computer can be assigned another task and so avoid being stymied by unavailability of a less important system device.

The realization of a computer system having the desired generic characteristics is totally dependent upon the development of a satisfactory data switching or inter-module communication system which is reliable, easily expandable and economical. Once such an interconnection scheme is adopted, the gross logical operation and some programming aspects must be specified in terms of the interconnection system.

The simplest approach to the interconnection problem is conceptually a space-divided or multilevel crossbar switching network as shown in Fig. 1a, wherein computer modules are connected to storage modules by controlling crosspoints of a switching matrix. Conceptual simplicity, however, is had at the expense of constructional and operational complexity. A controlled gating circuit is required at each matrix cross point (of each level) per bit per function, hence a product relationship exists between the number of computers, memories, peripheral devices and information bits. The excessive response time of physically realizable crosspoint gating elements severely limits the maximum rate at which modules can be switched. Moreover, additional time must be expended to insure that the connection can indeed be made and to perform other switch control logic functions. Thus, once a crosspoint connection has been established between two system modules it must be retained for an extended period of time in order to make' the time investment worthwhile. Furthermore, the system data rate is also dependent upon the dimensions of the crossbar network in much the same way that memory speed is sensitive to the number of words contained in the memory. Consequently system timing would require readjustment as the system grows. To circumvent these problems, the crossbar network is usually designed to accommodate a fully expanded system which is to say that it is not easily amenable to modularization.

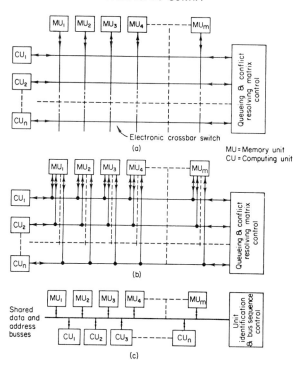

FIG. 1. Multiple computer interconnection schemes (input-output devices not shown for simplicity).

Also, additional hardware or programming or both is required to account for conflicting crossbar requests and to handle connection priorities in addition to the need for a crossbar scheduling routine.

In general, it is impossible for a multiple computer program to have arranged for all the data and instructions (or a large majority of such) for any given computer to reside in one memory module. Consequently, multi-memory accessibility for a multiple computer system must be achieved on a high-speed basis. A cross-bar switching system has the capability of multimemory access but *not on a high-speed basis.*

To overcome this difficulty computer access to several memories could be achieved by retaining already established computer-to-memory connections as required. To prevent all memories from responding to address requests the computer information must be coded so that only the particular memory specified by the code will respond. But if memory is coded it would not be necessary to establish computer-to-memory crosspoint connections, in other words a permanent connection might just as well have been made, consequently the system configuration could be reduced to that shown in

254

Fig. 1b. This arrangement would still require some type of queuing system to prevent simultaneous memory access by more than one computer in addition to a scheme for priority determination. In Fig. 1b several computers are shown having independent access to each and every memory, each by its own communication line. This is undesirable because each memory would require separate addressing circuitry for each computer. The cost of such an arrangement would be prohibitive and system growth would require hardware additions to each memory. To eliminate this problem, the clearest solution would be to share individual memory addressing circuitry among all the computers by some means. If this is done, the memory communication lines of each computer might just as well be shared also. The system could then be reduced to the configuration shown in Fig. 1c. Now however, both memories and computers must be coded to insure proper data flow, and queuing and priority schemes must also be employed as before so that one and only one computer can have access to the data bus at a time and to insure that only the specified memory(s) be receptive to information from any given computer.

A serious problem could arise with this configuration because of the possibility that one computer could completely tie up the communication medium (with the proper priority of course) for as long as required to execute its task. Such a possibility for locking out the remaining computers would severely limit the flexibility of the multiple computer system. This difficulty could be overcome by postulating that each computer be permitted access to the communication bus in a sequential fashion. This is possible because the logic operation time of a computer is significantly less than the duration of the memory cycle (a factor of the order of 20 or 30 to 1) so that the computer could address its memory, then relinquish the data bus for use by others, each in its turn, while it is waiting for its memory to generate a response. A memory cycle time later the response would be available from the memory, at which time the computer should again have access to the bus in order to receive the reply. Since each computer must have access to its memory (via the data bus) at least once every memory cycle time, a convenient scheme would be to permit bus access to each computer at least once each cycle and then for a time interval equal to the memory cycle time divided by the number of computers requiring bus access. This concept is really time-division of the communication medium and is an extension of well known time sharing techniques [4] which have been applied to transfer busses to permit the high-speed memory to be used as an input-output buffer. Computer identification would be established by the time of occurrence of its access to the communication line because at any given time one and only one computer is permitted bus access and it would be known beforehand which computer had access at that time. Data bus conflicts and queuing problems would be resolved automatically by this technique.

In retrospect there are really three basic ways of interconnecting the modules of a multiple computer system, namely, space-division (crossbar), time-division and frequency-division. The disadvantages of the space-divided method and the various degrees of refinement leading to the concept of time-dividing the communication medium have been discussed. Actually, these two methods could have evolved independently of each other with the greatest motivations for rejecting a space-divided scheme being the excessive transfer time and the hardware complexity involved as opposed to an expected savings of time and equipments when communication lines are time shared. The order of magnitude of the savings to be expected from employing time-division over space-division is easily calculable for any specific set of conditions.

A frequency divided scheme potentially offers the greatest flexibility for intermodular communication. However, for the data rates anticipated rough estimates indicate the need for a carrier frequency in the range of 100 to 200 Mc. Circuitry for modulation and demodulation in this range for a large number of information bits and the development of techniques for rapidly changing the center frequency of wide-band filters is felt to be presently beyond the state of the digital computer art. Hence the time-division scheme would be chosen as being more amenable to realization within the present state of the art.

For this hypothetical system, the number of computers can vary from at least two (in order to qualify as a multiple computer) to some predetermined maximum number limited by the physical circuit considerations which set the minimum time during which it is possible to transfer information successfully from one point in the system to any other point in the system. This time is related to the rise time obtainable from logic gates, the set time of a register, and response time of a transmission line (see Section 5.1.1).

The mode of time-division postulated thus far is sequential and is based on a segmentation of a unit reference time (the memory cycle time). It was conveniently chosen for the purpose of simple computer identification by time coincidence which eliminates the need of additional circuitry or programs to handle bus queuing or computer priorities. This form of time-division is highly desirable for computer-to-memory data transfer because of the determinate nature of both the memories and computers. However, the possibility of utilizing a nonsequential time-division scheme for transfer bus access should not be overlooked as a means for communication with nondeterministic devices such as peripheral tapes, discs, etc. Indeed such a method of time division would be more desirable in the case of input-output devices (see Section 5.3).

256

5.1 Some Important Aspects of Mechanization

5.1.1 Signal Distribution

It is important to observe that the computer-to-memory communication must occur within a time interval which is some integral fraction of the memory cycle time, i.e., T_M/n where T_M is the memory cycle time and n is the number of computers. The very problem with the space-divided crossbar which led to a time-divided concept was the excessive time required to establish the communication link between a computer and a memory (which is known to be several times greater than an average memory cycle time) but this was seen to be because the connection was established by means of a *gated* structure which is inherently speed limited and because special logic or time consuming routines or special addressing techniques must be entered to resolve crossbar conflicts, connection priorities, busy signals and selection of alternate paths. Time division of itself resolves all of these problems except for the physical limitation due to signal distribution.

Therefore, the realization of a bus distribution system over which high pulse rate information can be transmitted without appreciable deterioration is essential. The transmitted signal characteristics should be independent of the number of devices intended to receive the information. As pointed out above in connection with the crossbar communication method, this simple requirement precludes the use of a gated communication structure. The best known means of achieving the degree of performance necessary is the impedance matched, linear transmission line. Since many devices require access to the data transfer bus and since many receivers are possible, it would seem that a tree structured communication line with linear, repeater power amplifiers at each node of the tree would achieve the fan-out (in) required. This type of structure is such that any subsystem being interconnected can communicate with any other subsystem regardless of the relative physical location of the subsystem. A tree structure would insure that the transmission delay between any points of the system is the same and constant and consequently could be accounted for in the system timing. The physical layout of the entire system should be carefully considered to minimize cable delays to a tolerable amount. Either two or three dimensional structures could be used for the purpose, depending on the anticipated equipment complement and physical size of individual system modules.

For extreme reliability purposes, the entire data transmission system should be duplexed; otherwise only certain portions need be duplexed. This would also be required of the crossbar scheme but will be significantly cheaper for the time-divided system. Also, since the time-divided bus scheme employs fewer components than a functionally equivalent crossbar system the reliability should be correspondingly better.

With regard to system expandability, such a system is ideal. Since a transmission line system would be impedance matched (through appropriate line driving circuitry which connects system gating circuits to the matched line) a constant load is presented to the driving circuits regardless of the number of devices at the line termination. Thus system timing and driver circuit design is fixed for all possible system configurations. Equipments could be added to a minimum installation by supplying the necessary sections of transmission lines. The variation in cable delays as the system grows would be unimportant insofar as the delays associated with a maximum system were tolerable.

5.1.2 System Timing

Another critical aspect which requires detailed investigation is the system timing. The time sequencing feature would be provided by a master time generator which provides as many different phased pulses as there are computer units, one set of such pulses per computer. In effect a memory unit(s) is connected to that computer to whose time pulse it is receptive. The time pulses could be generated, for example, in Gray code order with the number of bits used depending on the maximum number of computers to be employed in the system. Since the Gray code is a unit distance code there would not be any ambiguity or transient disturbance when the time pulse changes. An n digit binary number code (there could therefore be a maximum of 2^n computers) corresponding to a time pulse code, would be stored in a register in each computer which would be permanently identified with that computer. The Gray coded time pulses from the time pulse generator would then be continuously compared with the number codes in each of the computers pulse time registers. When agreement is obtained a signal would be generated which would permit the proper computer to put a memory address, if any, on the common data transfer bus. A similar comparison procedure (accounting of course for propagation delays) would simultaneously be carried out in each memory and only those memories which have been assigned the proper time pulse code would permit information to be picked off the transfer bus. Because the total transmission line delay will not necessarily be integrally related to the memory cycle time it would be necessary to stagger (or delay) the coded time signals from the master time generator to insure this. The delays so introduced would necessarily vary for each function.

Since the time pulses are periodic there need not be a one to one correspondence between a particular reference pulse and the pulse which is actually used by the computer or memory. Therefore, only relative pulse positions would be of consequence.

The reference pulses could be delayed either at the computer or the memories, it being preferable to do so at the memories, since differences in memory timing characteristics due to tolerances would have to be accomplished in any event. A delay due to time pulse recognition was neglected in the preceding but could be accounted for in an actual system design.

5.2 Operational Features

The computer units should include facilities both for sequencing the instructions and for data manipulation and computation. Therefore, each computer should contain all the conventional equipment for instruction execution. It should be possible to program various computers to perform a wide variety of functions which precludes a built-in division of labor among the identical computers of a logical or arithmetic nature. The independently operating computers can communicate via memory transfer such that each computer acts under program control and memory transfer is on a request basis to prevent catastrophic interference between ·computers. Each computer, at any given time, would have access only to those memory units attached to it by the proper time-pulse assignment, and in general, may have several memories assigned to it. Multiple memories assigned to a computer could be distinguished from each other by a position number. A significant consequence would be that if several memories had been given the same position number within a time pulse they would form a stack of identical copies similar to carbon copies of ordinary typing. Data and instructions could, therefore, be duplicated with no additional time expenditure by the system. Stacking is also a convenient means by which a computer could collect and hold idle storage units. The number of digits needed to address any word in memory is no longer than the number needed for addressing in a single computer having the same memory capacity. Under program control, a memory unit could have its association with any given computer changed to another computer by changing its pulse time assignment, but this should only be achieved by the computer to which it would currently be assigned, so that no other computer could arbitrarily transfer memories to itself without the concurrence of the controlling computers. At this point, it should be emphasized that all memory modules should be identical in design so that they would be completely interchangeable with each other. Although at any instant of time, a limited amount of instructions or data is available to a computer (because of limited addressing capability) simple memory transfers between computers would provide almost unlimited capacity. In other words, any computer would have ultimate accessibility to all the system memory modules which would be far in excess of its inherent addressing capability.

A memory unit position within a time pulse could be changed (by the computer) by altering its position number and a memory unit could be transferred to another computer by changing the memory pulse time assignment.

Before a computer could send a memory to a second computer, it must insert the necessary identifying code words and other information into some portion of the memory reserved for such purposes. (The particular locations used would be agreed upon beforehand by programmers.) Thus a certain amount of computer time must be invested for a memory transfer. The actual number of instructions required will no doubt depend upon the complexity of the problem being worked on and the manner in which the computers are organized for its solution. Similarly, a computer receiving a memory must invest a certain amount of time to determine what type of data the memory contains, to obtain, if necessary, a set of operating instructions, and to assign it a position number. Again the time involved will, to some extent, depend on the problem being handled. Now since there is a double expenditure of machine time involved in memory transfer, the more words a unit contains the less significant is the bookkeeping time. On the other hand, short messages of a few words would also be sent from machine to machine and for these, very large memory units would be wasteful, just as very small memory units would be inefficient. Clearly a compromise of memory size must be reached for a system which is not to be restricted to use for one special problem type. Considerations of physical size, engineering problems of construction, etc., are important but at present 2^{12} or 4096 words would seem to be a reasonable size of memory unit module.

Since memories are not permanently assigned to any one computer and do not occupy permanent positions within a single computer's memory structure, some means of identifying an individual memory unit would have to be provided, perhaps by memory unit serial numbers which could be available to both computers and maintenance personnel.

5.3 The Input-Output System

The objective of any efficient input-output (i/o) system is to transfer economically, reliably and in an orderly fashion the largest quantity of data in the shortest possible time with a minimum of interference to other system operations. Thus, aside from the i/o devices themselves, the system philosophy regarding control and communication is of most importance.

For reasons of hardware economy, data transfer between peripheral devices and memories should also take place over time-multiplexed data busses. The real problem in this respect is not the time-multiplexing aspect itself but rather its control. Control and transfer of data could be exercised by a computer making use of its usual memory communication lines but this would result in excessive computer queuing by the input-output. Since there would be several memory positions available to each computer and since a computer would normally only be working with one of its assigned memories, the remainder could be assigned to input-output (if required). Queuing problems would be minimized by employing separate data transfer busses between memories and input-output devices. Input-output control could still be exercised by the computer on a pulse time basis but control transfer of data via a separate memory to i/o bus would require different considerations.

Because of parallel data transmission lines, the main objective should be to achieve the most efficient utilization of the time-multiplexed transfer bus. In other words, the bus should be fully occupied with data transfers 100% of the time, provided sufficient data is available for transfer.

Since the problem reduces to the physical information-carrying capacity of a transfer bus it seems reasonable to expect that the usage of the bus should be independent of programs and programmers. Thus the system should automatically control and optimize the traffic conditions on the bus such that the outside world is ignorant of the internal operation.

5.3.1 Input-Output Controller

Since data flow is between multiple memories and input-output devices it is clear at the outset that a controller or director would be required to perform the following general functions: to recognize the source of i/o requests, to handle i/o interrupts, to execute the i/o instructions and so on. The memory units could not serve in this capacity because they are passive by nature. Moreover, at any given time, the memories are intimately related to computers by a time pulse assignment and so could not be cognizant of i/o assignments of other computers. The assignment must then go to the i/o portion of the system but for similar reasons could not be delegated to specific i/o devices. Hence a new system unit, called the Input-Output Controller (ioc), should be introduced.

In addition to an input-output controller unit, each memory should be provided with a transfer control register, a word length i/o data register and associated control circuitry for both. These would complement the usual memory data and control registers used for computer communication purposes. Prior to any memory assignment to input-output the i/o control register in the memory would contain the assigned computer time pulse number and position number occupied by the memory.

5.3.2 Input-Output System Organization

The most significant reason for a different philosophy for i/o communications is that data flow is between a multiplicity of memories and a multiplicity of peripheral devices such that one could not assign a unique time pulse to either the memories or i/o devices. Since peripheral devices have widely variant characteristics, different control and identification problems arise which are not as easily handled by the sequential time pulse system employed for memory to computer communication. A more versatile organization for peripheral devices, based on a nonsequential time division scheme, is described below.

A typical sequence of operations in assigning a memory to an I/O device would be as follows: a computer request for data transfer to/from a memory under its control from/to an I/O device is directed to the IOC. Upon receipt of the service request, the IOC will fetch the specific peripheral device, if operable and not busy, and assign it a code number. Initially the IOC will communicate with the specified memory(s) by the computer time pulse code and memory position number. This information is specified in the computer service request and is always initially stored in the memory I/O control register. The IOC then directs a command to the memory which changes the contents of its I/O control register to the same code number given to the specified peripheral device. After receipt of a recognition signal, subsequent memory addressing is controlled by the IOC without further intervention by the requesting computer. In effect, the IOC has given a unique label (name, serial number, etc.) to one or more memories which have been designated for input-output service and they will thereafter be receptive to the proper peripheral device information until termination of the input-output operation, at which time the IOC restores the initial contents of the I/O control register.

It should be noted, however, that if the computer which originated the request wishes to address the memory engaged in input-output, priority and queuing problems arise which must be handled by either hardware or program. But since there is more than one memory position per computer, it is possible for the programmer to arrange for the computer to communicate primarily with memories in other memory positions which are not currently busy with input-output.

A fundamental difference is implied in the manner of handling peripheral devices and memories. Whereas memories are assigned to computers or transferred from one computer to another (by request or otherwise, but under program control), I/O devices should be pooled so that at any instant of time unused I/O devices do not "belong" to particular computers, but rather are available to any computer which might call for them. Consequently, a computer will call for a particular I/O device by name (or number) via the IOC which will fulfill the request (if the priority is proper) and "dispatch" the I/O device to a memory assigned to the requesting computer. The computer will retain control or cognizance over the assigned I/O device until the request is fulfilled or is interrupted by a higher priority request from another computer. However, the actual control would be exercised by the IOC and only supervised by the computer, if supervision be necessary.

The computer to IOC communication (control signals) could be on a sequential time pulse basis in the same manner as memories. Since discrete pulse times are associated with each computer, the IOC could easily establish the identity of a computer which has made a request by time coincidence, as in the case of the memories.

Note that a computer could easily specify many memories for stacking purposes and also could specify multiple I/O's to which data will be sent from a memory for I/O stacking purposes. Note also the possibility in such a system for one computer (only if it is acting as the executor) to specify a memory not controlled by it, thus easing the executive program. Memory stacking would be easily accomplished by the IOC by assigning the same peripheral device code number to several memories (those memories belonging to the requesting computer or those specified by the requesting computer acting as executor but assigned to another computer). Circuitwise when the code number is called, the appropriate gates are closed so that data on the transfer bus is simultaneously received by all the coded units.

I/O device access to the transfer bus is controlled by the IOC which would sense a flag indicating that the device is ready to transmit data. Access would be granted if and only if the line is not occupied and if the priority rating of the I/O device is proper. It is assumed, of course, that the I/O data rate to a *single* memory is less than the reciprocal of memory access time (T_M^{-1}). A slightly different approach would be required to handle memory to I/O data transfer. The memory readout would be serial at a maximum rate T_M^{-1} words/sec. But the slower I/O devices become buffer limited, hence the IOC must request the memory to transfer data depending on I/O buffer availability. The buffer must be located at the I/O and not at the memory since the same memory may be transferring data asynchronously to several I/O devices concurrently, under control of the IOC.

During the execution of the I/O request the specified memory is in direct communication with the selected I/O device regardless of any unrelated action taken by the requesting computer. For example, the computer could transfer that memory to another computer and to a different memory position. The memory unit, however, still retains the I/O code number (name, label, etc.) assigned to it by the IOC. Uninterrupted data transfer will continue from the selected I/O device unless, of course, an interrupt command were given to halt the process. Additionally, the original requesting computer may retain control of the I/O procedures (as would be desirable for an executor) or it may transfer the control to the new recipient computer and so notify the IOC. The program must, in any case, inform the recipient computer that its newly received memory is engaged in I/O proceedings.

The IOC would accommodate this control change command without interrupting the data transfer to the memory in question. The choice of which computer should control the i/o could be under program control, but it is important to note that the ioc would merely record the change of computer control, and upon termination of the request enter a modified termination routine.

With this input-output organization the programmer need never be aware that one input-output request were utilizing the i/o memory transfer bus more than another request.

In the computer memory communication scheme the time pulse duration is fixed and must be of sufficient duration to operate a predetermined number of logic levels and set electronic registers. In the i/o memory communication scheme the length of time devoted to data transfer from i/o can be determined by the ioc depending upon which particular i/o device is operating. This timing independence is an important characteristic because it allows virtually unlimited flexibility of the type and speed of i/o devices.

5.3.3 Input-Output Interrupt

All i/o interrupts would be handled initially by the ioc on a priority basis but reinstatement of interrupted requests should be accomplished by the computer which initially made the request. This method permits an unlimited depth of i/o interrupts with no additional burden placed upon the ioc.

Interrupt commands may be internally generated by the program or externally generated in a random fashion wherein the time of arrival cannot easily be predicted. In the latter case a control program subroutine must be available to direct and fulfill the external request which must be directed to the ioc which would have cognizance of all i/o status and priority ratings. Assuming the interrupt priority were proper, the ioc would record and transmit to the controlling computer the contents of an i/o device relative status register which would indicate what portion of the initial request had been completed. This would be simple to accomplish for absolutely addressable i/o devices but somewhat more complicated for block addressed devices. The contents of the status registers would be transferred to the *next* memory position which would have been filled by i/o; the i/o code number register at the memory would be automatically restored by the ioc to the time pulse and position number of the controlling computer; the ioc could then send a control signal to the controlling computer informing it of interrupt completion; the ioc would send to the computer the memory address where the computer can find the contents of the i/o status register. The computer could, at its leisure, by a subroutine, compute a new set of i/o orders which actually will be the old orders modified by the amount of i/o that had been completed at the time of interruption. Note that as far as the ioc is concerned reinstatement will

264

be treated by the ioc as if it were a new request. This follows because all pertinent information is known by the computer and absolves both the ioc and the i/o device in question of the responsibility of remembering any past occurrences. Moreover, memory space would, of necessity, be available since the space had already been reserved for the interrupted i/o data.

Two means of i/o service reinstatement are possible: namely, (a) the ioc could inform the interrupted computer that reinstatement is now possible; (b) the computer could attempt reinstatement at convenient times. If reinstatement is not yet possible the computer would be so informed by the ioc. The former method would not be desirable if the capability of unlimited depth of interruption were required since it would impose an extensive past history requirement on the ioc. The memory capability of the ioc should be restricted to necessary functions which cannot be accomplished elsewhere.

5.3.4 Additional Input-Output System Capabilities

Since i/o to memory transfers are asynchronous and since memories are available to the ioc either on an "idle memory" or "program interrupt" basis, special data gathering and transmitting capabilities could be provided for the system. For example, an ultrahigh speed memory, perhaps of low capacity to gain speed, might be tied to the i/o-memory bus under ioc control. Short bursts of data at multimegacycle rates could be directed to this adjunct memory for later transfer to a conventional i/o device or memory. Similarly, the adjunct memory could be loaded ahead of time for ultrahigh speed transmission of short messages.

In an expanded system, the adjunct memory (or memories) could store ioc programs for scheduling and other control decisions. Use of an ultrahigh speed memory is essential for this purpose to present ioc slowdown.

A space divided communication system (crossbar switch type) between i/o devices and the ioc is no more costly in terms of equipment than a time divided system. This is true only for the case when communications is between *one* unit (the ioc) and *several* units (the i/o devices) because the single unit ioc can communicate by transmitting an i/o unit selection code whenever communication is desired and only the selected unit will respond. But this is identical to the time-shared principle except that the selection is not made in time sequence.

5.4 Summary of the Features of the Hypothetical System

A multiple computer concept based on the gross implementation described above realizes the generic computer characteristics specified in the previous section by virtue of the intermodular communication scheme and memory computer organization. Its several unique characteristics, summarized below, would provide definite advantages over both conventional single processor systems and other proposed or existing multiple-computer systems.

(1) A high degree of concurrency in operation would be achieved by the multidimensional information processing inherent in a modular structure. Data processing and computational capabilities are elevated by several levels of parallelism within the system which is culminated in the concurrent operation of several computer units used either jointly on a common problem or separately for different problems. This is a significant step beyond the interrupt and priority control used in contemporary multi-programming schemes. The ultimate capability of the system is the truly simultaneous operation of all computer units under the programmer's complete control. This can be achieved by an executive control and scheduling routine which will minimize the over-all operating time.

(2) Ultrareliability, economy and easy expandability would be afforded by the time multiplexing of several identical units. System expansion merely requires the addition of standard communication facilities. No single unit could cause entire system failure, but rather decreased on-line capability. Faulty units could be easily removed for maintenance or routine servicing. Full time system operation would thereby be assured. In such a system organization separate machines could be employed in any desired manner and when one machine failure occurred, priority interrupts would take place (if necessary) and the entire program of the failed machine would be transferred to another computer by high-speed transfer of an entire memory unit or units. This operation would only require a few microseconds to execute under control of the executive routine.

(3) Such a system permits "memory stacking" by any one computer, simply by assigning several memory units to the same position within a computer time pulse. Data can then be read simultaneously into a group or stack of memory units just as if it were being read into a single unit. Thus, multiple copies of information could be produced at no increased cost in time and could be transferred to different machines as desired. This would increase the potential processing speed and enhance the flexibility of system programming.

(4) Another feature of such a system organization is the protection of one program and its operands from being altered or destroyed by another program. Because the memory units are addressed and reassigned to other computers only in their proper time pulses, privacy of information would be assured so that only one computing unit is working with the set of memory units associated with it in the same time pulse. However, while each memory unit would keep the

stored program and data within the confines of its sequestered subspace, the association of a memory unit with a computer unit would nevertheless not be a permanent one. The time divided communication bus provides the means by which a memory unit can be transferred from one computer to another so that an extremely high rate of transfer of data and/or program is obtained. The various computers in the system are thus tightly coupled for the best system performance.

6. Programming Considerations

Programming a multiple computer can only be accomplished when the logical operation and instruction repertoire of the system are known and will, in general, be quite different for various multiple computer organizations. However, in order to illustrate the potential power of multiple computer systems, a programming example will be presented for the hypothetical system described in the previous section. From the description given it is clear that the system will be highly efficient for problems involving frequent transfers of large amounts of data. Therefore, in this section, attention will be directed to a problem in which the net amount of information transferred between computers is still large but occurs in small units at a time (e.g., one word). In this case system efficiency is not obvious. The example chosen [5] will demonstrate that a modular memory structure can be quite efficient even for this type of memory transfer. It should not be inferred that this would be universally true but it will at least be shown that in cases such as that considered, high efficiency can be expected. It may be deduced that this would be true for a significantly large class of problems such that the hypothetical structure described and those based on similar communication schemes (e.g., a space divided or crossbar system) would be worthwhile.

In a multiple computer system composed of several general purpose processors, capable of performing independently of each other on various segments of the same problem, the processors must have previously obtained program instructions and data. In the hypothetical system, data or instructions (or both) are transferred in parallel between computers via high speed memory transfers. Hence, upon receipt of a memory unit, a computer must enter into a routine to determine what information is being transferred and what it should do with it. It is, therefore, appropriate for each computer to have two types of programs.

One program is a Reference Position Occupied program (abbreviated RPO) which is executed when a reference memory position of a computer is occupied by a memory that has just been transferred to that computer

267

from another computer. It should be pointed out that all memory transfers are always made to one predetermined memory position, i.e., the reference position to facilitate the control problem. In a program in which data transfer is frequent, this position should be cleared as quickly as possible so that the computer may be receptive to other incoming memories. Whenever the reference memory position of the computer is occupied, whatever the computer is doing will be interrupted so that the computer operating under the RPO program can absorb the incoming data and clear the reference memory position.

The other program is the main program which is that set of instructions that the computer follows when the reference memory position is not occupied. As long as this position is not occupied, the computer, following its main program, behaves like an ordinary computer.

The reason that there has to be an RPO program is that there are several possible routines that can be initiated when a memory has just been received in the reference position. Sometimes the incoming memory may be put into another position of the recipient computer. Other times it might be passed on to another computer or returned to the origin computer. The recipient computer will have to go through some operations before it can decide what is to be done with the memory—those operations are the substance of the RPO program.

The various computer units of the system will be referred to as $CU_1, \ldots,$ CU_n, and the memory positions of each CU will be referred to as P_0 (which is the reference position), $P_1, \ldots, P_{m-1}$.

6.1 One Method of Transferring Data

Several methods of effecting parallel data transfers between computers having a modular memory structure are conceivable. The basic instructions necessary for one method will be given here to illustrate more concretely the nature of a control program.

Suppose that CU_1 is transferring a word c to CU_2. In the hypothetical machine this transfer can only be effected by transferring the entire memory module containing c to CU_2. In some programs it would be convenient for CU_2 to keep this memory but it shall be assumed here that it is convenient for CU_2 to extract c and transfer the memory right back to CU_1 for that memory may have other words that are needed by CU_1. This kind of transfer would be useful when many pieces of data pass from CU_1 to CU_2 but not vice versa. Also, if memories were allowed to remain with CU_2 they would pile up.

At the point where CU_1 is to transfer c to CU_2, it must have the necessary transfer instruction in its main program. Let P_c be the position number of the memory containing c. For our purposes the transfer will be abbreviated

$$\text{TRANS } (\text{P}_c, \ 2)$$

which means transfer the memory in position P_c to CU_2. The main program can proceed after this instruction as if the transfer were complete.

But the RPO program for CU_2 must provide for transferring the memory containing c back to position P_c of CU_1 via P_0 of CU_1. If this memory is the only memory ever appearing in the reference position of CU_2 then the RPO program of CU_2 would simply consist of just one instruction that takes that memory, in reference position P_0, and puts it back into P_c. For the purposes of this section this instruction will be abbreviated as follows:

$$\text{POS } (\text{o}, \ \text{P}_c),$$

which means move the memory from position o to position P_c. On the other hand, if there are several memories that can appear in the reference position from time to time, then the RPO program would contain instructions for examining the serial number or some other identifying information of the memory that is there and the above instruction would be executed on condition that the examined serial number is the serial number of the memory containing c. Thus the RPO program for CU_2 will, on receiving this memory, do the following:

(1) read out c and read it into one of its other memories,
(2) make some sort of notation that it has received c, and
(3) execute the instruction $\text{TRANS } (\text{P}_c, \ 1)$

Again, if this memory is not the only memory that can pass through the reference position of a CU then the CU RPO program must begin by examining the serial number of the memory in the reference position.

The importance of step (2) above should be explained. In step (1) c is read into a storage position in one of the regular memories assigned to CU_2. Before c is read into that storage position some word or other is there, and there is no way that CU_2 can "know" that the word already there is not c. Hence the necessity for step (2). Step (2) might be accomplished, for example, by changing a *zero* to a *one* in some other place in storage. Or, in the event that c is one of a series of words transferred from CU_1 to CU_2, an index can be kept in some storage position that tells just how many such words have been sent. The storage position that is used to indicate that c has been sent will be called an *indicator*. Exactly how an indicator functions can be seen in terms of the sample problem presented below. The indicator is denoted by r_i and tells how much CU_i has computed.

Finally the main program of CU_2 when it uses c for the first time must check to see that c is really there by examining the indicator. If it is not, then it must either wait until c gets there and the indicator changes or do

269

something else. In this case an executor or scheduling program would direct subsequent action.

There is a necessity for having, for every transfer of information from one computer to another, an indicator which tells that this transfer has taken place. Since it has not been implied that there is any pre-established synchronization of the various computers, one computer could never be sure that a datum that it needs is available unless there is something to tell it that it is there. Thus the use of an indicator would be required in any routine in which data produced by one computer are transferred to another.

6.2 A Sample Problem

To illustrate data transfer from one computer to another, the following problem, which requires a tightly coordinated program, seems suitable. The problem involves computing an $(i \times j)$ matrix of numbers a_{ij}, where it is assumed: (1) that the initial values a_{i0} are given for all i and a_{0j} for all j, and (2) that there is a two-argument function F such that, for each i and j, each $\geqslant 1$,

$$a_{i,j} = \mathrm{F}(a_{i-1,j}, a_{i,j-1}), \quad \text{e.g., } a_{ij} = a_{i-1,j} + a_{i,j-1}$$

The computational assumption is that a subroutine for computing F exists and is available and requires an execution time that makes the time for transfer of data negligible. With this assumption, parallel computation seems to be called for.

To simplify the illustration, let it be assumed that a_{ij} are to be computed for $i \leqslant 8$ and $j \leqslant 100$. Then cu_1 can compute all the a_{1j}'s, cu_2 can compute all the a_{2j}'s, etc.

A copy of the subroutine for F must be loaded into a memory under the control of each cu. Assume for simplicity that eight computers are available. Then there are 8 copies of this subroutine in use. Let this subroutine in cu_1 be schematically described by the following formula:

$$\mathrm{F}(x_i, y_i) \to z_i$$

which means that the subroutine has working storage positions $[x_i]$, $[y_i]$, and $[z_i]$, operates on the contents of the first two of these storage positions, and puts the results of $\mathrm{F}(x_i, y_i)$ into $[z_i]$. Note that the different copies of the subroutine should have different notational descriptions differing in the index i on the variables.

Notational difference is necessary because "x_i" denotes not only a variable, but a storage position which differs for each i.

The programmer having decided to compute a_{11}, a_{12}, a_{13}, on cu_1, a_{21}, a_{22}, a_{23} on cu_2, etc., must write a series of instructions for each cu_i—a total of eight sets of instructions. In this particular computation the programs for the computers are quite uniform so only a flow chart for CU_i will be given, where i is any number between 2 and 7 inclusive. The programs for CU_1 and CU_8 must differ slightly, as discussed below.

A flow chart for the main program of CU_i is given in Fig. 2 and explained below. The RPO program is omitted, because it should be clear from the

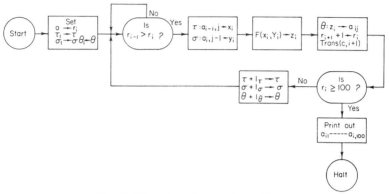

FIG. 2. Flow chart for sample problem.

previous discussion how it would be constructed, with the understanding that it is responsible (1) for placing $a_{i-1,j}$ and r_{i-1}, which both come from CU_{i-1}, into the correct storage positions in the memory permanently assigned to CU_i, and (2) for receiving back the memory that is the messenger to CU_{i+1}.

The memory in position P_c of CU_i must contain storage positions $[a_{ij}]$, for all j, and for the indicators $[r_i]$. This memory goes to CU_{i+1} and will read a_{ij} and r_i out into its own appropriate storage positions and pass that memory back to CU_i. Then the RPO program of CU_i will put it back into position P_c.

It may be convenient to have two copies each of r_i and the a_{ij}'s, one copy in a memory that remains with CU_i and the other in the memory that is the messenger to CU_{i+1}. In this way r_i and the a_{ij}'s will be available to CU_i even when the messenger memory is away, and perhaps CU_i's time will be saved, not having to wait until the messenger memory returns from CU_{i+1}.

Note that this flow chart has a main loop which CU_i goes through one hundred times. In going through it the kth time CU_i is calculating $a_{i,k}$ $(k < j)$. It does this calculation by using the subroutine $F(x_i, y_i) \rightarrow z_i$ but first it must read $a_{i-1,k}$ into x_i and $a_{i,k-1}$ into y_i; and after it comes out of the subroutine for F it must read z_i into $a_{i,j}$. r_i is the indicator that tells how much CU_i has computed. After $a_{i,k}$ has been computed, r_i will be equal to k. The importance of indicators was discussed above.

There does not have to be a storage position for j, since r_i serves as both

271

the indicator for the purposes of data transfer to cu_{i+1} and the clock in the main loop (i.e., the index that tells cu_i when to come out of the loop). τ, σ, and θ are variable instructions and must be modified each time before they can be executed. The method assumed here is a usual one for modification of instructions: each of these can be treated like a number, sent to the arithmetic unit, augmented by a certain constant; the result is a new instruction needed the next time around the loop. The three constants are designated as 1_τ, 1_σ, and 1_θ for τ, σ, and θ respectively. τ_1, σ_1 and θ_1, are τ, σ, θ as they must be originally.

The quantities cu_i uses but does not produce are $a_{i-1,j}$ (for each j from 1 to 100) and r_{i-1}. These quantities are obtained from cu_{i-1}. Before it goes into the loop for the jth time, cu_i must check that it really has $a_{i-1,j}$; that is, it must check that what it has in its storage position $[a_{i-1,j}]$ is what cu_{i-1} has computed. It makes this check by asking whether r_{i-1} is at least equal to j. The minor loop in the flow chart is there to make sure that cu_i has received $a_{i-1,j}$ before it goes through the main loop for the jth time. The function of the indicator r_{i-1} has been commented on above.

Note that the minor loop contains a decision box only. cu_i, when it gets here, asks whether r_{i-1} is greater than r_i. If it is not, then it simply asks the question again. This loop, which is as simple as a loop can be, could not have any useful function in an ordinary computer. For, in the case of an ordinary computer, if the answer to a question is "no" and if a negative answer causes it simply to ask the question again, then there would never produce an affirmative answer. Only in a multiple computer, where something can be changed by some other computer does this simplest type of loop have a use.

This flow chart will serve for all cu_i's except cu_1 and cu_8. The flow chart for cu_1 will differ in the absence of the minor loop. The program for cu_8 will differ in that there is no cu_9 to which to send a_{8j} and r_8.

The actual instructions are not presented here, first, because a suitable manner for transferring data has been given above, and, second, because a machine language for the hypothetical computer is not known.

6.3 A General Procedure for Programming a Multiple Computer

A general procedure for programming an ordinary computer is suggested in an article by Gorn [6]. Programming for a multiple computer involves new difficulties.

The first step in programming a computation on a multiple computer might involve constructing a schematic flow chart as if it were to be done on an ordinary computer. The next step would possibly be to decide how to make use of the number of available computers in performing the computation. In the case of the sample problem discussed above this decision was obvious, in fact, the problem was invented for the very purpose of illus-

272

trating as simply as possible, a tightly coordinated programming of the computers. The problem of deciding how to divide up a computation in an optimum manner is the scheduling problem which is discussed in the next section. The third step might be to make a schematic flow chart for each computer, and fourth make a detailed flow chart for each computer.

In both step 3 and step 4 the details of data transfer could be omitted. The final step consists in writing out the instructions, following the procedure suggested by Gorn. Here the exact arrangement of storage locations and the precise mode of data transfer from one computer to another must be decided upon.

In the past, automatic programming techniques have evolved after many years of human programming experience and usually little consideration was given to programming during the hardware development phase. For multiple computers, the success or failure of a hardware organization may rest solely upon the ease of programming and upon the completeness of a programming system. Consequently, programming and problem analysis should be an integral part of the total system development.

7. Multiple Computer Scheduling

Not until multiple computers are in use for some time and experience gained in their use will the exact nature of the scheduling problems be known. At present we can only speculate as to the scheduling needs for multiple computer systems, and extrapolate the ideas associated with the current conventional scheduling problems to anticipate some of the troubles and pitfalls which will face the user of a multiple computer system. While a solution to the problems of scheduling is not given here, the problems will be stated and in some instances point to a possible approach to a solution.

In the normal operation of a multiple computer configuration there will be several programs running concurrently. In order to maximize the operational efficiency it is necessary to have a plan for sequencing the programs and allocating computer components so as to obtain optimal processing of tasks. This plan is generally referred to as scheduling. There are two types of scheduling problems:

(1) The number of tasks to be performed have either deadlines and associated penalties or, equivalently, priorities which exceed the capacity of the computing facilities available.
(2) There are several subunits in the computer system, such as i/o and arithmetic units, each with a specialized capability and it is desired to minimize queuing on these equipments even though the various tasks use the subunits in different proportions.

Before a scheduling problem can be satisfactorily handled, a criterion for determining optimum operations must be established, preferably in mathematical-numerical terms. The main difficulties at the present stage of development of scheduling theory is the lack of a single definitive criterion. State-of-the-art theory assumes that the computing time for any task is known exactly. This actually cannot be so because there are many iterative subroutines which iterate to a tolerance and the number of iterations cannot be known in advance since they depend on the specific data. Furthermore, there are built-in instructions whose speed depends on the data as well as the command type. Consequently the computing time of a task can, at best, only be known on an average with perhaps an estimate of variance.

The second stumbling block to the scheduling problem is the fact that loss functions or penalties for failure to meet deadlines are generally unknown or at best only subjective estimates. Even then, these estimates are generally nonlinear. State-of-the-art theory cannot handle this kind of problem.

Lastly, the time taken to schedule and the time to reschedule when an interrupt occurs become appreciable with problems that occur in real life. This serves as a deterrent against scheduling since the loss of time may outweigh any theoretical advantages that may accrue.

Depending upon the system application it may be required to minimize either (1) the total cost of processing each task, including not only the cost of computation time and cost of set up time but also the penalties or "losses" for late delivery, or (2) the computer idle time, or (3) some combination of both.

The simplest type of scheduling occurs where several different tasks are independent of each other, and there is no advantage in using more than one computer on any of the tasks at any one time. The next level of scheduling arises when there are several tasks not independent of each other. Precedence relationships among various tasks must also be considered [7]. In some instances the program may contain within it a branch point, from which the task can go one of several ways. The system must be capable of responding rapidly and flexibly to external control signals whose arrival times cannot be predicted. The external signals may have their origin from high priority tasks or from removal of units for maintenance.

This section first summarizes progress made in deriving theorems and algorithms related to scheduling single computers and multiple computer systems under various constraints. Realizing that data used for scheduling are never accurate and that real-time situations have to be met in scheduling of tasks, the essence of an executive routine is introduced as a starting point for multiple computer scheduling.

274

7.1 Review of Scheduling Algorithms

The scheduling problem exists whenever several tasks are to be processed by either a single computer or a multiple computer installation. This section reviews the various techniques and algorithms developed so far in scheduling theory, at least as reported in the literature.

7.1.1 A Single Computer and Many Tasks

The simplest case is the one in which the tasks to be done have neither deadlines with loss functions, nor priorities associated with them. Then there will be no complication of any kind; simply run one task at a time until it is completed and proceed to the next.

If each task has a deadline of its own, the deadline may be either an absolute deadline in the sense that the task has no value at all if it is not completed by the deadline, or a relative deadline indicating that the task is by no means without any value if it passes its deadline. The first kind is designated as a priority task. The second kind implies that there is no loss of value of the task up to a certain point in time of completion; from that point on, the loss is a monotonic nondecreasing function of the time of completion, which may be linear or nonlinear, depending on the nature of the task involved.

Case (i): The first linear loss case is one in which no tasks can be finished before their respective deadlines. McNaughton [8] has proven the theorem: Let a_i be the amount of time required to finish task i and let p_i be the linear rate of loss function associated with the task i and define urgency $r_i = p_i/a_i$, then the total loss will be a minimum, i.e., the schedule will be optimal, if

(1) all tasks are scheduled without splitting in order of decreasing urgency r_i, and
(2) no time is unused before all tasks are finished.

Case (ii): A second linear loss case is where some of the tasks (say α, β, γ) have not yet passed their deadlines while others have. The solution to this case is to move the latest task α which finishes well before its deadline to a point later in time just before or bracketing its deadline (during γ) and advance all the intermediate tasks accordingly. A complete mathematical solution of this problem is given in a paper by Schild and Fredman [9].

Case (iii): If the loss function is nonlinear with respect to time after the deadline, the problem may be regarded as the same as that in Case (ii), except that urgency is now a variable depending on the average rate of increase of loss over the entire period from deadline to the time of completion of the task. Solution to this case consists of gradual elimination of more costly pairs, triplets, quadruplets, etc., until the least expensive solution is found. By pairs is meant the permutation of all tasks taken two at a time. Cross out the higher loss combination of each pair. Repeat the process by forming triplets with the surviving pairs and delete the two triplets with higher losses, and so forth. The process is described in another paper to be published by Schild and Fredman in Management Science.

Case (iv): The most nonlinear situation that can exist corresponds to the case where high priority tasks possess such high loss functions that they have to be done before lower priority jobs. The solution will be to arrange tasks in categories of decreasing priority and to compute the tasks in that order: within each priority category, either Case (i), (ii), or (iii) may apply; otherwise the tasks might just as well be handled on a first in, first out basis.

Case (v): Assume an interruption from "outside." If the interrupting task has higher priority than tasks in the system, then either store the status of the current task and proceed with the incoming task, or proceed with the new task without bothering about the status of the original task if this is warranted by the urgency of the interrupting task.

If the interrupting problem has lower priority than the tasks being processed, it gets routed to an input-output storage device or to an idle memory unit. An executive routine must be notified of the fact that a new task has come in and the task gets listed with other tasks with the same priority.

7.1.2 Many Computers and Many Tasks

There are five cases similar to those treated for a single computer. Regardless of the number of computers available, the number of tasks to be performed, and the nature of loss functions involved, there is no advantage in splitting tasks into segments unless the subtasks can be run concurrently in equalizing the workload of the computers.

Case (i): No deadline and no loss functions are associated with various tasks. The criterion for scheduling this case is to keep the system idle time down as much as possible.

Case (ii): If linear loss functions exist among tasks, it is necessary for optimal scheduling to arrange the tasks in order of decreasing urgency as for a single computer, predistribute the task assignment to the k computers in this order without splitting in such a way that the next task is assigned to the first computer that becomes free. Perform certain interchanges similar to those performed in the case of one computer, but using an algorithm due to Rubinoff [10] for swapping tasks among computers. This algorithm is based upon computation of total urgency $\sum_i r_{ij}$ of all remaining tasks on each computer $j = 1, 2, \ldots, k$ and swapping to advance larger total urgencies to an earlier computation time.

Case (iii): If the loss function is nonlinear, the scheduling problem is many times more complicated just as Case (iii) was more complicated than Case (ii) for one computer. More experience is needed for problems of this sort to determine whether this problem is worth handling or whether it is better to use priorities for assigning tasks.

Case (iv): This is the case in which hierarchies of priority are given for the tasks to be done. The approach is to arrange tasks in order of decreasing priorities and to process the highest priority tasks first, assigning them in any order (such as first come first served) as computers become available. Continue with tasks of lower priority in the same way. It is unlikely that equalizing the computation time among computers would be worth the trouble.

Case (v): When interrupts from the "outside" are received, treatment similar to the corresponding case for one computer is provided, except that the tasks are distributed among computers as in the previous cases discussed above.

7.1.3 Many Computers and One Large Task

The third type of scheduling arises when a large task can be partitioned into several subtasks to allow concurrent processing on several computers.

Case (i): If there are no deadlines, then advantage should be taken of the partitioning of tasks whenever some of the computers in the multiple computer system would otherwise be idle or working on tasks of lower priority.

Case (ii): In the case of linear loss functions after deadline, the algorithms of McNaughton, Schild and Fredman, and Rubinoff apply.

Case (iii): In the case of nonlinear loss functions, the problem becomes very complicated. If it should prove to be important in the future, algorithms will have to be developed for handling this case.

An example of an efficient algorithm for Case (i) with no deadlines is given by Codd [11]. Codd distinguishes between space-sharing and time-sharing in a computer system. Space-sharing refers to dividing the data processing equipments among the tasks in order to use the right amount of equipment at all times. The right amount can be shown to be close to the average amount of each type of data processing equipment needed to handle all the tasks on hand. For example, if the average amount of memory used by the tasks on hand is 100,000 words, the scheduling of tasks should aim at keeping approximately 100,000 words of memory in active use at all times even though 250,000 words are available. Codd has shown how to pack tasks onto a multiple computer system in a manner approaching optimal efficiency (minimum wasted facilities consistent with minimum queuing).

7.2 Environmental Factors

The environment in which a multiple computer system operates will affect the approaches to its scheduling. The scheduling methods described in the literature are applicable only to specialized types of environment. Three basic types of environments will be considered here, namely:

(a) the "Predetermined," which confronts the computer system with a given set of jobs on hand to be scheduled.

(b) the "Toll Booth," where the jobs to be scheduled are not known initially, but it is known about how many jobs will arrive and approximately when the jobs will arrive. Estimates of the probable nature and running times of the jobs are also available.

(c) the "Real Time," where jobs are scheduled as they come in, according to their priority.

Other environmental factors would include, for example, the physical surroundings and human elements associated with the computer system, for example, tape handling time for mounting a tape on a tape drive, and time needed for a machine operator to respond to on-line messages, etc.

7.2.1 Scheduling the Predetermined Environment

For a computing system the "predetermined" environment would have the form of a number of specific jobs to be run which are all able to be run immediately, e.g., an accounting or billing system. In some cases the jobs may have priorities attached or deadlines and associated losses if they are not done on time. These things, along with the characteristics of the computing system itself such as memory and input-output unit capacities and speeds, are what must be taken into account in scheduling the system. Most methods proposed in the literature for the predetermined environment are based on the techniques of the GANTT chart [12].

The GANTT chart consists of a graph with the available computing machines plotted along the vertical axis and time along the horizontal. Strips of paper are then made for each job whose lengths correspond to times needed on each machine, and width corresponds to the number of machines needed. These strips for all the jobs are then manipulated on the respective machines while preserving precedence relations until the least amount of time is wasted. If wasted time on one machine is more undesirable than that on another this could clearly also be considered in determining the best schedule. Many other factors could also be included but, of course, the more factors considered in the scheduling the fewer jobs one could handle by this method.

278

When the scheduling problem has the form of a linear equation for the quantity to be optimized and a system of linear inequalities for the restraint, the methods of linear programming may be applied. Unfortunately, methods based on the GANTT chart or linear programming can handle only a small number of tasks practically. The computation time and storage requirements for both methods increase rapidly, as the number of tasks to be scheduled increases.

7.2.2 Scheduling the "Toll Booth" Environment

The "toll booth" environment would exist, for example, in a company that rents out computer time where it is not known exactly what jobs are going to be submitted and consequently how many of what type of machines and personnel will be required. It is known, however, what time of the month it is, how busy its customers are, how many new customers it will probably get, etc. The size of the computing system at any particular time as well as how the jobs will be run on the system must be found from this type of information as well as possible.

One approach to scheduling the toll booth environment might be to assume that all the estimates of arrival time were exact and to use the techniques for scheduling the predetermined environment. Periodically, at preassigned time intervals, the scheduling information is updated and the tasks remaining are rescheduled in the light of "finer" data.

This approach would have the weaknesses and limitations of the methods used for the predetermined environment, and the need for rescheduling periodically can be very time consuming.

7.2.3 Scheduling the "Real Time" Environment

In the "real time" environment the system has jobs of varying priorities arriving in a relatively random manner. The system must be able to handle all the jobs efficiently enough so that a more than allowable backlog does not ever develop. The fact that the system may be idle most of the time is irrelevant. The whole object of the system is to be able to handle any condition that could arise. The airline's ticket reservation system is an example of a "real time" system. The fact that the spare time on such a system is often used for non-real-time jobs is not usually relevant either.

7.3 The Executive Routine and Program Segmentation

Multiprogram scheduling on multiple computers appears to require an executive routine. The executive routine is a program permanently stored in memory which has control over all programs and subprograms. The executive routine is brought into play whenever a computer unit finishes a task and a new task is to be assigned, or whenever an interrupt occurs. The tasks which the executive routine schedules need not be complete problems; rather, each problem may be partitioned into smaller segments. The segments (or tasks) should have the properties: (1) a task can be run independently of other tasks, once its input data are supplied; (2) a task is run on only one facility.

The size of segments is a critical point to consider. One desires to break a problem into pieces in order to make concurrent computation possible. But the smaller the segment size, the greater the number of segments. Since there has to be tabular entries in the scheduling tables of the executive routine for every task, very small segment size can make the tables for scheduling very large, and the time needed for scheduling very long. Also considering the time needed by the executive routine to load tasks, assign storage, and set up data links between program segments, it becomes apparent that segment size needs to be examined. Until further study is made on this topic and some experience gained, the segmentation will probably be made on the basis of the logical flow chart of the original problem. Each block of the flow chart will become a task or segment.

Some of the characteristics of an executive routine are:

(a) *Scheduling:* When a computing unit is finished performing a task and becomes available for work, the computing unit notifies the executive routine. The executive routine has tables which indicate what jobs are waiting to be done, the priority of the jobs, the running time, and due date for these jobs. Using the information in the table, the executive routine decides which job is to be done, and assigns the task to the available computer unit.

(b) *Program Loading:* Once the executive routine has assigned a task to an available Computer Unit, it has to place the programs and subprograms for the task into the memory of the available computer unit. Because a job will probably be composed of blocks of standard routines, which are on file in a bulk storage on-line to the computer system, the executive routine will have to allocate storage in the memory. If the memory of the computer is too small to accommodate all the routines needed for a job, the executive routine will have to load those which fit, and when the computer has performed these, the executive fills into the computer memory those routines which it still has to perform. The blocks of standard routines will have to be written so as to be usable in any memory position. This means that the programs stored in the bulk storage are not written in the basic machine language, but use relative addressing. At program loading time the executive routine has to perform address modification or relocation.

(c) *Input-Output Monitoring:* When a computer unit needs to perform input-output, it will notify the executive routine. The executive routine will assign and activate the peripheral devices and, after data transmission, test for accuracy, etc. If the transmission were error free, the executive routine will notify the computer unit that the transmission has occurred. If the transmission were not error free, the executive routine will try to retransmit or else correct the errors. If the executive routine cannot correct the i/o, the computer unit will be notified that transmission has occurred, but the data are suspected. By having the executive routine handle all input-output it is not necessary to have several copies of the "bookkeeping" programs needed for input-output.

(d) *Interrupts:* When an interruption occurs, the executive routine keeps track of what the interrupted computer is doing. When the job or task which caused the interruption is done, the executive routine restores the computer to the status it was in before the interruption and the computer can complete its assigned task.

(e) *System Checking:* The executive routine periodically checks various components of the system and if some components are failing, the executive routine reassigns the jobs to insure the successful operation of the high priority jobs.

7.4 The Executive Control Method and Simulation

Realizing that the data one uses to schedule is never very accurate, that a solution close to optimal is usually good enough and that "exact methods" are time consuming and can only handle a small number of tasks, a method has to be devised which will trade off accuracy for speed. The Executive Control method is formulated on the above premise.

The Executive Control method consists of an executive routine that decides by means of previously described techniques which part of which program is to be put on each facility as each task is completed. Clearly, if this is always done properly the scheduling problem is solved. However, which techniques to use and exactly how to use them, will have to be developed through analysis and much experience.

One way to determine which techniques to use is that of simulation. The input data to the simulator would be a list of jobs with all the necessary parameters, for example, running time of job, priority, partitioning, and so on. The simulator, using this data, assigns tasks to computer units and computes how long a job is on a unit(s) and the order of jobs. The output from the simulator would be a table or chart indicating the time each job started and finished. By changing the simulator rules and rerunning the input data through the simulator, a programmer could evaluate the effect that slight changes in the rules can have on producing a schedule, and select the most effective set of rules. When looking at several outputs from the simulator using the same inputs but different rules, a value judgment has to be made by the programmer which is dependent on the operational philosophy of the computer installation.

7.5 Features to be Incorporated into a Simulator and Executive Routine

In order to be realistic any simulation program should have secondary inputs to introduce disturbances into the system. The secondary input data would include, but not be limited to, at what time an interrupt occurs and the type of interruption, at what time a computer unit breaks down and for how long the unit is inoperable, and when human derived errors occur (e.g., poor estimate of running time given on primary input, operator has loaded wrong tape, etc.).

There will evolve several sets of decision rules each having some advantage over the others. From experience it may turn out that rule 1 is better than rule 2, p_1 part of the time and rule 2 is better than rule 1, $(1 - p_1)$ part of the time. The simulator should incorporate the ability to choose between alternate rules on a probabilistic basis. By having the simulator keep track of the alternatives tried and of the degree of success achieved using the selected rules, the probability of success associated with a set of rules can be kept updated. This feature of providing for a simulation program to test many sets of decision rules should, from a pragmatic viewpoint, yield an acceptable scheduling procedure.

The ability to select from several sets of decision rules, on a probabilistic basis, should also be built into the Executive Routine. By having the Executive Routine keep track of the rules it has tried and how effective they have been, the Executive Routine can "learn" and be "up to date" in its techniques even if the nature of the work load and interrupts change slightly. In order that the simulator be able to test a large variety of rules at the beginning, and that the Executive Routine be flexible in the event of a change in operating policy or nature of workload, the decision rules for the simulator and Executive Routine should be incorporated as subroutines which are easily inserted, modified, or deleted.

7.6 Summary

When the number of tasks to be scheduled is relatively small, and exact information about processing time is available, the techniques of linear programming (the simplex method, or the transportation method) can be used to obtain an optimum solution. Under the same conditions fitting techniques based on the GANTT chart can be used advantageously to realize usable schedules.

When the number of tasks is large the combinatorial nature of the problem renders the required computation of an exact solution prohibitive. For environments where the scheduling parameters are not known precisely the most practical approach to scheduling is the Executive Control method.

To determine which decision rules should be incorporated into an

Executive Routine, a Simulator should be constructed to gain experience and measure the effectiveness of the various possible sets of rules.

The technique of simulation can be used effectively in a predetermined environment where the number of tasks is large, without the use of an Executive Routine.

For maximum return the Simulator and Executive Routine should be adaptive, i.e., each should have the capability of measuring the effectiveness of the decision rules used, and alter themselves as needed.

Eventually multiple computers should be self scheduling so that one of the computers would be able to figure out a schedule for the computation and program automatically the other computers of the system. However, this will require extensive advances in the state-of-the-art of scheduling theory.

8. Existing Multiple Computer Systems

The gross operational features of four basically different multiple computer systems which are currently in operation will be described in this section. These are the PILOT, LARC, GAMMA 60, and RW-400 Systems.

The PILOT [13, 14] System reflects an organization in which gross computer functions such as input-output processing form the basis for the division of labor. The LARC System [15, 16, 17] realizes intercomputer communication via totally shared memory by application of a time multiplexing technique. Two identical general purpose computing units and a special purpose i/o processor are the main system modules. GAMMA 60 [18, 19, 20] is a system which is based on both of the above principles. In this system lesser computer functions such as arithmetic operations, comparisons, etc., are mechanized as physically separable devices all of which share one large memory via an asynchronously time-shared bus The RW-400 [21] is a crossbar organization wherein several identical general purpose machines and buffer storage units communicate with each other and with peripheral devices via the switching matrix.

Other multiple computer systems which have been built are variants of the above general schemes. Their internal operation and programming features may differ significantly from any of these four systems but this is incidental to the present topic. The B5000 [22, 23] and D825 [24] systems, for example, are essentially crossbar organizations and, as multiple computers, are functionally similar to the RW-400 although the specific methods of mechanization differ.

8.1 PILOT

The PILOT data processor has been designed and is operating at the National Bureau of Standards, and represents the first real attempt at the practical realization of a multiple computer system. The concept of satellite computers currently employed in large computing installations is an outgrowth of the techniques first developed in the PILOT machine. Some of the more recent sophisticated system designs, to be described later in this section, may appear to far exceed PILOT capabilities but it should be borne in mind that this merely represents expected later progress. For example, a recently announced system, the Control Data Corporation 3600 Systems [25], has the same basic organization as PILOT except that it provides for numerous modular units to enhance the total capacity of the system, i.e., it gives a growth potential feature to the PILOT organization which is to be described below.

The basic organization of PILOT provides for three different and independent processors each structured to optimize the performance of key machine functions, namely, computing (arithmetic operations), housekeeping, and input-output operations, with special emphasis on the latter task. The three basic units can operate together concurrently and cooperatively on the solution of one problem. Each unit possesses memory and may be independently programmed to perform its unique function. Intercomputer communication is provided for by control and data linkages such that messages can be exchanged between units. Since the specialized functions of the three PILOT computers are quite different, the form of the messages exchanged between them must also be different; hence special exchange and control instructions have been designed into the instruction repertoire of each unit. Messages which reflect the programmers solution approach must be written into the program but other messages are generated automatically when certain prescribed machine conditions occur. Such conditions would, of course, occur as a result of the program but the occurrence is recognized automatically and acted upon by the machine without any prior planning on the part of the programmer. There are generally four types of messages exchanged, namely,

(a) Data Transfers,
(b) Direct Commands,
(c) Status Inquiries,
(d) Requests for Action.

Data transfers refer to the routine transfer of information between the various storage units (internal and external) of the system and require no immediate action on the part of the recipient of the information. Direct commands on the other hand do require immediate action on the part of the recipient since the command information becomes part of the current program of the receiving computer and usually requires direct program intervention. Status inquiries are merely the sharing of branching information between system units. The computer inquiring of the status of another would modify its action according as a yes or no answer to its query were received. Action requests provide the mechanism by which a computer notifies a recipient that it needs additional information before it can proceed with its task. This differs from a direct command in that the sending computer does not dictate what the recipient should do next.

The structural organization of PILOT, as shown in Fig. 3, realizes highly versatile external control capabilities, compatible operation with a great

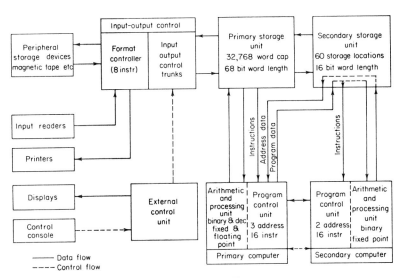

FIG. 3. PILOT block diagram.

variety of either local or remote peripheral devices and the ability to accept random external commands on an unscheduled basis. How the system achieves these features will be evident from the description of the functional operation of each major unit.

Before describing subsystem functions, it is important to consider the control problem. The control trunks, shown in Fig. 3, regulate data flow between the internal storage units and peripheral storage devices and between the various internal storage units themselves. The necessity of such an over-all control function is evidenced by the fact that all system processing units may have access to any internal or external storage unit which implies that some means of avoiding and/or resolving conflicts is mandatory. Otherwise nonconflicting and concurrent operation would be virtually impossible. The control trunks for input-output and intermemory data transfers are equipped with automatic interlocks which eliminate the need for programmer intervention, and insure that all operations take place in sequence even though they are capable of being executed at

285

completely unrelated rates. The automatic interlocks detect and resolve three basic types of conflicts:

(a) Time conflicts—several units simultaneously demanding access to the same storage unit.
(b) Space conflicts—several units attempting to utilize the same storage locations for logically inconsistent purposes.
(c) Command conflicts—program requests for busy peripheral devices.

The control feature built into PILOT by means of the control trunks permit the system to cope automatically with these possibilities and to establish unambiguously which machine has the right of way at points of program intersection.

The Primary Computer is a three address, general purpose, stored program computer which executes the main program of the system. It consists of a primary storage unit and a program control unit which interprets and controls the sequencing of the program instructions. The primary computer instruction repertoire contains seven arithmetic instructions, five branch instructions, two logical processing instructions and two control instructions. The two control instructions provide the control linkage to the other two computers of the system and as such effect data transfers between system storage units and regulate the secondary computer. The primary storage unit is a high-speed modular structure of 256 sixty-eight bit words per module and has a total storage capacity of up to 32,768 words (128 modules). The modules may have different random access times ranging from 1.0 to 32 μsec although the initial installation consists of only a few diode-capacitor memory modules [26] of 256 words each and 1.0 μsec access time.

A single word or the contents of an entire memory module may be transferred to one of the other computers. The use of relative addressing techniques permit program determination of addresses by the recipient computer. While the data transfer is in progress, the primary program control unit will automatically prevent addressing of the locations being transferred (or of the entire memory module) by other system computers. Alternatively, the primary storage capacity can be supplemented by the secondary storage facility since this memory is also directly addressable by the primary computer.

The primary computer instruction word format provides for three 16 bit codes which specify the addresses in memory of two operands (16 bits are required to address up to 65,536 words in memory) and usually the address in memory where the result of the operation (as specified by the operation code bits of the instruction word) should be placed. A unique feature is provided by four bits in the instruction word which specify any one of sixteen locations in the secondary memory where the address of the

286

next instruction will be found. These locations are referred to as base registers and provide a diversity of ways by which the program can branch. Since the base registers are located in the secondary memory, they may be manipulated by the secondary computer and so permit regulation or control of the primary computer by the secondary computer under program control. By this means, for example, the result of counting the number of iterations can be used to alter the next instruction of the primary program which in effect diverts the main program to a path conditioned by the secondary computer.

The Secondary Computer is a two address computer which serves as system housekeeper. All control-instruction processing and transforming are accomplished here. The main functions of the secondary computer involve the execution of specialized procedures such as automatic indexing, address modification, counting iterations, etc., for the primary computer. It also is composed of a processing and control unit and a secondary storage unit. The processing and control unit sequences and executes programs composed of sixteen basic instructions of which six are arithmetical, four are branching, one logical processing and five control. The five control instructions constitute the control linkage with the primary computer and involve checking and regulating the primary, replacing primary instructions, and accepting inputs from the primary computer.

Of the two addresses in the secondary computer instruction word format, one always indicates the location of an operand while the second specifies the location of a second operand or the address of the next secondary computer instruction. The secondary computer may effect a data transfer from the primary computer to the secondary storage or from the primary storage unit to the primary control unit. Thus the secondary computer can examine each instruction of the primary program and, depending on the secondary program, cause any particular instruction to be executed or not. If it is not executed, the secondary computer will replace that instruction with a new instruction (whose address would be in the appropriate base register) which is specified by the secondary program.

The secondary storage unit is a diode-capacitor memory having a capacity of sixty 16-bit words with a random access time of 1.0 μsec. Both primary and secondary computers have access to this memory. Sixteen of these locations are the base registers referred to above. Actually, the contents of the base register selected by the primary computer are added automatically to the address specified in the primary computer instruction word. Hence the base registers are actually index registers to the primary computer whose contents can be modified by a completely independent program.

The Format Controller is the third independently programmed processor which is specifically designed for inspecting, editing, interpreting, and modifying the data that enters or leaves the system. It also consists of a processing and control unit and a storage unit. The function of the processing and control unit is to control the transfer of data, under primary computer control, between the internal system and the peripheral devices. It also performs all code and format conversions on words and characters from the peripheral devices in addition to the operations of extraction and shifting. With these capabilities, a wide variety of noncompatible peripheral devices can be employed with the system.

Different programs for the Format Controller are stored on a variety of removable plug boards which are selected under the control of the primary computer. These are the storage unit of the Format Controller. Up to four such plug boards can be made available on-line each containing up to 64 words of 16 bits each at a random access time of 1.0 μsec. Eight basic instructions are available to construct the plug board programs of which three are for branching, three for processing and two for control. The branching instructions are used to compare input data against the contents of a fixed storage register in the Format Controller and depending on the outcome of the comparison branching occurs to appropriate programs. The processing instructions regulate the transfer of characters from the input-output devices and control the input-output buffers. The control instructions set and reset the input-output control logic. The Format Controller accepts initial commands from the Primary Computer which effect execution of one of the plug board stored programs. For example, the primary computer will select the plug board on which a program for word length conversion is located in order to convert characters from a peripheral device to a word which is compatible with the internal word length of the machine.

The External Control Unit provides a facility for PILOT to communicate with the outside world. This unit is a transfer channel between a control console and displays and the internal machine and is different from other peripheral devices in that various switch settings (set by local or remote means) on the console insert coded action signals into the machine. This unit decodes the switch settings to produce specific computer control signals which are delivered to the computer by the external control unit when it recognizes that specified transfer conditions exist. By this means, external instructions from the console may effect an interrupt from current machine proceedings and cause branching to occur from the scheduled program to perform the control operations requested by the console. The control signals usually indicate the kind of console operation to be performed, the condition under which it should be accepted and the storage locations involved.

8.2 LARC

The Remington Rand LARC (Livermore Atomic Research Computer) computer system is closely analogous to the hypothetical system described in Section 5, primarily in the method of computing unit to memory communications but also in the method of handling input-output devices.

The basic modules of a fully expanded LARC System are: two main computing units (CU), up to thirty-nine independently addressable banks of high-speed core memory and an input-output processor which controls a basic peripheral device complement of up to forty magnetic tape stations and twenty-four magnetic drum storage units. The interconnection of these units is shown in the fully expanded block diagram of Fig. 4.

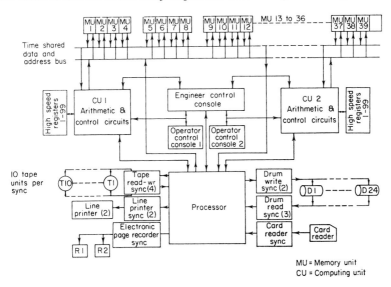

FIG. 4. LARC system block diagram.

A LARC computing unit is a single address decimal machine but can be made to simulate a three address machine by utilizing two of its 99 independent high-speed registers (1 Mc repetition rate). These registers are used as accumulators or index registers and are logically interposed between the memory units and the arithmetic section of the CU. The instruction repertoire consists of 75 instructions, many of which are variants of a few basic types or are small frequently used subroutines which have been mechanized to speed up machine operation. This technique also reduces programming time since fewer instructions are used than would otherwise be required. There are no direct input-output instructions as such; rather a set of variable pseudo-orders are employed as summary commands to the Processor Unit via the totally shared memory. Thus a program need only provide for the summary orders to be placed in storage, alert the Processor to their presence, and finally, provide for checking their completion by the Processor after some period of time. Additionally, the Processor itself may be programmed, at the programmer's option, to generate and issue the summary orders, thereby completely relieving the CU program of any concern for input-output operations. It is a programmer responsibility to insure that the CU be informed of the memory locations where input information has been stored and to which output information should be transferred.

A CU has the capability to address uniquely any high-speed memory location plus its 99 fast registers. Each module of magnetic core storage has a capacity of 2500 words of 12 decimal digits each—giving a total core storage capacity of 97,500 words for 39 modules. In addition to serving as the primary storage medium of the system, a secondary usage, made possible by the memory sharing feature, is buffer storage for magnetic drums and other peripheral devices. Thus, for example, information could be assembled from numerous peripheral devices in a memory unit and transferred in toto to another peripheral storage device without any intervention by a main CU.

The main feature of LARC and that which accounts for its high-speed capabilities without an attendant cost increase, is the time divided memory bus. The mode of time division used is based on segmenting a 4 μsec memory cycle time into 8 equal time intervals, called time slots, of 0.5 μsec each. Each time slot is allocated to a system unit as follows. During time slot 1 the Processor or Processor Computer has access to the bus and operands or instructions are transferred for input-output programs. During time slot 2, CU-1 may obtain instructions while CU-2 utilizes time slot 3 for obtaining operands. The Dispatcher section of the Processor utilizes time slot 4 and time slot 5 is not used. Time slots 6 and 7 reverse the sequence of slots 2 and 3 while time slot 8 provides the Processor an additional access. Actually, a complete read-regenerate or clear-write operation of the memory takes 8 μsec but the reading and clearing operations may be overlapped with the core selection and regenerate functions respectively, so that the effective cycle time is 4 μsec. Two slot times are required for a given unit to receive or transmit information from or to the memory since the memory must first be addressed (during the first time slot) and subsequently (during the second time slot) operands or instructions are received or transmitted. Consequently, it would appear as if the memory cycle time, as seen by a CU, were 8 μsec. However, as a consequence of the memory overlapping feature it is possible for a computing unit to process several instructions simultaneously and to perform different phases of these instructions in parallel. Thus while one instruction is being executed the operand of another instruction can be transferred

290

to/from memory while the operand address of yet another instruction can be modified. Although one instruction actually takes longer than 4 μsec to execute, the effective execution rate of a series of such instruction approaches 4 μsec. Thus, the time multiplexing feature increases rather than decreases the speed of the system by providing for concurrency of operations.

Normally the system is programmed to avoid simultaneous reference to the same memory unit by more than one CU or by the Processor but complete protection cannot be had by programming alone; hence some hardware protection is also provided. This is in the form of interlocking logic in each memory unit so that, once addressed, the memory is unavailable for further use for at least the duration of the current memory cycle. Furthermore, it would be possible for one CU, for example, to continually tie up one or more memory units unless some priority determination scheme were employed. Logic for this purpose is built into each memory module and gives equal priority to each CU but higher priority to the Dispatcher such that when the Dispatcher addresses a busy memory unit it will be assured of access no longer than one memory cycle time later and the CU and Processor Computer will be locked out from that memory unit until the Dispatcher has been serviced.

The Processor Unit has three main subdivisions of control, viz., (a) the Central Processor or Processor Computer; (b) the Synchronizers; (c) the Dispatcher.

(a) The Central Processor (CP) is a two address, general purpose, stored program machine which has its own independent instruction repertoire for executing its own programs. It is, however, much less elaborate than the main CU, its primary use being to serve as I/O editor and interpreter and to execute the details of the CU generated I/O summary orders or to perform this function itself. The CP is not required to monitor and control every step of I/O operations as this is more conveniently delegated to the synchronizer. The CP possesses the means for interrupting either of the CU and force a transfer of control to a CP routine. Upon completion of such a routine, control is restored automatically to the CU program at the point where it was interrupted. The existence of a CP greatly alleviates the CU of the burden of directing I/O operations and obviates the need for mechanizing any peripheral device instructions in a CU.

(b) A Synchronizer, under the direction of the CP, controls the serial information flow between the peripheral device it services and any one of four word length buffers contained in it, checks for errors, and performs format and code conversion functions. Although a different Synchronizer is required for each type of on-line peripheral equipment, one Synchronizer is capable of servicing several identical I/O devices.

The CP directs the Synchronizer to process a small fraction of the total summary orders which it will do without further intervention by the cp. Also, while it is processing this, the cp can alert the Synchronizer to process the next block and so on.

(c) The Dispatcher merely controls the transfer of data from the synchronizer buffers to the main memory units. When a synchronizer completes the transfer of a word from its i/o device it signals the Dispatcher to effect the data transfer, during its time slot, to a memory location specified by the cp program.

The maximum on-line peripheral equipment complement of a fully expanded LARC System includes 24 Magnetic Drum Units, 40 Magnetic Tape Units, Two Electronic Page Recorders, Two High-Speed Printers, a High-Speed Card Reader, an Operator Console per cu and a System Control (Engineer) Console. Figure 4 shows the number of each device which may be serviced by one Synchronizer.

Each magnetic drum is a self contained unit capable of storing 250,000 words of 12 decimal digits. Under cp program control, any drum can be connected to any drum synchronizer and with a full complement of synchronizers three reading and two writing operations can be executed concurrently. By operating two drums alternately with one synchronizer a data transfer rate of 330,000 decimal digits per second can be achieved.

The four tape synchronizers can operate in parallel with each other as well as in parallel with any other synchronizer and while a reading or writing operation is being executed on one tape unit, the remaining tapes connected to that synchronizer may by rewound. Interchangeability of tape units and synchronizers is effected manually by changing plug boards.

The Electronic Page Recorder displays information on the face of a cathode ray tube which is recorded by a high-speed, self developing, program controlled camera. It can operate at an average rate per film frame of approximately 15,000 numeric or alpha numeric characters per second.

The High-Speed Printer is an electromechanical device capable of printing at 600 lines per minute with 120 characters per line. The High-Speed Card Reader can process 450 eighty-column cards per minute.

8.3 GAMMA 60

The GAMMA 60 multiple computer system is designed and manufactured by Compagnie des Machines Bull, Paris, France. The gross system organization of GAMMA 60, shown functionally in Fig. 5, consists of a variable number of independent and different processors which share common two-way distribution busses. The number and type of processors which would be so interconnected is a function of the particular application. Control over bus access is exercised by a Central Control Unit on a non-sequential time basis, i.e., each request for data and/or instruction transfer from any processor is examined by the control unit and access is granted

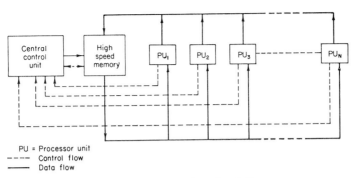

PU = Processor unit
---- Control flow
—— Data flow

FIG. 5. GAMMA 60 gross functional diagram.

on a predetermined priority basis. All permissible data transfers between the various processor units are via the high-speed memory unit which stores both program instructions and data. The contents of the memory are available to all processors and as such represents one possible realization of the "blackboard memory" referred to in Section 3. The processors themselves do not possess buffers (except to match their speed with that of the high-speed memory and in GAMMA 60 these are called Liaison Registers) but simply registers in which information is stored during operation. The high-speed memory acts as the buffer element between the different processors. Each processor unit is capable of performing one type of specialized operation (with variations) and so must be functionally different but, of necessity, certain common functions must be provided such as interface control logic with the common central control unit. Each processor must also contain a processing section which contains all the information handling logic to execute its specific task.

A more detailed explanation of how the GAMMA 60 system realizes these gross system characteristics is described below with the aid of the more detailed block diagram of Fig. 6.

The Central Control Unit is seen to be composed of two major subunits, the Transfer Distributor (TD) and the Program Distributor (PD), while the main busses are termed the data collecting and data distributing busses. Since each processor is autonomous, some means of requesting data and instructions must be provided for each processor. These must be separate communication links since each processor can make requests at random which precludes the use of time-sharing that communication medium. Data transfer requests are directed to a priority determining unit of the TD which examines the request and, using a pre-established priority chain (or queue table), determines which processor of the many which have made requests would benefit most from the next allowable data transfer. Once this determination is made, the TD will allocate the

293

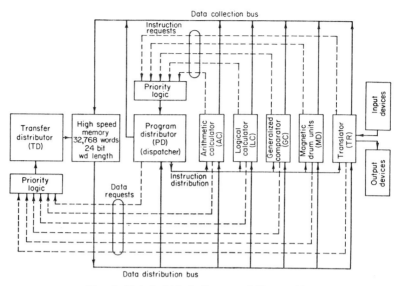

FIG. 6. Detailed block diagram of GAMMA 60.

bus to the selected processor and notify the high-speed memory of this decision. Selection logic in the high-speed memory will in turn select, according to the program, the address to which information will be transferred or from which it will be extracted. Thus, the major functions of the TD are: to receive requests for data transfers to or from the high-speed memory, to select that request (of many) which will effect the fastest processing time, and to allocate the data busses to the selected unit. The TD by its predetermined priority rules resolves the problem of conflicting requests. An example of· how such priority determination reduces total processing time follows. With reference to Fig. 6, suppose the arithmetic calculator (AC) and the magnetic drum (MD) have both requested a data transfer. In the TD, the MD has been given the higher priority of the two devices. If this were not the case and its request were denied in favor of the AC then the MD transfer would have to be delayed a full drum revolution or about 20 msec (average drum access time). On the other hand if the MD request were honored immediately, the AC data transfer need only wait for the next memory cycle or about 10 μsec (high-speed memory random access time). This large reduction of waiting time is possible because the data in the AC waiting to be transferred can be held in its data register and extracted immediately upon command whereas for the MD one must wait for the desired data to appear under the drum reading heads before it can be transferred.

The Program Distributor of the Central Control Unit receives instruction requests from the processing units and functions in the same manner for instructions as the TD does for data transfer requests. It is possible for several instruction requests to be received simultaneously (via separate lines from the processors) and to resolve conflicts by servicing that request with the highest priority. The essential PD functions are: to obtain from high-speed memory the instruction requested by the selected processor, to interpret this in part and transfer the instruction to the processor control unit via the instruction distribution bus. It is important to note that the PD itself must direct all of its memory access requests to the TD which will examine the priority of the PD request relative to processor requests already in the queue. This would also include PD generated requests for memory access for address modification purposes and so on. If it should happen that both an instruction request and a data transfer request occur from the same type of processor, the data transfer will have the higher priority. Thus, a tape unit request for data will be serviced before that of a PD request for an instruction to transfer data from another tape unit. If conflicting requests from different processor types are encountered, the instruction request of the PD for one processor could, in some cases, be honored prior to the data transfer request of another processor as in the case when the PD is providing instructions to a peripheral device, and the AC, for example, is requesting a data transfer. This would inhibit halting the peripheral device for lack of an instruction.

GAMMA 60 provides for five types of processors in addition to a variety of peripheral devices as shown in Fig. 6.

(a) The Arithmetic Calculator (AC) executes the usual arithmetical computations on numeric or alphanumeric characters. All calculations are performed in the decimal system on a word length of 24 bits. Numbers in the system are represented in the binary coded decimal (BCD) format, i.e., four binary bits are required to express one decimal digit. Alphanumeric characters require 6 binary bits to represent the twenty-six letters, ten numerals and miscellaneous punctuation marks. Thus one machine word may represent six decimal digits or four alphanumeric characters. Numbers processed in the AC require two machine words (i.e., 48 binary bits) which permits arithmetic operations on twelve decimal digits in fixed point arithmetic or on ten decimal digits in floating (programmed) point arithmetic, both in BCD format. In floating point arithmetic, two four-bit characters are used to express the exponent of 10 for decimal point location.

(b) The Logical Processor (LP) performs arithmetic operations on strictly binary operands as well as carrying out all logical operations, e.g., logical OR, logical AND etc.

295

(c) The Generalized Comparator (GC) can execute either one- or two-way comparisons on variable length alphanumeric operands. The one-way mode merely compares two operands and stops automatically when a difference is detected while the two-way mode compares a variable length operand x with two other operands A and B and determines the magnitude of x with respect to A and B.

(d) The Translator (TR) performs all code and format conversions of information from peripheral devices into internal GAMMA 60 format and vice versa.

(e) The Magnetic Drum (MD) provides additional medium speed storage for programs and operands. One or several magnetic drum units may be used, each having the following characteristics: A capacity of 25,600 words and an average access time of 10 msec. Data transfers to and from the drum are variable in length (increments of one word) and the read or write time for one word in 100 μsec (the time to extract or enter data from/to the drum via the reading or writing heads). The drum is word addressable and transfers between drum and high-speed memory are one word at a time.

The initial instructions which indicate what a processor must do and the addresses of the operands on which it must operate originate in the Central Control Unit (TD and PD). Since each processor is mechanized to perform a unique function, once an instruction is given to it and the operands are available, it will execute its operation without further programming. Hence, specific instructions do not exist for each processor as such but rather a set of generic instructions are used to control the over-all operation of the total system. These are called canonical instructions of which there are four types.

(a) Cut (C) Instructions

These instructions designate a processor and initiate its operation by loading its Instruction Address Register (IAR) with the address of the first instruction of the program it is to execute. Note that if a previously active processor had been interrupted then a cut instruction is required to specify the instruction to be executed immediately following the cut.

(b) Address (A) Instructions

Every address instruction designates one of a processor's operands by loading its Current Address Register (CAR) with the address of the operand.

(c) Directive (D) Instructions

Directive instructions inform the processor what operation (within its mechanized repertoire) is to be performed on the operand contained in its CAR. Receipt of this type of instruction is sufficient for the processor to initiate its operation.

(d) Branch (B) Instructions

Each processor contains an Actual Instruction Address Register (AIAR) which is loaded with the contents of IAR by a command from the PD. A B instruction modifies the contents of AIAR to an address designated by the B instruction itself and so effects a branch or jump condition to a new program.

Generally, a set or sequence of these canonical instructions is necessary to initiate a processor function. Such a set is called a complete instruction and must always be terminated by a D instruction. Each canonical instruction requires one full machine word. The canonical instructions in themselves do not specify to which processor they refer. This is an additional function of the Program Distributor. A set of complete instructions for a given processor constitute an elementary program sequence and a subroutine (in the usual sense) or complete program is an orderly collection of such elementary sequences.

High-Speed Memory Characteristics. The high-speed memory is a magnetic core memory device capable of storing 32,768 words of 24 bits each at a random access time of 10 μsec. The memory is addressable by a 15 bit binary code in the instruction word. Although GAMMA 60 is designed to handle variable length operands, one word must be read in or out for each memory access.

Peripheral Device Complement

(a) Three Card readers at 300 cards per minute.
(b) Any number of paper tape readers can be used. They can read 5 and 8 channel codes at a speed of 200 characters per second.
(c) Magnetic Tape Units with a total capacity of 1,600,000 words in blocks of 128 words can be used at a speed of 22,500 numeric or 15,000 alphanumeric characters per second (3750 words per second). Two direction reading and unidirection writing is possible. Each tape unit must be limited to 12,500 data blocks.
(d) One 300 line per minute printer.

8.4 RW-400

The RW-400 multiple computer system is a product of the Ramo-Wooldridge Corporation and is more widely advertised as a Polymorphic Data System. It is basically a crossbar connected system of the general type discussed in the introduction to Section 5. By virtue of its modular construction, it possesses a large majority of the features deemed necessary to satisfy the needs of the information systems outlined in the Introduction to this paper.

The heart of the system is the Central Exchange (cx) unit which is a modular, high-speed, electronic switch [27] utilizing transfluxors [28] as the switching element.

Two basic module types are interconnected via the cx, namely, general purpose computer modules (cm) and buffer modules (bm). Interconnections between these units and a large variety of peripheral devices completes the essential properties of RW-400. The number of such units which can be interconnected is expandable, by design modifications, due to the quasimodular nature of the electronic crossbar switch; a basic switching unit can provide for 16 computers and buffers to be connected to up to 64 peripheral input-output equipments. However, either a cm or bm must *always* be one of the modules of an interconnected pair. Therefore, one magnetic tape unit could not be connected directly to another magnetic tape unit, for example, but rather each must be connected to an intermediate bm. The connection control may be initiated, on a request basis, by either cm or bm provided one or the other of these (or both) is directly involved in the connection. One exception exists when any one of the cm is manually designated to be the master computer and in this case it will be permissible for that computer to effect a connection between two other modules not including itself. The connection requests are under program control but the option to accept or reject such a request resides with the recipient module. The responsibility for resolving conflicting crossbar requests and connection priorities belongs to the cx itself. If the alert signal is accepted, the current proceedings of the recipient module will be interrupted automatically at some convenient point in its program. If the request is rejected, a busy signal is generated by the cx and is sensed by the requesting module. Special subroutines, which have been stored in the modules memory, are entered to determine what course of action to follow, if any. Non-honored connection requests to busy or otherwise unavailable modules are not stored automatically by the cx, hence the requestor must periodically and at convenient points in its program continue repeating the service request until it is honored or rejected as not being currently possible. When a connection is established the information transfer is, as noted above, bit parallel but word serial (actually only half-words are transferred). Thus, at any instant of time, any cm connected to bm or i/o equipments behaves as any ordinary single computer. One obvious advantage of this organization is that a computer can request a bm to retrieve information from a slower peripheral device in anticipation of its actual need. When the information is needed by the processor it will be transferred serially directly from the bm memory to the cm storage at one-half the memory access speed. In this mode, the bm are truly acting as buffers, but as will be seen later, they have more powerful capabilities.

298

An over-all block diagram of the RW-400 is shown in Fig. 7. The grid-like matrix represents one plane of the central exchange crossbar switch. Actually the crossbar switch is many levels deep, at least one plane per bit to provide for bit parallel data transfer, in addition to other planes

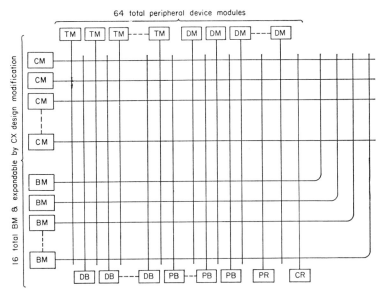

FIG. 7. RW-400 system block diagram.

for control purposes. The CX matrix provides for multiple path routing so that system modules can communicate without delay or interference due to malfunction of a crosspoint connection, for example. In this case one or more available buffer modules would be employed as intermediate stores in the data transfer. The average switch connection time is of the order of one instruction execution time, or about 65 μsec. This time expenditure includes not only the physical response time of the transfluxor gating elements but the time required for the switch logic to test for busy conditions and to examine connection validity. The latter task is realized by an Interrogation Module which is essentially another plane of the switch in which nonpermissible switch connections are stored and inhibits such connections if and when requested. A switch look-up table (in switch memory) is provided so that symbolic switch addressing techniques may be employed by the programmers. This avoids the necessity of having the address in the switching command correspond to the physical location on the switch matrix. The look-up table is another function of the Interrogation Module.

A computer module is a general purpose, two address digital machine completely capable of autonomous operation. It has an internal random

299

access memory of 1024 words capacity. The word length is 26 data bits plus 2 parity bits. Information transfer between modules is parallel by half-words. The basic instruction repertoire of a CM provides for 39 instructions of which 24 are the usual arithmetic type, 10 program control (jump, shift, compare, etc.), and 5 for input-output operations. Several options are possible within these classes to provide for over 300 different operations. The five external instructions are those required for intermodular communication and control. Each instruction is multipurpose and so is functionally equivalent to several conventional I/O instructions. It should be noted that all of the instructions to be executed by the CM must be stored within the confines of its own memory and cannot be obtained directly from any buffer storage locations. A CM has access to any or all BM memories for the purpose of either obtaining peripheral device data or for utilizing the buffer memory as an adjunct to its own internal memory capacity. This is an important aspect of buffer usage although this is not its primary purpose. This function is more aptly served by a number of Magnetic Drum Modules (DM) each of which can provide a storage capacity of 8192 words. Conventional usage of a DM is as an intermediate storage device to minimize magnetic tape handling time. The CM effects data transfers from the buffer storage by an indirect addressing technique wherein if the address field of a CM instruction word contains the number 1023 (the highest internal memory location of a CM) then data is to be obtained from a buffer read register. Since the CM is a two address machine, an extended addressing feature is possible. In this instance the second address will be specified by the contents of the buffer read register incremented by one. After each instruction is executed the read register is incremented automatically by the appropriate amount.

A Buffer Module can initiate and control peripheral equipments either by instructions from a CM or from its own internally stored program. In effect, a BM is a small, special purpose, stored program machine rather than a strictly passive storage device. Since it is capable of autonomous operation and has control capability, a BM can carry out a large majority of peripheral device operations thereby relieving the CM of performing these routine operations. The CM is therefore allowed to execute more efficiently those tasks for which it is best suited, namely those of an arithmetic or computational nature. In this sense, a BM is akin to a satellite computer. A BM is actually composed of two logically independent units, say A and B, each having 1024 words of random access high-speed storage in addition to logic and internal registers for executing its own internally stored programs. The two back-to-back units are interconnected by a switching mechanism which permits the two units to alternate functions. Thus, for example, information can be read from a magnetic tape into unit A while unit B simultaneously transfers a previously obtained word to a CM. Then unit A transfers a word to a CM while unit B assembles a word from the tape and so on. This alternating mode of operation lends itself to concurrent reading and writing from peripheral devices or computers as required and so accounts in part for the high degree of parallelism within a polymorphic structure.

The peripheral equipment complement of the RW-400 includes Magnetic Tape Modules (TM), a Tape Adaptor Module (TA), a Peripheral Buffer Module (PB), a Display Buffer Module (DB), a Printer Module (PR), and a Punched Card Reading Module (CR).

Several TM can be utilized simultaneously in the RW-400 via the CX switch. The reading/writing rate is 15,000 words/sec. Data may be recorded in variable length blocks up to a maximum of 1024 words per block, i.e., the size of a BM or CM memory. The Tape Adaptor operates in conjunction with a TM and is an independent unit to convert RW-400 format to IBM 704 and 709 formats.

The PB is actually a magnetic drum storage device wherein fixed segments of the drum are allocated as buffers to very slow speed external devices such as Flexowriters, Plotters, Punched Paper Tape Handlers, Teletype lines, and Keyboard Operated Equipment. Each PB can accommodate 4 external devices and provides to each device 8 buffers of 64 words length for both input and output functions.

A DB is a storage device for cathode ray tube and numerical displays etc., in a Display Console. It also is a drum storage device in which bands have been allocated to each display tube.

The PR is a 160 column, 900 line per minute printer which utilizes a 6 bit alphanumeric format—4 characters to a computer word.

The CR is capable of reading 80 column punched cards at 2500 cards per minute and is connected into the CX via a PB since it is a relatively slow-speed device.

9. Conclusions

The multiple computer art is presently in the adolescent stage and considerable effort must yet be expended on the theory and organization of these systems. This should be coupled with an intensive analysis of many current and anticipated applications to serve as a guide for bringing to fruition the potential advantages of truly concurrent processing along with ultrareliability, expandability, and economy. Programming systems and techniques, particularly executive control programs, will require new thinking and should be an integral part of the total system development. The efficient use of any multiple computer installation will be critically dependent upon scheduling routines which far exceed what state of the art theory has been able to produce. Consequently, scheduling theory must be broadened considerably and should also be closely coordinated with both hardware and programming efforts.

Several topological approaches to the mechanization of multiple computers have been proposed, but subject to the above considerations, a modular system of computers, storage elements and peripheral devices which provides for the transfer of information within the system at memory access speeds, emerges as the most promising organization. Time-divided and space-divided systems utilizing general purpose machines with special control features have been successfully mechanized but the prospects of the time-divided method toward realizing the ultimate advantages of a multiple computer currently exceed those of the space-divided system.

ACKNOWLEDGMENTS

The author gratefully acknowledges the work of many associates from whose unpublished reports information has been freely extracted and presented in this paper. In particular, credit is extended to Dr. Oliver Aberth and Mr. Herbert Nishino for their early contributions to the basic concepts of the system described in Section 5, to Dr. Robert McNaughton for his contribution to the section on programming and to Dr. Morris Rubinoff for his valuable suggestions on this topic while serving as consultant to the Radio Corporation of America.

The author also wishes to thank the management of the Systems Engineering, Evaluation and Research division of the Radio Corporation of America for permission to publish this paper.

REFERENCES

1. Theory of Switching Circuits, *6th Quarterly Progress Report*, Moore School of Electrical Engineering, Univ. of Pennsylvania, Philadelphia, Pennsylvania, December 15, 1957.
2. Bauer, W. F., Why Multi-Computers?, *Datamation* **6**, pp. 51–55, September, 1962.
3. Gotlieb, C. C., Programming a Duplex Computer System, *Communications of the ACM* **4**, pp 507–513, November, 1961.
4. Strachey, C., Time Sharing in Large Fast Computers, *Proc. of International Congress on Information Processing*, UNESCO, Paris, pp. 336–341, June, 1959.
5. McNaughton, R., Internal RCA Report.
6. Gorn, S., Standardized Programming and Universal Coding, *Journal of ACM* **4**, pp. 254–273, 1957.
7. Prosser, R. T., Application of Boolean Matrices to the Analysis of Flow Diagrams *Proc. of Eastern Joint Computer Conference*, Boston, 1959, pp. 133–137.
8. McNaughton, R. F., Scheduling with Deadlines and Loss Function, *Management Science* **6**, pp. 1–12, October, 1959.
9. Schild, A., and Fredman, I. J., On Scheduling Tasks with Associated Linear Loss Functions, *Management Science* **7**, pp. 280–285, April, 1961.
10. Rubinoff, M., Private Communication.

11. Codd, E. F., Multiprogram Scheduling of Electronic Computers, Tech. Report No. 69, Management Sciences Research Project, Univ. of California, Los Angeles, California, February, 1961.
12. Churchman, Ackoff and Arnoff, *Introduction to Operations Research*, Wiley, New York, 1957.
13. Leiner, A. L., Notz, W. A., Smith, J. L., and Weinberger, A., PILOT—A New Multiple Computer System, *Journal of ACM 6*, pp. 313–335, July, 1959.
14. Leiner, A. L., Notz, W. A., Smith, J. L., and Weinberger, A., PILOT, The NBS Multicomputer System, *Proc. of Eastern Joint Computer Conference*, Philadelphia, 1958, pp. 71–75.
15. Eckert, J. P., Chu, J. C., Tonik, A. B., and Schmitt, W. F., Design of Univac-LARC System: I, *Proc. Eastern Joint Computer Conference*, Boston, 1959. pp. 59–65.
16. Lukoff, H., Spandorfer, L. M., and Lu, F. F., Design of Univac-LARC System: II, *Proc. Eastern Joint Computer Conference*, Boston, 1959, pp. 66–74.
17. Univac LARC System, Sperry Rand Corp., Remington Rand Univac Div., General Descriptive Bulletin U-1797, Rev. 1.
18. Dreyfus, P., Programming on a Concurrent Digital Computer, "Frontier Research on Digital Computers," Vol. I, Univ. of North Carolina Summer Institute, 1959, Section V.
19. Dreyfus, P., Programming Design Features of the GAMMA 60 Computer, *Proc. Eastern Joint Computer Conference*, Philadelphia, 1958, pp. 174–180.
20. Dreyfus, P., France's GAMMA 60, *Datamation* 4, pp. 34–35, May/June, 1958.
21. Porter, R. E., The RW-400—A New Polymorphic Data System, *Datamation* 6, pp. 8–14, January/February, 1960.
22. Lonergan, W., and King, P., Design of the B5000 System, *Datamation* 7, pp 28–32, May, 1961.
23. The B5000 Concept, Burroughs Corp., Descriptive Bulletin.
24. Anderson, J. P. et al., D-825—A Multiple-Computer System for Command and Control, *AFIPS Conference Proc.* 22, Philadelphia, 1962, pp. 86–96.
25. Casale, C. T., Planning the 3600, *AFIPS Conference Proc.* 22, Philadelphia, 1962, pp. 73–85.
26. Scott, W. F., and Wasserman, R., Diode-Capacitor Memory, Digital Computers and Data Processors, Univ. of Michigan Special Summer Session 1956 (J. W. Carr and N. R. Scott, Editors), Section V.4.12, pp. 1–8.
27. West, G. P., and Koerner, R. J., Communications Within a Polymorphic Intellelectronic System, *Proc. Western Joint Computer Conference*, San Francisco, 1960, pp. 225–230.
28. Rajchman, J. A., and Lo, A. W., The Transfluxor, *Proc. IRE* 44, pp. 321–332, March, 1956.

Author Index

Subject Index

A

Accreditation, 151
Adjunct memory, 265
Administration on campus, computer, 140
AIMACO, 4, 5
Algebraic Data Systems Language, 24–27
ALGOL, 15, 17, 24
Algorithmic method, 149, 157
All-magnetic circuits, 54, 62
American University, 145
Amplifier, free jet interaction, 199–202
   turbulence, 202–205
   vortex chamber, 224–229
   wall interaction, 210–224
Analog computers, 136
AND-gate, 175, 190, 196, 205
Area (in information algebra), 42
   set, 44
Arithmetic calculator, 295
Arizona, University of, 145
Arrays, generalized, 39
   rectangular, 30–32
Automated classrooms, 161

B

B5000, 283
Ball elements, 187–194
Base register, 287
Binary adder, 177, 184, 234–236
Binary counter, 179, 182, 192, 222
Bistable element, 176, 188, 196
BIZMAC, 20
Boolean algebra, 154
Boundary layer control, 198, 202–205
Branching, 9, 10
Buffer module, 298
Bundles, 44, 45

C

California, State of, 152
Calling, of a procedure, 12
Carnegie Institute of Technology, 145
Case Institute of Technology, 145
CDC *1604*, 145
CDC *3600*, 284
Central control unit, 293
Central exchange, 298
Central processor, 291
Change packets, 18
Circuit engineering, 156
Clauses, 6
COBOL, 5, 14, 15, 21, 22, 23, 28, 29, 31, 36
Codasyl, 14, 21
   language structure group, 39, 40
Communication Sciences, 143, 144
Compagnie des Machines Bull, 292
Computer accessibility, 147
Computer and Information Sciences, 143
COMTRAN, 5, 15, 16, 29, 36
Conditional clauses, 6
Console button pushing, 148
Control Data Corporation, 284
Control trunk, 285
Coordinate set, 40
Core-diode circuit, 70
Core-diode schemes, 62
Core-wire circuits, 54, 70
Correspondence courses, 158
Cost of student problems, 148
Credit versus no-credit issue, 148
Crossbar switching network, 253
Crowder Tutor-Texts, 161
CSX-1, 144
Curricula, 143
   undergraduate engineering, 141
Customer education, 138

D

D*825*, 283
Data division, of a program, 5, 28
Data organization and description, 27–38
Data processing, problems, formulation of,
   1–52
   theory, 38–49
Data Processing Management Association, 153
Datum, 39

309